Elements of Writing

Peter Lindblom

MIAMI-DADE COMMUNITY COLLEGE

ELEMENTS OF WRITING

MACMILLAN PUBLISHING CO., INC.
New York

COLLIER MACMILLAN PUBLISHERS
London

Macmillan Publishing Co., Inc.
866 Third Avenue, New York, New York 10022

Collier Macmillan Canada, Inc.

Library of Congress Cataloging in Publication Data

Lindblom, Peter D., 1938–
  Elements of writing.

  Includes index.
  1. English language—Rhetoric.   2. College
readers.   I. Title.
PE1408.L559   1983   808'.0427   82-7804
ISBN 0-02-370910-3

Printing 1 2 3 4 5 6 7 8   Year: 3 4 5 6 7 8 9 0

The author makes grateful acknowledgment for permission to reprint the following:

"Barbed Wire," by John Fisher. From *The High Plains* by John Fisher. Copyright ©
1978 by John Fisher. Reprinted by permission of Harper & Row, Publishers, Inc.

"Listen! The Wind," by Anne Morrow Lindbergh. Reprinted by permission of
Harcourt Brace Jovanovich, Inc.

ISBN   0-02-370910-3

Preface

Audience. Elements of Writing is directed to students in first-semester freshman composition and to those who need a preparatory course prior to taking that course. Those who read poorly will benefit especially from this book because they will be able to learn the basic principles of writing in the first two units before they go on to write essays based on readings in the third unit. Even those who read fairly well will find the study skills and reading skills review in Unit Three useful for their other college courses. The first seven assignments, based on observation or recollection, may be adjusted to students of all levels of sophistication.

Theoretical assumptions. Three assumptions serve as the foundation for this book:

1) Writing is a process. All writers, whether they consciously identify the steps or not, follow a process when they compose and revise. Those who do not write well can learn this process best by learning it one step at a time. After they have mastered the process, they will begin to work naturally and easily through the process and may even begin to do some of the steps subconsciously. People who have mastered the process of writing can apply it to every type of writing assignment, and they thus have a method for working on any writing project that they confront.

2) Personal writing, or writing based on observation and recollection, provides the easiest, most natural subject matter for

beginners to use when they learn to write. Personal writing does not demand attention to readings; nor does it develop analytical skills that expository writing demands. Nevertheless, students can learn all the elements of writing from carefully structured assignments in personal essays.

3) Because writing provides a way to discover ideas and insights, personal writing often improves students' understanding of themselves and their past experiences. When they begin to make discoveries, students become motivated to write. They begin to see writing as a valuable experience in itself.

Objectives

1) To teach the students the steps needed to take a project from conception to completion.

2) To teach them to apply these steps to various types of writing.

3) To make writing a valuable, intelligent experience that provides the students with insight into their own experiences.

Organization.   The book, divided into three units, begins with the smallest complete unit of composition, the paragraph, and moves to longer essays—first to personal essays and then to essays based on readings. The progression through the composing process moves from the whole to the parts, from the planning and conception of the entire piece, through its organization, and finally to the paragraphs and sentences. The second half of the writing process, revision, is also taught from the largest elements to the smallest, beginning with content and organization and working down to editing and correcting. Each of the three units has two sections, one on composing and one on revising. The first unit thus teaches basic elements of composing paragraphs, and then teaches the qualities to look for when revising a paragraph. The second unit teaches the organization and development of longer essays, and then deals with methods for checking and revising these elements. Unit Three teaches basic expository techniques and deals with the final stage of revision, editing and correcting. The book also contains a brief handbook with simplified rules and drills to illustrate the rules, and it closes with an appendix which explains basic principles of language functions.

Content Features

1) *Step by step instruction, with the steps repeated and incrementally expanded.* Revision is covered in small logical divi-

sions. An appendix discusses in non-technical terms the logic and organization of the language.

2) *Three types of sample essays.*

Professional examples of almost all essays are joined with a "typical student's" version of many essays, and with occasional essays by students to illustrate each assignment. Readings accompanying most assignments vary in difficulty so that all students can read at least one example fairly easily. The examples provide models, as well as examples of finished versions, for intermediate steps in each assignment.

3) *Exercises and journal-keeping projects to promote scribal fluency.* Exercises in sentence-combining, sentence building, and error-recognition and correction follow each assignment.

Pedagogical Features.

1) Free-writing and journal-keeping to develop freedom to write.

2) Writing exercises—in sentence combining and sentence building—to develop flexibility in structuring sentences.

3) Editing exercises to develop the ability to recognize and correct errors.

4) Incremental approach: writing is taught step by step, with early steps reinforced by repetition in later assignments.

Contents

To the Student, A Few Introductory Words

You are beginning a program in writing, a course of study designed to make you a capable, confident writer. At the end of this program, I hope you will know how to handle any writing project, whether it is a letter to a loved one in which you express a deeply-felt emotion, a paper for an important class in college, or a business report that might help you on your way to success in your career.

Learning to write requires two steps before you even begin to work on a specific project. First, accept the idea that writing is hard work. It requires you to use muscles in ways you probably don't ordinarily use them, in ways that will be tiring at first. The effort involved in writing for a twenty- or thirty-minute period might be difficult at first, just as the first quarter mile of a conditioning program for running or swimming might be difficult. But if you will work on the beginning exercises in the book, you'll find that very soon the work becomes a little easier, just as running or swimming becomes easier as you get in condition.

Second, decide that you will write when it is time to write, in spite of the hesitation that strikes when you first look at a blank page. Every writer has that same feeling when the time comes to start writing. John Steinbeck reported essentially that same feeling in the preface to *Travels with Charlie*. In his book, Steinbeck sets out in a truck to tour the entire United States. Just before he leaves home, he contemplates the extent of the proposed trip and feels a kind of panic that is familiar to every writer.

1

And suddenly the United States became huge beyond belief and impossible ever to cross. I wondered how I'd got myself mixed up in a project that couldn't be carried out. It was like starting to write a novel. When I face the desolate impossibility of writing five hundred pages, a sick sense of failure falls on me, and I know I can never do it. This happens every time. Then gradually I write one page and then another. One day's work is all I can permit myself to contemplate, and I eliminate the possibility of ever finishing.

John Steinbeck, *Travels with Charlie*

You can overcome your hesitation in the same way Steinbeck did: begin to write a word, then another, then one sentence, then a paragraph, and then finally a whole page. Start. Pick up your pen, put it on paper. Write something—anything—just to get yourself started. The more you write, the easier it will be for you to write. Writing will never be easy, unlike naptaking or eating, but it can be easier for you than it is now. All you need to do is to bury your reluctance and begin to write.

The course uses some strategies to help you get started:

- Exercises to build your strength.
- Free writing to loosen your mind up a little.
- Focused writing to help you record information more easily.
- Journal writing to make writing a regular part of your life, at least for now.

In addition, the first few writing projects in the course will come straight from your own experiences, rather than from reading. You will write paragraphs based on observations, and essays based on recollections of your past. Through those assignments, you ought to be able to learn a great deal about the process of writing. This approach to writing will allow you to focus on writing and on developing writing skills before you must work on more academic papers.

Perhaps most important, you will learn a process for writing, a process that will be usable for any writing project. You will learn where to start and how to carry through step by step to the completion of the project. Later on, you may even learn how to change and vary the process, or to shorten it for certain projects. Knowing the process will give you both a starting point and a set of directions to follow, so that you will always have a way to get started and a method for proceeding whenever you receive a writing assignment.

I hope that these efforts will make the course manageable for you, and that by the end of the term you will be well on your way to becoming a capable, confident writer.

WHY FRESHMAN COMPOSITION?

It is highly likely that freshman composition is a requirement for graduation from your college or university, and you are enrolled in this course to meet at least a part of that requirement. Such requirements are not set by some timeless law or by some decree of educators long since dead. The requirement was established because you need to be a capable writer in college, and later, in your career.

In college, quite obviously, you need to write capably so that you can produce papers, write tests, and do other types of written work required in your courses. You will demonstrate your knowledge of many subjects almost entirely by writing paragraphs and essays, rather than by answering objective tests. The further you progress in school, the more you will find yourself writing to demonstrate your knowledge. You need to write capably to fulfill your assignments.

In your career, you will also need to write capably to do your job and to advance in your career. "Perhaps in some jobs," you might say, "but not in mine. I'm going into engineering, or accounting, or computer technology." The truth is that a surprising amount of writing is necessary in each of those professions. Accountants must explain what they learn about a business by examining its records. Engineers must explain their ideas, and, in the case of consulting engineers, must write proposals before they even get a consulting contract. Programmers and analysts must write instructions into their programs so that others can follow the procedures called for. In almost every occupation, communications within the organization and permanent records of all sorts are written. Writing skills are especially important in big organizations where you might not be well-known to all of the officers. "My boss knows me," said a bank officer to me one day, "but the big chiefs do not know me well. They know only my work, my written reports and proposals.

Much of my progress in this institution depends on my skill as a writer." Skilled writing is valuable at work.

But writing is valuable in a different way, a way more important than the practical ways mentioned above. Writing is a way of learning, a special way of focusing your mind on important matters and learning about them. Writing helps you learn in two ways. First, writing about an idea or concept helps you to understand and control the idea. If you need to understand and remember something for a test, write it out in your own words. Writing will help you master ideas and facts. Second, writing helps you to connect one idea to another in a way that doesn't happen unless you write. Psychologists tell us that writing puts together ideas that haven't previously been connected in your mind. This special way of learning works for school subjects, and it also works on more personal matters. If you are confused, if you have a problem, write about it. The very act of writing will help you to clarify your thinking, to learn in ways not possible through other means.

Becoming a capable writer is, therefore, valuable at school, in your career, and in the act of learning.

UNIT ONE

Writing Based on Observation

BEGINNING TO WRITE

Daily Writing/Journal

It is important for you to develop the habit of writing. For the next four weeks you should keep a journal in which you will write one page for each day that this class meets. Writing every day will increase your ability. You will develop your strength and will become more relaxed about writing. Most of us have at least a little anxiety about writing. Regular practice will increase your confidence.

You can also use the journal writings as a way of working on the assignments. Practice the strategies for observation taught in Unit One. Use the journal entries to collect information for the essays in Unit Two. Those three essays will focus on your past experiences, and you will need to recollect and record a great deal of information to serve as the raw material for the essays. Along with the exercises included with this unit, you will find suggestions for journal entries. In general, the suggestions will follow the patterns discussed below. The exercises are located at the end of the unit. Do one exercise for each day of class.

SUGGESTIONS FOR JOURNAL ENTRIES

1. *Free writing*. Start by trying to cover paper. Try to write enough to cover one sheet of paper with anything that comes to mind.

Write about the weather, school, work, the appearance of clouds, the antics of a dog out on the track, anything or anybody that comes to mind. The objective here is simply to cover paper, to develop the ability to write rapidly without fatigue for several minutes at a time.

2. *Observations of daily life.* Take a moment to look around you. Write a page describing the people, places, actions, or whatever else you can see.

   Recount what you did on a given day. What did you accomplish? How do you feel about that day?

3. *Focus on single incidents.* Describe things that took place in school, or encounters with people. Try to write about each incident in a way that will outline what happened, but concentrate mostly on your reactions and feelings about the event.

4. *Recollections from the past.* Focus on some time of your life, perhaps on a time when you were developing new attitudes or taking new directions. Write about those times, telling what was happening, what you were thinking, who your friends were, who your enemies were, or anything outstanding that you remember.

5. *Focus on a specific person or place.* Write a description of that person or place. Tell what you did with that person, what sort of place it was, what you did there. Include in your writing some observations about what you were thinking, how you were reacting, and how you were changing at that time.

6. *Yourself today.* In a slightly different way from the work you did in observations on daily life, try to discuss your current life, your situation, and your attitudes. Describe a typical day. React to that typical day. Start a page by writing, "I'm in a time of my life when . . ." Take an inventory of your desk top or dresser top. Comment on the items you find there, and explain their importance to you or their contribution to your life. Write about one or two special places in your life. Write about one or two special people. Write about things you do by choice rather than by assignment or requirement.

7. *Yourself tomorrow.* Write about your plans, hopes, dreams, and goals. Tell where you hope to be and what you hope to be doing in ten years. Describe a perfect day for yourself in 1989. Name four things not related to work that you would like to

accomplish over the next twenty years. Explain what t things are and why each one is important to you.

8. *Copy work*. Once or twice during the course, select a pa writing that seems to be good or interesting. Copy that passage word-for-word in your journal. Notice the choices of words, the sentence structure, and the general feel and rhythm of the passage. Such copying was one way Benjamin Franklin worked to improve his own writing. He used to suggest this method as standard practice for students in his time.

WRITING EXERCISES

You need to do two kinds of exercises as you begin to improve your writing skills. First, you need to do the writer's equivalent of weight lifting to develop your strength. Second, you need work which will develop in you a relaxed response to putting words on paper.

For strength and conditioning, try the following exercises when you are preparing for class.

1. Write your name—your signature—on a sheet of paper as many times as you can in two minutes.
2. Sign your name, last name first, as many times as you can in ninety seconds.
3. Write the title and number of your English course as many times as possible in the next minute.
4. Write the word *sunrise* as many times as you can in two minutes.

Take a brief rest between each of those exercises, but try to write without stopping while working on each exercise.

On a clean sheet of paper, write for ninety seconds, putting on paper whatever comes into your mind after you read each of the following words:

1. Sunrise.
2. Strawberries.
3. Singing.

Simply begin to write after reading each word. Write about each word, without stopping, for ninety seconds. Then take a brief rest.

Write without editing your writing. Don't worry if you drift from the words of your assigned topic. This exercise is designed to help you drift, to allow you to put thoughts on paper whether or not they seem important to the topic. You will find that some of your most valuable ideas on a subject come after you seem to have wandered from the assigned topic. Don't concern yourself at this time with neatness or correctness. This is a free-writing exercise, not an exercise in editing. Do these exercises each day as you prepare for class.

SENTENCE COMBINING

In addition to the free- and directed-writing exercises, which are designed to get you in shape to write and to give you freedom to write, you need to do some exercises to introduce you to different ways of putting together sentences. This practice will help you to increase your flexibility as a writer.

When you first began to read, you practiced with a reader that used extremely short sentences.

> Jane sees the dog. The dog is white. The dog has brown spots. Jane calls the dog. And so on.

The writing is clear, and it is correct. But it lacks any life, and reading very much of this kind of writing would very soon put most of us to sleep. It would be more interesting to read

> When Jane sees the white dog with the brown spots, she calls it.
> or
> Upon seeing the dog, which is white with brown spots, Jane calls it.

There are other ways of writing these four short sentences, but what is obvious about the two new versions is that they combine the short sentences into one longer and more graceful sentence. You already write in sentences longer than the "Jane sees the dog" variety, but you can improve the style—that is, the rhythms and sounds and flow of your writing—by doing some exercises that focus specifically on ways to combine several short sentences into a single longer sentence.

You will find additional exercises with each chapter. As you work on the writing assignments, do the exercises as well. Here is a sample: Join these sentences by using the word *and* or *but*.

Jim walked down the hall.
He entered the last classroom on the right.

Jim walked down the hall, and he entered the last classroom on the right.

Follow the same pattern:

The office building is seven stories high.
It has a long circular drive in front of it.

Jim and the girls parked the car in the student parking lot. They made the long walk to the library.

The bus arrived late.
George didn't mind waiting for it.

The tall boy looks like a basketball player.
He would rather study nuclear physics.

The Student Union is a wonderful place.
I spend a great deal of time there.

We went to the soccer field.
Then we walked into the picnic area.

The entire class left early.
Every member went to the tennis courts.

Joan picked up her purse.
She picked up an umbrella.
She picked up a set of keys.

She walked slowly down the stairs.
She got into her car.
She drove happily off to work.

Jim opened the windows.
Jean turned on the fan.
They both began to work on the test.

When you join three or more items in a series, use this pattern:

Joan picked up her purse, her umbrella, and a set of keys.
She walked slowly down the stairs, got into her car, and drove happily to work.

Jim opened the windows, Jean turned on the fan, and they both began to work on the test.

ASSIGNMENT 1.

Writing Directions

Your first writing assignment for this term is very practical and yet very important. You must locate your teacher's office, the school library, and the bookstore. Write a set of directions for walking from this classroom to the other three locations. In your directions, try to give the reader a glimpse of some of the sights along the route.

Note that the assignment asks for two things. It asks for a set of directions from one location to three other locations on the campus. You will need to check these locations before you begin to work. Look at a campus map or ask directions of someone who knows the campus well. Then make a tentative decision as to the best route from the classroom to the other locations. Your directions will lead the reader along that route. In addition to the directions, you also need to provide the reader with visual details that will be seen along the way. These details will serve as checkpoints, and they will also provide a little of the flavor of the campus.

Next, gather your tools and get to work. You will need a pen and paper, preferably a pad of some kind. Set out, going from the classroom to the first location. Take notes as you walk.

> Leave class. Turn right. Take first stairs. Downstairs, turn right and go about 200 yards. When past swimming pool take walkway to the left. . .

Take notes for moving between the three locations by noting down the directions between places on separate sheets; that is, write the directions from the classroom to the English office on one page, and to the other two locations on separate pages. On each page include a few notes about the sights along the route.

When you finish taking notes, you need to make two decisions. First, have you selected the most efficient route to take in walking to all three of these places? Do you suggest to your reader that the library is the best first stop after leaving the classroom? Or is the best first stop the bookstore? What is the next place on your route? There are some fairly obvious alternatives here for choosing a route from the classroom to the other locations. One route would start from the classroom and go to the nearest location. You would then continue from there to the next spot, and finally to the place farthest from the classroom. Another choice is to go first to the farthest location and work back to those nearer to the classroom.

You might choose a route because it provides the easiest access to the places, or to avoid important obstacles that stand in the way. There is an easy, logical, natural way to move from one location to the next. Your job as a writer is to find it and to give your reader directions for that route.

Second, you need to decide what details to include in your instructions. Some details are extremely important. A left turn omitted from the directions might cause your reader to end up on some far corner of the campus.

Other details, sights, and sounds encountered along the way are not vital to the success of the instructions, but they can be helpful to the reader and can add a little of the flavor of the campus. In your choice of details, you will mention some things you saw but will omit others. The selection is strictly up to you. One of the privileges you enjoy as the writer is the right to select what you put in the paper. You have the right to create an impression that suits you and your feelings about the campus.

After you have decided upon

a. an order for presenting the materials and
b. a selection of details to be included,

simply arrange the notes in order, and write out a first version of the paper. When you finish the first version, lay it aside for a time and then read it through carefully to be sure that you have

a. followed the order, the actual directions, very carefully.
b. included all the necessary instructions.
c. provided enough visual details to assist the reader and give the flavor of the campus.

When you have checked these items carefully, recopy the paper neatly so that you can turn it in to your teacher.

Your set of instructions might be similar to the following:

It is a little difficult to find your way around our campus, so a set of directions from our English class to the English offices, the bookstore, and the library is a very useful tool. First, go down the stairs outside the classroom and take the hallway to the left at the bottom of the stairs. Go out the last door on the left and take the walkway past the fishpond, which leads to the Humanities Building; go back past the fishpond and turn right on the gravel path. About a hundred yards down this path you come to the library. To get to the bookstore, go around to the back of the library, past the rose garden and the patio. The bookstore is in the back of the library building.

COMMENTARY

You should notice two important points about composition, both of which appear almost naturally in this assignment. First, every written project has an order for presenting materials. This project has a built-in order; when you select the most efficient route to the three places, you also select the order of presentation for the materials in the essay. Any presentation that jumps around out of that order would be confusing to your reader. Other types of writing projects will use different orders of presentation, but you will learn these when you need them. Simply remember that every written project does have some order for presenting materials.

Second, the selection of details to support your topic is a vital part of good writing. The details you supply in the paper explain and clarify the topic. Much of the art of selecting details is based on seeing, whether the details are visual, part of a set of directions for finding locations on a campus, or are important items to be found by very close reading of a complex passage. As you work on these instructions, begin to develop your ability to see and select details.

The following selection contains a set of instructions in the art of stringing a barbed wire fence. The author has included additional information about the invention of barbed wire, but once he leaves the history, he moves into the same pattern you used in your directions. Note that he also uses great care in his selection of details.

BARBED WIRE

by John Fisher

[1] If you grew up in a city, it is possible that you have never had occasion to look closely at a barbed wire fence. In that case, it might be fun to try to invent it, in imagination, for yourself. It sounds easy. You only have to set two posts in the ground and string between them wires, fitted with barbs at about six-inch intervals. The problem is to fix the barbs so firmly that a heavy animal brushing against the fence will not break them off, or slide them along the wire. If they slide, you will soon have all the barbs shoved up against one post

or the other, with a naked wire in between. Another problem is to figure out a way to make your wire cheaply and fast—that is, with machinery requiring a minimum of hand labor.

[2] You might think of soldering on the barbs, but that quickly turns out to be a poor idea. The soldered join is inherently weak, and since each one has to be made by hand, the process would be prohibitively expensive. Another possibility is to take a ribbon of steel about one inch wide, cut zigzags along one side to form sharp points, and then twist the ribbon as you string it. This, too, has been tried and found impractical. The ribbon can be rolled, and cut by machinery, but it is too heavy to handle easily, uses too much expensive steel per foot, and is too weak to resist the impact of a charging bull. Another abortive scheme involved spiked spools strung on a wire.

[3] According to the Bivins Museum in Tascosa, Texas, 401 patents for barbed wire have been recorded, and more than 1,600 variants have been catalogued. Out of all these attempts, only two proved successful. Both were patented at nearly the same time by two neighbors in De Kalb County, Illinois; Joseph F. Glidden and Jacob Haish. Whether they got their ideas independently, and who got his first, are questions that have provoked much expensive litigation. Their concepts were quite similar. Each involved clasping barbs around a wire at appropriate intervals—and then twisting that wire together with another one, so that the barbs are tightly gripped between the two. The only essential difference, to the eye of anyone but a patent lawyer, was in slightly variant methods of clasping the barb.

[4] Whether or not Glidden was the original inventor, he certainly was the more successful businessman. He made his first wire in 1873, forming the barbs with a converted coffee grinder and twisting the twin wires in his barn with a hand-cranked grindstone. He sold his first wire, and took out his patent in 1874. That same year he formed a partnership with a neighbor, I. L. Ellwood, and built a factory in De Kalb. Before the end of the next year, their factory was turning out five tons of wire a day, using improved, steam-operated machinery. In 1876 Glidden sold a half interest in his invention to the Washburn and Moen Manufacturing Company of Worcester, Massachusetts, which had been supplying him with plain wire: in payment he got $60,000, plus a royalty of 25 cents for every hundred weight of barbed wire sold.*

[5] How profitable this deal proved to be can be glimpsed from the following figures. In his first year of manufacture, Glidden sold 10,000 pounds of wire. Two years later, Washburn and Moen sold 2.8 million pounds. Within the next five years, sales mounted to more than 80 million pounds a year—yielding Glidden an income of more than $200,000 annually, the equivalent of at least $1 million today and that was before the era of income taxes. The manufacturer's profits amounted to many times that.

*Washburn and Moen eventually merged with the American Steel and Wire Company, a subsidiary of U.S. Steel. American Steel and Wire's museum in Worcester is the prime source of information about barbed wire.

[6] Much of his wire was being shipped to Texas. Glidden and his money followed it, leaving a permanent impress on the settlement of the High Plains and especially on its main city, Amarillo. There I came across his traces nearly sixty years later.

[7] But in the meantime I had a chance to become well acquainted with his product. When I was eleven years old, my grandfather John Fischer taught me how to string wire during a summer I spent on his homestead near Apache, Oklahoma. To my eyes he seemed a very old man, but he was still wiry, lean, hard-muscled, and accustomed to working from sunup til long after dark.

[8] Like inventing barbed wire, stringing it is a more complex business than you might think. First you find your posts. My grandfather insisted that they be either cedar, locust, or bois d'arc, also known as Osage orange. These woods will last in the ground for many years, while cottonwood or pine will rot quickly unless creosoted—and we had no creosote in those days. Some he cut himself along a little creek that ran across one corner of his 160-acre farm; others he bought or bartered from neighbors. Each post had to be exactly six feet long.

[9] When the posts were all collected, with a mule team and wagon, he stacked them near the edge of the pasture he planned to fence, and then marked his line. This he did with a borrowed surveyor's transit, a handful of stakes, and a few rolls of binder twine. At thirty-foot intervals he scratched a mark on the hard prairie soil to indicate where he wanted each post to go. One of my jobs was to make a hole in the ground with a crowbar at each mark, and fill it with water from a five-gallon, galvanized-iron milk can, thus softening the earth for my grandfather, who followed me with his post-hole digger.

[10] The first post set, to a depth of precisely two feet, was of course at a corner of the tract he was going to enclose. It had to be braced in both directions of the future fence lines. For braces he used two other posts planted diagonally in the earth with their feet anchored against heavy stones; their top ends he sawed at the proper angle and fastened to the corner post with tenpenny nails. Then we set about the weary labor of digging holes and setting intermediate posts until we came to the place he had marked for his next corner. We had to do only three sides of the forty-acre pasture, because the fourth side abutted a field enclosed years earlier; but at that, the post-setting took us the best part of two weeks.

[11] Then we drove the wagon into Apache to get a load of wire. It came on big wooden spools, so heavy that the hardware dealer had to help us load them. Grandfather let me drive back, a proud and nervous assignment for me, although the mules—named Pete and Repeat—were gentle enough.

[12] At the rear end of the wagon bed he rigged a pole, crosswise, to serve as a spindle on which a spool of wire could be mounted and easily unwound. We drove the wagon close to a corner post, twisted the end of the wire around it one foot above the ground and stapled it fast. Next we drove along the line of posts for about 200 yards, unreeling wire on the ground behind us. There

Grandpa stopped, unhitched the team, blocked three wheels of the wagon with rocks, and jacked up the fourth wheel, the rear one next to the fence line. He cut the wire and twisted the loose end around the axle of the jacked-up wheel, fastening it to a spoke for additional security. By turning the wheel, we wound the wire around the axle until it was taut. (There were patent wire-stretchers, but Grandpa did not own one. The wheel-stretching method worked just as well, and saved money.) After he had lashed the wheel to maintain the tension, we went back down the line and stapled the wire to each post. Then we repeated the process, time after time, until we had the pasture enclosed with a standard fence of four strands, spaced a foot apart. We finished up by making a wire gate at the corner nearest the house.

[13] Three tips for fence-stringers:

—Wear the heaviest leather gauntlets you can find. Even so, you are bound to get your hands and arms torn, so carry some iodine and bandages with you.

—Staple the wire on the side of the posts facing into the pasture. When a heavy animal runs into the fence, he will press the wire against the posts, not the staples. If the wire were on the other side, the staples might pop out.

—Hang the expense, and use two staples for each fastening of the wire. One of them might someday rust or work loose.

[14] I haven't seen that fence in decades, but my brother told me a few years ago that it was still standing and tight. Probably it is the most nearly permanent thing I have ever worked on. Certainly its useful life has been far longer than that of any article or book I have written.

ASSIGNMENT 2.

Describing a Place

The second assignment in Unit I asks you to describe a place. Your first aim will be to show your reader how the place looks. Your second goal will be to explain the importance of this place to you. Paint a word picture, but add some of your feelings about the place, and suggest its meaning to you.

The most important part of a description is the visual details that make up the scene. Since we often ignore details when we look at a scene, it might be a help to practice a special method of observation and note-taking for descriptions. You can look around you at any time to practice this special technique for observation. Start your practice, therefore, by observing the front of the classroom in which you take English. Later, you will select another place as the subject for this project.

First, scan the front of the room from left to right, and then back from right to left. Take note of the objects on the wall. Observe also those objects standing near the wall. Be aware of the general shapes and colors in that part of the room. When you have scanned the room for a moment or two, list the visual details on paper by following these directions:

Take a clean sheet of paper and fold it in half from top to bottom. Number from one to fifteen down both halves of the page. Above the columns write the following phrases and fill in the blanks with words that fit naturally into the blanks:

This room has ———————————   This room is ———————————————

This room has	This room is
1. a front wall	1. light green in color
2. a blackboard on the wall	2. all squares and angles
3. a table	3. cold—the temperature is too low
4. a podium on the table	4. cold—the colors are dull, institutional in nature
5. a movie screen hanging from the ceiling	5. messy—papers on the floor
6.	6. starkly lit by fluorescent lights
7.	7. filled with uncomfortable desks—chairs
8.	8.
9.	9.
10.	10.
11.	11.
12.	12.
13.	13.
14.	14.
15.	15.

The words that fit naturally after the word "has" are nouns, the names of items in the room. Those words that follow naturally after "is" are adjectives, words that describe colors, shapes and other qualities. Continue to work on both lists until you have listed all the important items and qualities in the scene being described.

These two lists make up the raw material for a description. Select those items that seem most important and most interesting, and then decide on an order for presenting those items in your own paragraph. Select details that generate an impression of the room.

The average classroom seems to be plain in appearance. It may be cold, both in its color and its temperature, but it is useful and functional. The details that support such an impression are the colors, the tone or feeling in the room, the temperature, and the equipment. Note especially the straight lines and sharp angles found on the kind of furniture customarily used in schools and colleges.

Your order of presentation ought to take the eye of the reader in a specific direction across the room. It is possible to start on one side—the right, for example—and go across to the left; or you may choose to go from left to right. It might be useful to start in the foreground, with the central pieces of furniture, then move to the background on one side and across the room looking at the objects on the wall, such as the blackboard with its chalk tray. Such a paragraph of description might read this way:

> At the center of the room, and the center of attention, is a table, dull gray in color, with a darker gray top made of formica. It is the plain, sharp-cornered table found in a million classrooms across the country, all made of the same materials by the same company, or so it seems. On the table is a small lectern, a little shelf for the teacher to prop up books or lecture notes, and to hide behind, if necessary. Over against the wall to the left of table stand some maps, rolled up and apparently never used. A blackboard, which is actually green in color, though nobody calls it a greenboard, fills the entire wall from floor to ceiling. The board has a chalk tray running across it about waist-high. The tray has one eraser and three tiny nubs of chalk lying on it. The rest of the wall beyond the end of the blackboard is taken up with the door and a small panel of light switches. The whole thing is very businesslike and functional and also a little dull and cold.

This brief exercise ought to provide a working strategy for the second assignment.

Assignment:	Describe a place that is important to you. Give the reader a picture of the place and a sense of its importance to you.
First.	Select a place. Since you only have about one page to present the entire picture to your reader, choose a place that is not very large. Don't try to describe a whole neighborhood. One room in a house or one corner of a field would be a suitable size.
Second.	Collect the visual details by performing the detail-gathering exercise you learned in class. Be sure to do a thorough job, going over the scene several times to be sure you have not missed anything.
Third.	Express your feelings about the place, and try to choose the visual details that will make your feelings clear to your reader.
Fourth.	Decide on a direction to lead the eye of your reader around the place, and write a draft of the paragraph.

In the following brief paragraph, Anne Morrow Lindbergh describes the cockpit of her small plane. The place is important to her because she spends a great deal of time there. It is also a place of security and warmth for her, a place where she is able to be quietly at work and where she is accomplishing something both pleasant and important, the business of flying.

LISTEN TO THE WIND

Anne Morrow Lindbergh

This little cockpit of mine became extraordinarily pleasing to me, as much so as a furnished study at home. Every corner, every crack, had significance. Every object meant something. Not only the tools I was working with, the transmitter and receiver, the key and the antenna reel; but even the small irrelevant objects on the side of the fuselage, the little black hooded light, its face now turned away from me, the shining arm and knob of the second throttle, the bright switches and handles, the colored wires and copper pipes: all gave me, in a strange sense, as much pleasure as my familiar books and pictures might at home. The pleasure was perhaps not esthetic but came from a sense of familiarity, security, and possession. I invested them with an emotional significance of their own, since they had been through so much with me. They made up this comfortable, familiar, tidy, compact world that was mine. . . Outside the night rushed by. How nice to be in your own little room, to pull your belongings around you, to draw in like a snail in his shell, to work!

Now it is time for you to write your assignment, a description of your special place. Remember to follow the process you used in the exercise. Record the visual details, generate an impression, select an order, and write the first draft. After you finish the first draft, lay the paper aside and come back to it later to check it and copy it over neatly.

COMMENTARY

It is important here to follow the steps listed above rather than to rush aimlessly into the job. The use of the two-sentence exercise to collect visual details emphasizes the importance of gathering materials for use in writing. In this case, the materials for writing are simple visual details; in later assignments, the materials will be other types of details and facts. In every type of assignment it is

vitally important to collect as much information as possible before you start to write.

Also, you should begin to see that every paper creates an impression or has a statement to make, and that the impression or statement governs the choice of details used in the paper.

ASSIGNMENT 3.

Describing an Action

Describe a brief event from your life, an event that is in some way
interesting or important to you. The description should focus
closely on the action in the event so that the reader will be able to
see that action and get an impression of the feelings you had during
the event.

This project requires the same close attention to detail that you
used in Assignment 2, but in this case you will be looking closely
at an action rather than a scene. As a warm-up for this project, do
the following group exercise in class.

The teacher, or another student, will leave the room and re-enter
by the front door so that you can observe the actions as the person
opens the door, walks across the room, and sits down in one of the
chairs. Watch very carefully as the door opens. Begin at this point
to make brief notes about the action. Note the hand movements,
the walk, the body movements, and the facial expression as the
person enters the room and takes a seat. On scratch paper write
down as many of these details as possible. These guides may help
you to pick up the details more easily:

1. Does the person swing the door open boldly and let it close of
   its own weight? Does he or she hold the door and close it slowly?
2. What do the hands do? Do they swing boldly? Hang loosely?
   Droop?
3. Watch the feet. Are the strides long and bold or are they short?
   Is the person tentative and nervous about entering the room?
   Can you hear the footsteps, or are they muffled in the person's
   attempt to slip into the room unnoticed?
4. Is the body upright and stiff? Is it relaxed but straight? Does the
   posture suggest nervousness? Does the person attempt to sneak
   in?
5. Pay careful attention to the movement into the desk. Is it grace-

ful, a gradual swing into the seat? Is it a turn like that of a ballet dancer? Or is it just a flop down into the seat with no concern for appearance or grace?

6. What facial expressions and changes of expression occur? Are the eyes steady? Do they flit about the room nervously? Does the person look at the floor? The class? Only at the desk? Do you see a smile? A frown? A nervous laugh?

Watch carefully, and take additional notes as the person repeats the action. Then compare your notes to the following notes taken by a typical student:

1. The man eases the door open   holds it   moves through it slowly closes it behind him   tries to keep noise down
2. Hands move slowly, hang loosely at sides seem to want to avoid notice. One fist is clenched the other hand is full of books.
3. He hardly moves feet they slide over floor sneaking along, make no noise on the tile floor
4. Bent over,   not upright   shoulders rounded to make himself seem smaller
5. Sits down quickly   speed seems most important   motion awkward flops down pulls himself into seat desk   shifts from sudden jolt
6. His eyes never leave floor, face is a big frown of concentration; he looks a little scared, like he wishes he hadn't come today if he had to be late.

Now review your notes and, in your mind, examine that walk again. Try to develop a general impression of the way the person walked, of the mood he or she was in.

Write a sentence in which you describe the action. What was the impression you gained of this person as you watched him or her in action?

The notes recorded above might yield a general sentence such as this one:

The man slipped quietly into the room, trying to get to his seat unnoticed.

or

Obviously embarrassed, the man slipped quietly through the door, trying to get to his seat without being noticed.

or

> The man opened the door very quietly and walked to his seat, trying not to call attention to himself.

Write your sentence on scratch paper. You might need to make several attempts before you are satisfied with the sentence.

Concentrate most on expressing the action and the mood of the person. Grammar, spelling, and punctuation can be corrected later on.

Now look again at the notes. Select important observations on the entry, the walk, and on the act of sitting down. Look especially for items that will show the person's attitude or mood as he or she enters the room. Write two or three sentences describing these actions and expressing the mood of the person.

The notes might yield sentences such as the following:

> He eases the door open very slowly, and he tries not to make any noise as he lets it close behind him.

> He walks very slowly toward a desk. His steps are very short, and he puts his feet down very carefully and very quietly.

> He sits down very quickly, just flops into the desk because he wants nobody to notice him.

Now write your sentences on the scratch paper.

Finally, review the notes one more time. Try to find small details that will develop a clear picture of the person's mood and attitudes.

The smaller items in the notes are the best source for these details.

Two or three sentences that capture these small impressions will round out the description:

> His eyes are fixed on the floor as he slips through the door. He lets the door close without a sound and clenches his books tightly. Sitting down, he slips the text open on the desk and sneaks a look at the next desk to get the page number. Locating the page, he smiles eagerly at the teacher, pretending he had been there all the time.

Write these last sentences on the same sheet of paper with your other sentences.

You have now written a general sentence describing an action, two or three sentences describing the larger elements of action, and two or three that fill in smaller details. Now combine these sentences into a paragraph. Use the general sentence first, then the larger elements, and finally close the paragraph with the sentences that convey smaller details. The sentences written in the examples can be combined into the following paragraph:

SNEAKIN' IN LATE

The man slips quietly inside the door, trying to get to his seat without being noticed. He eases the door closed behind him and moves slowly, one careful step at a time, into the room. He begins to crouch as he approaches the desk and glides quickly into the seat, pushing the desk a little out of place in his haste. His eyes look only at the floor, his hands hold tight to his books. He opens the text on the desk, finds the page, and mission accomplished, smiles eagerly at the teacher, pretending he has been there all along.

This exercise in describing action ought to prepare you for the work needed in Assignment 3.

Describe a brief event from your life. Let the account make clear the importance of the event.

Select a subject. Use two guidelines for choosing an event for this assignment:

First.   The event ought to be interesting to you, the writer. It might be exciting, amusing, embarrassing, or frightening. It might be a very pleasant experience. Whatever your choice, be sure that you are able to generate a good bit of interest in the event.

ONLY IF THE SUBJECT INTERESTS THE WRITER CAN IT HAVE ANY HOPE OF INTERESTING THE READER.

Second. The event ought to be fairly fresh in your memory. The details must stand out in your mind, or must be readily available for you to recall them. This guideline probably rules out anything so emotional that you do not want to recall the details.

ONLY AMPLE KNOWLEDGE OF THE SUBJECT WILL ALLOW YOU TO MAKE IT VIVID AND INTERESTING TO YOUR READER.

Review your possibilities and select an action that meets the two requirements.

Favorite topics for this assignment include:

High school graduation—receiving the diploma.

The first meeting with a special person.

Some action in a sport or game, such as an exciting rally in a tennis match.

A frightening or embarrassing moment.

The steps in the assignment are almost exactly the same as the steps for Assignment 2. After you select a subject, let your imagination work through the action. Next, record the details of the action, exactly as you did in the classroom exercise. After you have recorded all the details and have arranged them in chronological order, write several sentences describing the action. Then write an opening sentence to set the scene and a concluding sentence to record some of your feelings. Set the work aside for awhile and then copy the opening sentence, the action, and the conclusion neatly, so that you can turn it in to your instructor.

Before you write your own paper, it might be useful to read the following examples, two by students, and one by a professional writer.

MOTORCYCLE RACING: HOW TO TAKE A TURN

by Kevin Kraus

As you sit on the bike you keep your eyes fixed on the next point of challenge along the course. This time it is a tight left-handed turn connected to a long straightaway. The turn has an embankment, like that of the Indy 500 track. It also has a berm high up at the top with a few ridges halfway up. At the bottom of the turn the dirt is not dirt but mud, and with the passing of many bikes around it, it has many deep ruts. The berm is powder and looks solid, but could give away, the midsection is good but has few places to get extra traction. You approach the turn and as you do so you change your body position, slide up onto the gas tank to give the bike more stability. Your gloved hands pull in the clutch and front brake levers while your feet in their special boots activate the rear brake and click down a gear. You do this while the rest of your body gets into position, lean the bike over, keeping the body vertical, tilt the head, put out your foot for extra stability, pull back on the throttle, tilt the bike some more. The tires dig into the ruts as you choose the line you think to be the fastest, your foot slides along the mud helping to keep the bike stable. You tilt the bike more, add more throttle, click up a gear, slide back onto the seat, bring the bike back up to a vertical position as you exit the turn and go flying down the straightaway. The total time it took to execute the turn. . . just over one second.

THE LONG SKATE

by Tom Neal

I caught the puck on the end of my stick as it came careening across the ice. I immediately dug my skates into the ice and pumped as hard as I could. As I crossed my own blue line the opposing left-winger came at me intent on laying me on the ice. He made the fatal mistake of watching my stick and not my body. I gave a quick fake to the left with my stick and then I quickly moved to the right allowing him to glide by me with a groan. I could hear the screech of the skates on the ice as he stopped to turn around and chase me. As I crossed the center line in full-stride I knew a goal had to be scored on the play or that would be the end of our team for another season. I was skating hard. I could feel my chest pads every time I inhaled. Behind me I could hear the biting of skates on ice and the heavy panting of the players behind me trying to catch-up. Ahead of me I could see the defensemen skating backwards, positioning themselves to halt my advance. As I swooped by the first defenseman I felt a surge of confidence. There was only one man between me and the goalie. As I maneuvered around them he unexpectedly stuck out his hip. I went over him in a mid-air cartwheel. I lay on the ice on my side with the defenseman lying on the ice behind me put there by the impact of my weight. Miraculously the puck was there beside me as I got up and headed toward the goal. I took a low shot at the net and hit the post. To the goalie's and my astonishment the puck came back to me. I barely put it in the top corner as the goalie was out of position. The buzzer ending the game went off and I could not help thinking that it was about time. As I skated behind the net, stick held high, I felt a relief knowing that we had won the game and an excitement at scoring that important goal. I realized that I had the ability to do what I was required and that I could keep up with the rest of the players.

THE EIGHTY-YARD RUN

by Irwin Shaw

The pass was high and wide and he jumped for it, feeling it slap flatly against his hands, as he shook his hips to throw off the halfback who was diving at him. The center floated by, his hands desperately brushing Darling's knee as Darling

picked his feet up high and delicately ran over a blocker and an opposing lineman in a jumble on the ground near the scrimmage line. He had ten yards in
the clear and picked up speed, breathing easily, feeling his thigh pads rising and
falling against his legs, listening to the sound of cleats behind him, pulling away
from them, watching the other backs heading him off toward the sideline, the
whole picture, the men closing in on him, the blockers fighting for position,
the ground he had to cross, all suddenly clear in his head, for the first time in
his life not a meaningless confusion of men, sounds, speed. He smiled a little
to himself as he ran, holding the ball lightly in front of him with his two hands,
his knees pumping high, his hips twisting in the almost girlish run of a back in
a broken field. The first halfback came at him and he fed him his leg, then
swung at the last moment, took the shock of the man's shoulder without break-
ing stride, ran right through him, his cleats biting securely into the turf. There
was only the safety man now, coming warily at him, his arms crooked, hands
spread. Darling tucked the ball in, spurted at him, driving hard, hurling himself along, all two hundred pounds bunched into controlled attack. He was
sure he was going to get past the safety man. Without thought, his arms and
legs working beautifully together, he headed right for the safety man, stiff-
armed him, feeling blood spurt instantaneously from the man's nose onto his
hand, seeing his face go awry, head turned, mouth pulled to one side. He
pivoted away, keeping the arm locked, dropping the safety man as he ran easily
toward the goal line, with the drumming of cleats diminishing behind him.

COMMENTARY

This brief passage, the opening paragraph of a fine short story by
Irwin Shaw, demonstrates clearly three very important techniques
for describing action. Perhaps the most noteworthy aspect of this
passage is the great attention Shaw pays to the details of the action.
Shaw describes here a single play in football practice, an action
that covers eighty yards and no more than ten seconds in time.
Notice the number of details in the first two sentences:

1. The pass and the jump to catch it.
2. The flat slap of the ball against the hands.
3. The shake of the hips to throw off the halfback.
4. The dive of the halfback.
5. The center floating by.
6. The hands of the center brushing Darling's knee.
7. The feet picked up high.
8. The delicate steps over the blocker and opposing lineman.

Shaw shows us eight specific, distinct pictures of parts of the action. He focuses our attention on small, isolated, but very important parts of the whole picture of the action. This action involves twenty-two men, eleven on each team, but Shaw shows us only very specific details of selected parts of the action. He does not try to present the entire picture. Notice in the third sentence how the use of details appeals to our five senses:

breathing easily
feeling his thigh pads rising and falling
the sound of cleats

The first two sentences also use this type of appeal in the use of the words "feeling (the ball) slap flatly against his hands," an appeal to the sense of touch and to the sense of hearing, and in the center's hands "desperately brushing" Darling's knee. Even more often in these first sentences, Shaw appeals to our sense of sight, to produce a vivid picture of the action. The runner shakes his hips, the half-back dives at the runner, the center floats by, the hands are desperate in their reaching for the runner, the feet move high and the steps are delicate as he moves over the tangle of blocker and runner. The tangle itself represents another appeal to the eyesight, even though it is not described as part of the action, but is simply identified as being part of that particular focus.

The essence of what Shaw does here is his selection of a rather large number of small details. He enables us to focus our attention on these rather than on the larger picture of the field and the general movement of the two groups of eleven players. You are familiar with this difference in focus if you have watched any sport on television. A view from the top of the stadium that shows the entire field and the patterns of the specific play, the initial formation, and the movements of all the players, provides us with one kind of knowledge, the overall movement and direction of the play. Such a view is a favorite of coaches and commentators who want to demonstrate how and why a specific play worked or didn't work. We gain mostly technical knowledge from such a perspective.

But for a sense of being there, for the down-inside feeling of what it was like to make that run, we need to see the small details, details that focus on things felt, heard, seen, smelled, and thought by the runner. Close-up camera work, shot in slow motion, is what we need in order to get the feeling of the play, if we are to understand what the experience was like.

In addition to his very close attention to detail, Shaw also employs action words to carry the sense of the passage. Count the number of words that specifically identify actions, and you will find a large number of them: jumped, felt, shook, and so on. Only three times does Shaw rely on verbs that are forms like *was* or *were*, forms that stand still rather than provide motion. He uses the word *was* only at the beginning of the passage and twice at a point where there is a transition in the action: "There was only the safety man," "He was sure he was going to get past the safety man." Note that the last use of *was* is part of a longer verb form, "was going to get," and so this is in reality an action word. He does not try to use these static forms to convey a sense of action.

A third basic method for portraying action, for providing a sense of motion or speed, is the use of *-ing* forms of the verb to add pieces of the action to a shorter sentence. Look at the third sentence, "He had ten yards in the clear and picked up speed," to which Shaw adds five *-ing* forms:

breathing
feeling
listening
pulling away
watching

These words describe the actions of the runner. In addition, Shaw uses five more *-ing* forms that attach themselves to other players on the field. If you examine the core of short thoughts that make up this longer sentence, you read something like this list of very short sentences:

He had ten yards in the clear.
He picked up speed.
He breathed easily.
He felt his thigh pads.
He listened to the sound.
He pulled away from them.
He watched the other backs.

We could scarcely bear to read this series of short sentences if Shaw had left them in this form. Only when he converts several of them to *-ing* phrases and constructs one long, flowing sentence do we get a real feel for the movement and action of the play.

There are many other devices Shaw uses to make this action vivid, but the basic steps are to

1. Use close-up focus, providing many details that appeal to the senses.
2. Use action verbs and other action words, and avoid using forms such as *was* and *were*.
3. Use *-ing* phrases to add to the flow of the passage.

SUGGESTED EXERCISES TO ACCOMPANY THE SHAW PASSAGE

You might find it useful to copy this passage, or a few sentences from it, word-for-word into your journal. Read it over aloud several times to establish the sounds, rhythms, and constructions in your mind.

It would also be useful to take another action, such as chopping a tree, washing a car, or making a play in baseball and describe it, following as closely as you can the methods Shaw uses in his passage.

ASSIGNMENT 4.

Writing About an Idea

The fourth in this series of short assigments focuses your attention on an idea, and asks you to write a brief reaction to that idea. Tell the reader whether you agree or disagree with the idea and explain why.

In a fine film on his life and works, Woody Allen, the comedian and writer, says

It is important for the writer, the artist, to fail. Or maybe not to fail, but to be willing to fail, to run the risk of failure by pushing out into untried areas, uncharted territory, so to speak. To avoid working only in areas where he knows of strength, where success is a reasonably sure thing. A person who is not willing to fail will never know his limitations and never develop any new capabilities. He'll remain always in the same old rut.

The following article expresses pretty much the same idea. It says "Failure is a beneficial experience, necessary to growth and development, unavoidable and even desirable if one is to discover capabilities and develop both personality and skills to the fullest extent possible."

NEED TO FAIL? IT COULD BE STEP TO SUCCESS

by Cheryl Pilate

The most successful people have suffered the most monumental failures.

And those who think they've never failed don't have any reason to be smug. They're often the biggest failures of all.

"Every person who is a success is also a failure, and every person who is a failure is also a success," said Bob Atkison, clinical psychologist and assistant director of the Wichita Guidance Center.

"If you're not failing pretty regularly," he adds, "you're working so far below your potential, you're a failure anyway."

Failure is ubiquitous, but that doesn't mean we're comfortable with it. We avoid admitting failure and avoid association with those who do.

After all, we're the folks who "dress for success" and "aim for the winner's circle."

We either want to be a rising star or hitch our wagon to one.

And if we want to add more oomph to our image, more zeal to our spiel, we get pumped up at "positive thinking" or "win" rallies.

No one wants to be a dud, a loser, a washout or a has-been. We may not all aspire to fortune and fame, but neither do we want flop and fiasco.

"In our culture, failure is to be avoided," said Brooke Collison, associate professor of student personnel and guidance at Wichita State University.

According to Atkison, anyone who sets goals is destined to have some failures.

"If you're working, trying to achieve, trying to change things, you're going to fail," he said.

Many folks hide from their failures or refuse to acknowledge them. Usually, said Collison, they depend on two common coping mechanisms: denial and/or blame.

"They say things like: 'I didn't care, anyway I wasn't trying.' Or, 'It's his fault,'" explained Collison.

Atkison said these exercises in self-deception can be dangerous, or at least a hindrance to future success.

"To ignore failure and your part in it," he said, "leads to making the same mistakes over and over again."

"I use everday failures as well as big failures to evaluate how well I'm doing things."

And, in assessing failure and success, Collison and Atkison agree that we should depend on internal judgments, not those of others (though this doesn't mean we should be completely oblivious to external standards).

Atkison said it's only natural to feel pain and disappointment when we fail. If we blithely rush onward after a major setback, he said, we haven't been honest with ourselves.

"If something is important and we don't achieve it, we're going to feel awful." But, he added, we usually throw ourselves as soon as possible into a new task because the best medicine for failure is another shot at success.

"Failure is always the first step in success; success is always the first step in failure," Atkison explained.

"I have never considered failure to be anything but a guidepost."

This idea seems perfectly reasonable when a successful writer/comedian/actor says it. It sounds good when a newspaper writer quotes an expert on the subject. But it does not seem to be quite as easily managed when we begin to talk of our failures. Probably we all have the same reaction. We're taught to avoid failure at any cost. People cheat on tests and buy term papers to avoid failing in school. Failure is almost always made out to be a bad and destructive experience. We either avoid failure, refuse to admit that it exists, or blame the failure on other people.

Allen and the experts quoted in the article by Pilate agree: failure comes to everyone, or to everyone who is trying to accomplish anything. Since it will come to us if we are normal, active people, we must learn to see failure in a positive light, to convert its effects from a destructive force to constructive experience. How can we do this? Write about the idea. Start by writing a simple reaction. In about a half page, state your reaction to the idea of failing. Pick a failure from your recent past. Discuss your reaction to the event and its outcome. What have you learned from that experience? What have you learned from other unsuccessful efforts? Go beyond "I learned not to do that any more." You probably learned of an area in which you are not extremely strong, or you may have learned to approach certain types of experience from a different direction, to take a different approach or tactic in the particular circumstance. Write about a strategy for coping with failure. How can you approach failure constructively? The next time a project or a relationship falls apart, what strategies will you employ to gain from the experience?

Finally, try to define on paper what your attitude toward failure ought to be and what effect failure ought to have on you.

After you have done this background writing, your assignment is to write a paragraph in response to Allen's statement that it is important for the artist (for everyone) to fail. Read the following typical responses to that idea:

"Failure is important," says the famous comedian/writer. "Easy for you to say," I respond. "You have no teachers, no average to maintain, no parents to satisfy, no future to build." I can't afford to fail, at least not in school. I must play it safe, get the work out, get the best possible grades by doing what I think the teacher expects. I know this policy keeps me pretty much in the same track, that I never get to experiment or fool around in any areas where success is not assured, but I can't afford anything else.

"It is important to fail, to be willing to fail, to put yourself into situations where the success of the venture is not assured because your skills and competencies in that area are already proven. You need to get out, to move into new areas, areas in which you have not tested yourself so that you can discover new skills and strengths." I think that is a fair summary of the article, and a fair paraphrase of what Woody Allen says in the movie. It sounds like a reasonable idea, one that almost anyone would agree with—in theory. But when it comes to putting the idea into practice, I'm not sure. If I do something simple, like trying a new sport, I feel really dumb because I don't pick it up quickly. If I take a course in a subject that's totally unfamiliar to me, I might get lost and either fail or have to withdraw. The risks are too great, my average will suffer, my chances for transferring to a good school will drop, my father will tell me I am a jerk. I just don't believe that I can take the risks that Allen suggests. I'd better stick to the safe, sure path.

How did these writers produce these paragraphs? What steps did they follow, and what kind of work did they do before they set these paragraphs on paper? The steps in the writing process are the same for any kind of project:

- Select or identify the subject.
- Write down what you know about the subject.
- Settle on a specific statement.
- Select items out of your knowledge to illustrate your statement.
- Choose an order for presenting the information.
- Write a draft.

The unusual aspect of this assignment is that you must state a re-action and an opinion on a subject which you may not have thought about very much before now. You are not recalling an event; you are not observing an action or a place. The information is not out there in front of you, available as either memory or observation. Somehow the work on this assignment seems to be different.

In one sense the work on this project is the same as the work on the earlier projects. The process you used on the earlier assignments will work on this project also. One step after the other, with a bit of retracing, will get the job done. But there is a difference, and the difference lies in the collection of information, in the answer to the question, "What do I know about this subject?" The difference works itself out like this.

When you begin to write down information on the subject, you will be doing two things. First, you will be recording your immedi-ate reaction to the idea, probably as it has developed out of your past experiences of success and failure, and out of your reactions to these successes and failures. But as you write, you will be doing something in addition to recording. You will be doing a kind of thinking on paper. You will be expressing your opinions and reac-tions as you hold them at the moment, but you will also be formu-lating additional, perhaps even new opinions, as you write. Writing, in this situation, is very much a way of learning. You have an opin-ion, and you record it. In the act of recording it, you also develop new opinions, because your mind makes additional connections to other ideas and opinions. Some of these connections will be totally new to you. All these connections occur in the act of writ-ing. Writing about a subject helps you to formulate new ideas on that subject.

Since it is the act of writing that fosters learning, it stands to reason that you must write extensively and freely if you are going to produce anything valuable out of this assignment.

A Few Suggestions

1. Begin by writing, not by sitting and thinking.

   You probably tend to wait for worthwhile thoughts and don't write until you get them. Don't wait. Writing—any writing—will produce thoughts. Put something on paper, and worthwhile ideas will follow.

2. Let your writing ramble.

    Write a definition of failure; write about a person who failed; write about a time when you failed; write about a time when you didn't undertake something because you were afraid you might fail.

3. Be a little philosophical.

    Write a definition of failing and a definition of being a failure. Differentiate between failing in an individual undertaking and being, generally speaking, a failure.

4. After you have rambled and philosophized, try to express, in a single sentence your reaction and your attitude. This sentence is the goal of all the free-writing, but if it doesn't come easily, don't despair. Just keep on writing and trying, and eventually you will formulate an idea.

When you have written a sentence stating your idea, you are ready to begin writing the paragraph explaining the idea to your reader. The short papers you have written for the previous assignments have provided a built-in form for the final version of the assignments. The three assignments were based on observation or recollection, and so the content was dictated by the collection of details you put together. A set of directions can contain only points involved in those directions. "Go from here to there and then on to the next place and so on." A *description* contains the details of what you have seen. A *narrative* describes an action using details from the event. "This happened and so on."

Just as the content of each of the earlier essays was set by the observation or recollection, the order of presentation was set by the nature of the essay. A set of instructions has a built in order—Step 1, Step 2—in your earlier assignment, locations on a campus. "Turn right at the bottom of the stairs and then go to the door across the patio." Giving those directions out of order would pretty well destroy the usefulness of the directions. Zigzagging back and forth across the campus is no way to get from one place to the next in good time. Telling a story or painting a word-picture in zigzag fashion is just as destructive to the story or the picture. A story probably works best when told from beginning to end; a description goes best when the eye is led in some orderly fashion around the scene. Thus both the order and the details of content for the first three papers were established almost automatically.

In this paper—a paper discussing an idea—order and content do not automatically suggest themselves. Instead, there is an infinite number of possibilities open to you as writer. Later on, as you become a more practiced writer, you will want to try out some of those possibilities. For now, the easiest way to develop a paragraph on an idea is to use a very simple formula.

First, write out your statement, the one that expresses the idea for the paper.

> I understand Allen's statement, "It is important to fail," but right now I can't afford to take the risks.

Now, write a few sentences of definition and discussion. Explain Allen's statement and discuss the reasons why you cannot take any risks at this time.

> Allen means that it is important to try projects or activities that are new, where success is not assured. If I don't do this, take this risk, then I will never know whether I can do that thing. Moving into new, uncharted territory produces growth, even if the move is not successful. Risk or failure, even failure itself, brings growth.

> I can't take the risks now. A failure in school would mean a lower average, would mean a lot of static from my father, who doesn't believe failure is ever acceptable, might mean I miss out on transferring to State or some other good school.

Then, after you have explained yourself, it is a good idea to give your reader a concrete example of what you mean. You need to supply a specific instance in which failure or risk of failure opens the opportunity for growth.

> My Aunt Jo followed Allen's advice, even though she had never heard of him, when she went back to college last year. At that time she had two kids in high school and could have made an awful fool of herself if the whole thing had failed. But she got up her courage and went back, and now she's almost ready to take a job on her city's newspaper. That risk opened up a whole new world for her.

For the second part, a shorter example might do.

> I'd like to take a course in music, simply because I love it, but I can't because the grade might turn out bad, or I might have to use too much time to make a good grade, and I can't afford any low grades if I want to transfer. So the risk of a bad grade in that course, plus the loss of time I need to

use on my chemistry and math simply means I can't take any risks at this time.

The formula for the content of the paragraph should include

a. A single sentence stating the idea of the paragraph.
b. Some definition and discussion of what you mean by the idea.
c. An example or two used to clarify the discussion.

The discussion for this idea comes in two parts:

Allen means . . .
I can't . . .

and the example really is in two parts also:

My Aunt Jo . . .
I'd like to take . . .

Certainly the most obvious and straightforward order is to provide the controlling sentence first:

I understand what Allen means . . .
but I can't afford to take risks now.

Then provide both discussion and example for the first half of the controlling sentence.

Allen means . . .
My Aunt Jo . . .

And then provide discussion and examples for the second half.

I can't take the risks now . . .
I'd like to take a course in music . . .

Read the paragraph written in that order.

Failure may be good for Woody Allen, but at this time I just don't think I can afford to take any risks. The idea Allen presents is clear: each of us needs to test various areas of our personalities and our skills so that we can find out what we can do. I watched my Aunt Jo start to attend college at forty-four. She tried a completely new experience and did well at it, and so she has grown a great deal. But I am in my freshman year and I want to transfer to State in the School of Business, which demands better than 3.2 grade point average. I can't afford much experimentation or risk now. Suppose I did take that special music course or try some new job. I might make a low grade, or I might use so much time that my grades in other subjects would drop. I'd like to be able to do that, but right now, I'm just not able to take the risk. I'll save the experiments for later on, when I'm better-established.

Paragraphs:
Quality and Quantity

The short essays you have written so far in this course have in reality been rather long paragraphs. While each essay makes a complete statement and thus can stand alone, the paragraphs should have the same qualities found in the paragraphs of a longer essay. The following definition and discussion will help you to see the qualities a paragraph should possess.

A paragraph is a unit of composition; that is, it is one of the ways we mark off sections in the development of a written piece. We use sentences, paragraphs, chapters, and even volumes to mark off divisions within a written work. A sentence contains a thought or single statement about an idea. A paragraph ordinarily contains several sentences expressing and developing an idea. Chapters are groups of ideas focused on a general theme or topic. For our purposes, since you will be writing short essays, the paragraph is the major division for written work.

Centuries ago when the Greeks began to write extensively, they wrote without any divisions into sentences or paragraphs. All written work carried on line after line without any break or division to help the reader keep track of thoughts and ideas. Finally, writers began to place dots (·) in the middle of the space following the word where a thought ended. Today, we use the same mark (.) to show the ends of sentences. We simply put our mark on the line of writing or type rather than in the middle of the space. Later, another helpful person began to mark off groups of sentences that treated a single idea; this writer placed a mark (¶) in the margin to the left of the place where discussion of the new idea began. We still use this sign as a proofreader's mark to indicate the start of a new paragraph.

There is one sense, then, in which sentences and paragraphs perform similar functions. They both mark off a kind of section for the reader. The sentence marks off a group of words that are a single thought. A paragraph marks a group of sentences that make up the discussion of an idea.

None of this marking is intended to be secret, or tricky, or even difficult. The writer marks the beginning of a paragraph by indenting a few spaces from the left margin, and leaves an indentation at the other end of the paragraph following the end of the last sentence. The sentences between the indentations—one paragraph—are simply the writer's way of saying, "The sentences in here talk about the same idea. When you finish reading this paragraph, file the idea mentally and go on to the next paragraph. You will be better able to control the reading if you do so."

By definition,

A PARAGRAPH IS A GROUP OF SENTENCES SET OFF AT THE BEGINNING AND END BY WHITE SPACE INDENTATIONS.

A PARAGRAPH PROVIDES THE READER WITH DEVELOPMENT OF AN IDEA WITHIN THE WHOLE COMPOSITION. THE DEVELOPMENT IS SINGLE, FOCUSED AND COMPLETE.

A PARAGRAPH DEALS WITH ONE IDEA.

A PARAGRAPH PROVIDES ENOUGH INFORMATION TO TELL THE READER EVERYTHING NECESSARY TO UNDERSTAND THE IDEA WITHIN ITS CONTEXT IN THE ESSAY.

This definition provides a clear statement of one of the important qualities of a paragraph:

A PARAGRAPH TREATS ONE, AND ONLY ONE, IDEA, OR PART OF AN IDEA, WITHIN THE ENTIRE WRITTEN COMPOSITION.

Again, there isn't any trick here. The paragraph handles only one item at a time. This way, the reader is able to keep track of the whole composition—letter, story, argument, discussion—by dividing it into manageable parts. Paragraphs that contain two or three different discussions are ineffective because the reader can't click a single unit into a mental file at the end of the paragraph. Two ideas taken at the same time can't be managed as easily as they might be if the writer presented them one after the other in some kind of sequence.

You can easily grasp the idea of singleness if you look at the topics for the first four assignments. Suppose that the first topic, "Give directions to three places on your campus: the library, the English Department, and the bookstore," started off with a set of instructions.

> To go quickly from this classroom to the library, turn right as you leave the door and walk down the stairs, go outside the building, and take the walk that goes past the gym. The gymnasium was built in 1976 in honor of Walter W. Samuels, a founder of the college, whose family donated...

"Wait," you would respond, "I was prepared to find directions to three locations on this campus, but I get confused when the writer begins to give me the history of yet another building."

Or imagine the writer of a description of a beautiful farm who begins the description by showing you horses in a pasture and suddenly moves to a discussion of the care and feeding of these horses:

> As beautiful as those horses are, keeping them healthy is almost a full-time job. They do not eat what is good for them; instead, just like humans they can be counted on to eat foods that are horribly fattening if they can find them.

"I'm not ready at this point," you say, "for a discussion of the eating habits of horses. I'm expecting a visual tour of a pasture, orchards, a pond, and a barnyard, but I can't file the information on what horses eat under any of those categories. It just confuses me. Talk about the horses and their diet later, if you want, but don't do it when I expect word-pictures of the farm."

Read this paragraph written as a response to the fourth assignment, to Woody Allen's comments about the importance of being willing to fail.

> Allen's comments in the film, that people do not grow unless they try new experiences and perhaps fail in the attempt, really interest me a great deal. I have watched my cousin Seth in a number of those growth experiences. He tries all sorts of wild schemes and fails in every one of them. Just last

year he spent two weeks trying to develop a milking stool with a heated
seat for people who had to milk cows on cold mornings. He didn't sell a
one, because everytime somebody sat down on it, the darn thing shocked
them. Probably he didn't know enough about electricity to know that pressure on the heating element would cause a short and shock the user. This
problem almost defeated the man who invented the electric stove also. The
element worked just fine, heated up just beautifully until he put a pot of
water on it. Then the weight of the pan shorted out the electricity and
ruined the pan. . .

"Stop. How did we get from crazy Cousin Seth and his heated
milking stool to the problems involved in the invention of the
electric range?" "Easily enough," is the answer. The problems
with the two inventions were the same, so the writer slid quickly
from one to the other. The connection is logical, but the discussion
of the two different inventions ought not to occur in the same
paragraph. Two ideas in the same paragraph confuse the mental
filing system of the reader. One thing at a time is a much more
easily handled presentation.

The second major quality of a paragraph is most clearly expressed
in the question that automatically pops into your mind whenever
you are given a writing assignment.

HOW LONG SHOULD THIS PIECE BE? HOW MUCH IS ENOUGH?

The answer is similar to the answer Abraham Lincoln gave the man
who questioned him about his height. "How long should a man's
legs be?" "Long enough to reach the ground." And that's how
long a paragraph should be—long enough. But for what? Long
enough for what? And how long is long enough?

You can answer the question in this way: a paragraph ought to
to be long enough to express what is needed in the composition.
And what is needed in the composition is information on the idea
within the paragraph. The reader ought to get enough information
from the paragraph to learn everything needed to understand the
essay. A paragraph should supply sufficient information on the
idea so that the reader can cope with the rest of the composition;
or, the paragraph should supply enough information so that the
reader will not have questions left at the end of the paragraph about
the connection this idea makes with the rest of the composition.
Think of the set of directions you wrote at the beginning of this
term. If the directions took your reader only halfway to the library

and then began the directions to the bookstore, your reader would have some questions to ask you, if not while he or she read the instructions, then certainly if he or she tried to follow them. Your paragraph would not be long enough, because it would leave the reader with the question, "Now which way do I go?"

It is probably more useful to think of complete development rather than about length. Length—125 words, 183 words—is simply an arbitrary figure, something pulled out of the air. Instead of asking "Is this paragraph long enough?" ask, "Does it say enough—enough for my reader to know all that is needed about the idea, enough to be useful within the rest of the essay or paper?" Complete development is a more important goal than reaching a certain number of words.

Check this idea out against the compositions you have written recently. In a description of a street, it is possible to provide a general overview

> The street, lined with old brick buildings, swung down toward the river and came to a dead end in the park, a large splash of green dotted with cherry trees that bloomed a glorious pink in the spring. All the buildings were of that wonderfully warm old brick so popular as reclaimed brick in stylish subdivisions, except this brick was the original material and had been weathering and softening on this street for almost a hundred years.

or to give an incredibly detailed technical description, of the sort a tax assessor might produce:

> The street has seventeen buildings on it, eight on the left and nine on the right. All but one are commercial buildings, the one is a small hotel. The construction of the buildings is brick. . .and so on, building by building.

Perhaps you begin to get the idea. Each description is correct, each is useful in its own context, and yet they differ markedly from each other. The length of the second paragraph would far exceed the length of the first, because the second one must provide many kinds of visual and technical details for official purposes. The first can be much shorter because it is designed only to produce a general visual impression.

Look briefly at the short narrative paragraph (Assignment 3) you wrote earlier. A narrative paragraph of about 150 words on the subject of high school graduation presents a problem typical of narration. Suppose that you write such a paragraph, deciding that you will describe the day. At which point should the story start?

>When the alarm rings?
>After breakfast?
>When you arrive at the auditorium?
>When you start across the stage to get the diploma?

Any of those starting points is workable, but the point you choose for a beginning will depend on

a. The point of the story.
b. The details your reader must see to understand that point.

It is possible to to give great attention to getting dressed for the ceremony and trying on the cap and gown. You might also include details of the drive from your home to the auditorium. You might talk about getting in line to march into the auditorium. All of these descriptions could be used to make your point.

But one specific event surely must be included: the walk across the stage and the actual presentation of the diploma. The choice of including or leaving out other parts of the day depends on the length of the project—if you can write 750 words, you can surely include more details than you would if you were writing 150 words on the same subject. If you are limited to a short paragraph of about one page, then the right strategy is to select the most important part of the whole event and concentrate on that, providing just enough background to tell your reader what was happening. Read this sample paragraph and notice where the focus of the action is, and notice where the writer gives you the most detail:

>Graduation would be just like any other day, I had thought. What was the big deal anyway? Just getting the diploma, and just from high school at that. Same people, same old auditorium, no big deal. I'd be cool through it all, not like those dumb girls who cry at every little thing. I got dressed, tried on my cap and gown and let my mother take a bunch of pictures. Then I drove to the school. We all stood around for a while and then organized so we could march in and sit in the right order. The whole thing went down smoothly enough. Songs, speeches, the major speaker, some politician from upstate, none of those bothered me. Finally, we stood and began to file across the stage one at a time. Finally, they called my name, with my stupid middle name included. I took the diploma, and shook hands with Mr. Hampton. As I came down the steps from the stage, as my foot hit the auditorium floor, something hit me. Graduated. GRADUATED.

My hands shook just a little. My throat tightened. Twelve long years completed. A whole new world opening before me. Graduated.

In a paragraph of discussion or explanation, a paragraph which attempts to state an idea and explain it—such as the paragraph explaining your reaction to the Woody Allen statement on failure—the use of the three-part formula for paragraph development will almost certainly guarantee that you have written a well-developed paragraph. Start with a single sentence in which you state the idea of the paragraph. This is often called a topic sentence. Follow the topic sentence with two or three sentences, or more if necessary, defining the terms in the sentence. Don't use a formal definition unless you are involved in a rather formal paper; simply write out an explanation of what the terms in the sentence mean. Follow that definition with a discussion or application of the idea. Show how the idea works, discuss its importance, and limit it in some way. Tell your reader what must be known about the idea in order to understand it. Finally, provide a very concrete illustration of the statement. You can select a true incident or a hypothetical example that gives details as to the meaning of the idea. Open the illustration by saying, "Once," or "Just last April," or if the example is hypothetical, "Imagine that. . ." Here is a topic sentence for a paragraph discussing safety problems at major intersections in a town:

> Some of the intersections in this city are engineered or designed in ways that seem to cause traffic hazards.

A discussion of the same statement:

> One problem is that traffic patterns must cross each other and cars are forced to move across the path of other vehicles to make a turn or take another direction. A second type of problem occurs when the right of way is not clearly defined when cars are turning left across a line of traffic. The third important hazard occurs when cars merge into fast moving traffic on expressways that do not have an adequate approach lane on which to develop speed.

Finally, an example of each type of hazard:

> Cars coming off I-11 are forced to merge with cars on Eighth Avenue, and any car needing to turn right from Eighth onto West Avenue must cross the path of cars moving off the exit ramp of the interstate.

When Northside avenue crosses Jones Boulevard most of the traffic comes out of the subdivision on the west side of the boulevard and turns left. Any car crossing the boulevard moving west must face all those cars turning left. Even though westbound traffic has the right of way, those turning seem to take the right of way because there are so many more cars coming out of the subdivision.

All the access roads onto the old part of the downtown thruway have no merging lane for cars entering the thruway to use to build up speed. Each car must stop and then start from there trying to build up speed quickly to enter into the flow of traffic. A car unable to gain the proper amount of speed runs the risk of being hit from behind.

The discussion of the specific problems and the concrete examples of the problems can be arranged in at least two ways, but in either arrangement the complete paragraph will provide a topic statement, discussion and explanation, and examples.

Some of the intersections in this city are engineered in ways that seem to cause traffic hazards. One problem is that traffic patterns must cross each other, and cars are forced to move across the path of other vehicles to make a turn or take another direction. Cars coming off I-11 are forced to merge with cars on Eighth Avenue, and any car needing to turn right from Eighth onto West Avenue must cross the path of cars moving off the exit ramp of the interstate. A second type of problem occurs if the right of way is not clearly defined when cars are turning left across a line of traffic. When Northside Avenue crosses Jones Boulevard, most of the traffic comes out of the subdivision on the west side of the boulevard and turns left. Any car crossing the boulevard moving west must face all those cars turning left. Even though west-bound traffic has the right of way, those turning seem to take the right of way because there are so many more cars coming out of the subdivision. The third important hazard occurs when cars merge into fast moving traffic on expressways that do not have an adequate approach lane on which to develop speed. All the access roads onto the old part of the downtown thruway have no merging lane for cars entering the thruway to use to build speed. Each car must stop and then start from there trying to build up speed quickly to enter the flow of traffic. A car unable to gain the proper amount of speed runs the risk of being hit from behind.

You have now completed the first unit of this text, four short writing assignments, several exercises in sentence combining and development, and some very informal writing in a journal. The goals for this unit are rather simple. First, you should now feel much more relaxed about writing, and more confident of your ability to find something to say and say it understandably. Second, you should now understand at least a little bit about the process of writing a paper, and you should be aware of some of the qualities of a well-written paragraph. Finally, by writing on a regular basis in your journal, you should have collected some materials that will be useful when you move into the second unit.

WRITING EXERCISE 1

1. Write the word REGISTRATION as many times as you can within 90 seconds.
2. Now write *about* registration for two minutes.
3. Record your thoughts and reactions as you left home this morning. Give yourself two minutes.
4. Fill 5 lines on a sheet of notebook paper with the word WRITING.
5. Write a few sentences in which you discuss your abilities in writing.

Combine the following short sentences into one longer sentence.

The weather was hot.
It was rainy.

The men searched for the buried treasure.
The tall woman searched for the buried treasure.

We walked down the trail.
We looked at the beautiful waterfall.

Journal Writing

A suggestion for a journal entry will occur at the end of each exercise. Feel free to write anything else you prefer, but use these suggestions if nothing better comes to mind.

Write about a place where you used to play when you were ten years old. Try to include the story of one incident that occurred there.

WRITING EXERCISE 2

Write the word *weather* as many times as possible for the next ninety seconds.

Describe the weather this morning as you left for class. Use as many "color" words as you can.

Write the name of your favorite month 20 times.

Explain in four or five lines why it is your favorite month.

Fill half a sheet of paper by writing the date of your birth over and over. Write as rapidly as possible.

Describe what you did on your last birthday. Fill about a half page with your recollections.

Combine the following groups of sentences into a single, longer sentence for each group.

The two boys walked.
They were tall.
They walked slowly.
They walked down the street.

The sun rose.
It burned off the fog.
The fog was in the valley.

We ate breakfast.
We ate in the cafeteria.
The cafeteria was crowded.

Journal Entry

Write a page discussing the reasons why you chose to attend this school.

WRITING EXERCISE 3

Write an account of a conversation you had yesterday. As much as possible, use the exact words that were spoken.

Write a few sentences that state your reaction to that conversation.

Write as much as you can of the lyrics of one of your favorite songs.

Try to tell why that song is one of your favorites.

Combine the sentences in each group into a single, longer sentence.

In the fall people go to football games.   (but)
In the spring their fancy turns to baseball.

I enjoy watching football.   (but)
I enjoy baseball even more.

I enjoy watching football.   (Although)
I enjoy watching baseball even more.

Tom went to the basketball game.
Sue went to the basketball game.
They sat at mid-court behind the team.

Journal Entry

Write a page describing the physical appearance and the personality of a person you met since you came to school this term.

WRITING EXERCISE 4

Describe your feelings when you entered this class today.

Briefly discuss one thing you have learned in a class other than this one.

Write the name of your favorite subject as many times as you can in two minutes.

In about five sentences, discuss the appeal this subject has for you.

Sentence Combining

The girl walked toward the car.
She was tall.
She was slender.
She inspected the tires very carefully.

She finished inspecting the tires.   (After)
She opened the door and checked the speedometer reading.

The tall slender girl opened the hood of the car.
Then she took a wrench out of her toolbox.
She removed a spark plug so she could check it.

The girl looked very carefully at the tip of the plug.
She shook her head sadly.

She replaced the plug.
She closed the hood.
She walked slowly away from the car.

Journal Entry

Write a description of a school you attended between the seventh and the tenth grade. Start with the outside of the building, and include in the description a view of one of the rooms.

WRITING EXERCISE 5

Write a physical description of the right front corner of this classroom.

List the items sitting on the kitchen counter in your home the last time you saw it.

Write everything you know about an important event that was in the news yesterday.

Tell some good news and your reaction to it.

Sentence Combining

The boys walked.
They were both short.
They both wore brown shirts.
They walked down the street.

The carpenter picked up his hammer.
He walked slowly to the ladder.
He climbed carefully to the roof.

The mechanic looked carefully at the engine.
She located her socket wrench.
She removed the distributor.
She replaced it with a new one.

Journal Entry

Write an account of something enjoyable you did last summer.

WRITING EXERCISE 6

Watch a sporting event, such as a basketball game, either in person or on television. Write a description of the action.

Try to describe the mood of the people watching that event. Describe the actions that suggested that mood to you.

Write a set of instructions for some action connected to a sport; for example, serving a tennis ball, or throwing a football.

Choose a topic from the general area of sports and for three minutes write anything that comes to mind about that topic. Continue to write even if your thoughts move from that topic. Try to write without stopping for the entire three minutes.

Sentence Combining

The lifeguard sat in the tower.
He scanned the water carefully.
He was looking for people in distress.
There was no sun that day.   (because)
The water was very cold.
The sky was a dull gray.

Only a few people were at the beach.
They sat on the sand.
They listened to their radios.

About noon the lifeguard closed his stand.
He walked slowly across the sand.
He was carrying his umbrella and his suntan lotion with him.

He sat quietly at the lunch counter.
He ordered a hot dog with onions and pickles.
After lunch he took a short nap.

Journal Entry

Select a person who went to high school with you, and write a full page about that person. Try to record specific details of the person's appearance and at least one account of an incident you remember about that person.

WRITING EXERCISE 7

It is useful to be able to enrich your writing by careful use of modifying words and word groups. Follow the steps used to enrich the following brief sentence.

The boy walked.

Add two one-word modifiers.

The short, muscular boy walked.

Add an *-ing* phrase.

>   Carrying a large package, the short, muscular boy walked.

Where did he walk?

>   Carrying a large package, the short, muscular boy walked into the room.

How did he walk?

>   Carrying a large package, the short, muscular boy walked slowly into the room.

Follow the same pattern of development for the two brief sentences below. Use colorful, imaginative word choices.

The man ran.   The child slept.

Journal Entry.

Write two stories about your experiences in seventh and eighth grade. Describe the action of the stories in great detail.

WRITING EXERCISE 8

Record on paper some idea for improving the school you attended last year.

Write for three minutes about the best thing that has happened to you this term.

Sentence Combining

The pass was high and wide.
He jumped for it.
He felt it slap flatly against his hands.
He shook his hips to throw off the halfback.
The halfback was diving at him.

He had ten yards in the clear.
He picked up speed.
He breathed easily.
He listened to the sound of cleats behind him.
He pulled away from them.

The spectators were in the stands.
They stood and cheered wildly.

They waved their white handkerchiefs.
The power of the white handkerchiefs overcame the power of the Terrible Towels.

Journal Entry

Write a page telling about an adult who was important to you when you were fifteen. Use at least one incident that illustrates the importance of that person.

WRITING EXERCISE 9

Add words and phrases to the following brief sentence.

The woman saw the boy.

Add two one-word modifiers.
Add an -*ing* phrase telling what she was wearing.
Tell where the boy was.
Combine these groups of sentences, putting them in the most logical order.

The girl wrecked the car.
It was her mother's car.
The night was cold and rainy.

The batter swung at the first pitch.
He dug his spikes into the ground.
He fouled the ball into the stands.

Journal Entry

Write about your activities last summer. Simply start to write on that subject, and continue to write until you have filled one page.

WRITING EXERCISE 10

Sentence Combining

Friday finally came.
We all left school.
We all went to the beach.

All afternoon the clouds built up in the west.
Then it rained in great torrents.
The family stayed in the house and played chess.

Football season is about to start.
Soon we will be going to the stadium.
We will carry a picnic lunch and a full cooler.

The students came to class.
They were alert.
They were eager.
They worked very hard throughout the whole hour.

The man parked his car in the shade of a tree.   (After)
The tree was tall and leafy.
He washed the car.
He waxed it so that it looked like a new car.

Journal Entry.

Discuss an adult among your acquaintances who is happy with life. Describe his life—work, recreation, family, and so on—and try to figure out what makes the person happy.

WRITING EXERCISE 11

Sentence Enrichment

Add the specified pieces of information to the basic sentence.

The men cleaned the garage floor.

How many men?   The floor was covered with oil
  Two   and grease.   (which)
Wearing?
  Blue uniforms

The horse jumped the fence.

The horse was a beautiful chestnut color.
The fence enclosed the pasture.

The team won the game.

When? Last Saturday
How? By kicking a field goal.

Journal Entry

Try to remember the first career choice you ever made (as in, when I was five, I wanted to be a firemen). Write down what you think attracted you to the career then, and discuss how you feel about that job now.

WRITING EXERCISE 12

Sentence Combining

Last night three guys came to visit Jim.
The three guys had played on his high school soccer team.   (who)
The four of them sat and talked until 3:00 A.M.

One of them is studying accounting.
He had been a weak student in high school.   (who)
He now works very hard on his courses.

He had never enjoyed school work very much.   (but)
He finds several of his courses extremely interesting now.

He had never enjoyed school work very much.   (Although)
He finds several of his courses extremely interesting now.

Note: In each version a comma follows the word "much" at the end of the first sentence.

The second guy is in the Air Force.
He is a year older than the others.   (who)
He is studying to be an electronics technician.

The third intends to enroll at the state university in the fall.
He has been working construction since he graduated from high school.
  (who)

Journal Entry

Write a page about a person who attended high school with you. Try to compare what he is doing today with what he expected to be doing after high school.

WRITING EXERCISE 13

Sentence Enrichment

Add the specified pieces of information to the basic sentence. Follow the pattern in Exercise 11.

The woman is studying commercial art.
She had been interested in art for many years.   (since) or (who)
She is studying *at the art institute downtown.*   (use this phrase)

Their horse won a first prize.
They had raised the horse from a colt.   (which)
Their horse is a quarter horse.
The horse is a beautiful steely gray.
The prize was in the local horse show.

My grandfather is a farmer.
He is *a relatively young man*.
He starts his work every day at 4:30 A.M.   (who)
He has done this all his life.   (just as he has done. . .)

Journal Entry

Write a page in which you discuss the best thing you did in high
school. Recollect a pleasant or successful experience and tell how
it occurred.

WRITING EXERCISE 14

Sentence Combining

The two men installed the antenna on the building.
They found a small suitcase filled with money.

The girls were walking slowly down the hall.
They stopped to talk to the other students.

The clouds built up slowly in the west.
They brought lightning and thunder early in the evening.

The players saw that defeat was certain.   (Although)
They played even harder for the rest of the game.

I am not finished with today's assignment.   (Although)
I think I will go play some racquetball.

Now continue to the following exercise to see how these sentences
should be punctuated.

Punctuation of Combined Sentences

The two men installed the antenna on the building.
They found a small suitcase filled with money.

The two men, installing the antenna on the building, found a small suitcase filled with money.

Punctuation rule: When an *-ing* phrase interrupts a sentence, set it off with commas.

The girls were walking slowly down the hall.
They stopped to talk to the other students.

The two girls, walking slowly down the hall, stopped. . .

The clouds built up slowly in the west.
They brought lightning and thunder early in the evening.

The clouds, after they built up slowly in the west, brought lightning and thunder early in the evening.

Punctuation rule: When a clause opened with *when, etc.*, interrupts a sentence, set it off with commas.

The players saw that defeat was certain.   (Although)
They played even harder for the rest of the game.

The players, although they saw. . ., played even harder. . . .

I am not finished with today's assignment.   (Although)
I think I will go play some racquetball.

I think I will go play some racquetball although I am not finished with today's assignment.
(no comma needed when the *when*, etc. clause is the last element of the sentence)

In the five sentences you used in Exercise 13, convert the *-ing* phrases to *when* etc., clauses and put them within the sentences. Set them off with commas.

UNIT TWO

Writing Based on Recollection

INTRODUCTORY WRITING EXERCISES

The short projects you wrote in the first unit were based almost entirely on observation and recollection. You wrote a set of directions in which you described a walk from place to place and noted the important landmarks. You wrote a description of a place based on your observations of the visual details. You wrote a brief narrative, an account of some incident in your life, and that account was based on the recollection of details lodged in your memory. Finally, based on past experiences with success and failure, you wrote a reaction to a comment by Woody Allen. All four of these projects were short, and they focused on very limited topics.

In this unit you will get involved with slightly longer writing projects. These projects will be longer, about four or five paragraphs, but you will still be writing based on recollections from your past. Not much changes when you move from shorter to longer projects. The goal of the project is still the same: to write a paper that makes a statement about you and your background. The process you will follow is identical to the set of steps you followed in the shorter projects. The biggest difference is that you will be using more than one paragraph to make your point, so you will need to collect more information about your subject. You will also need to learn some techniques for selecting content to help your reader in very specific ways to understand what you want to say. Beyond this enlargement in the scope of the assignments, you will find little that is new and different in this unit.

The three assignments in this unit are projects that ask you to focus on your background, on the places where you lived when you were younger, and on the people who were important to you during those years when you were forming many of the attitudes and directions that have made you the person you are today.

There are two reasons for using your past experiences as source material for writing projects. First, such materials ought to be readily available to you. The information is in your memory, and it needs only to be retrieved by writing randomly about it. To use information out of your past does not take any special skills. You do not need to read especially well, nor to do library research, nor to perform any advanced analysis of other written materials. All that is necessary for generating the content of these essays is a willingness to sit down with paper and pen to record experiences and discuss people. You must think of your background, and put on paper whatever comes to mind. You have already been involved with this work if you have been keeping your journal through the first few weeks of this course. Everything you have recorded up to this point is potentially useful in the projects you will work on in this unit.

Second, when you write about your past experiences, you have a chance to learn something about yourself, both your past and your future. You learn about any subject in a special way when you write about it. You organize the subject and open it up for examination. Further, you make new connections when you write. Your mind is given an opportunity to process and organize what you know and to make new assumptions and conclusions.

If you came to college after some other experiences—perhaps work or family responsibilities—rather than coming from high school directly to college, you may wish to write about the past few years of your life rather than about the years from thirteen to eighteen. These recent years are important to you, for out of these experiences you decided to come to college and to take yourself in a new direction. Writing about these experiences might provide insights into your motivation and direction for such an important step.

It is necessary, then, to summarize in a single, clear statement the scope and purpose of the next assignments. The work for the next three projects is to look back at a place and a time in your life when important things were happening to you: a time when you experienced growth and change, made decisions about the future, and developed attitudes about yourself and other people, about education, work, and life in general. This look back ought to focus on the place where you were living at that time, to determine what kind of place it was, to think about the people who lived there and the incidents that made up your life, to see what kind of influences worked on you while you lived there. Writing about the place, the people, and the experiences will help you to see them clearly, and seeing them clearly will help you to understand more about your life.

BACKGROUND WRITING

The first part of this project ought to be a general look at the neighborhood where you lived at an earlier time of your life. You will remember that in the first series of projects you wrote a description of a place. Most likely you went to the place and recorded a series of notes. For this project you will need to do the same kind of description, and you will need to use exactly the same notetaking procedure you used earlier to collect visual details for your descriptive paragraph.

Write the two sentences

The place is ———————————————
The place has ———————————————

which should read *was* and *had* because we are now looking back at an earlier time in your life. Turn back to page 16 if you need to review this exercise.

The only change in the procedure for gathering material for this description is caused by the movement back in time: you must look at this place in your memory rather than right before your eyes. Take notes at random, now, as the place comes back into your memory.

The place was ———————	The place had ———————
a *little* farm in southwestern Minnesota.	*a farmhouse*, very old but recently rebuilt by my parents.

small.

outside of town about two miles.

old; the original house is over 100 years old. One of the beams has Indian arrowheads buried in it.

sagging a little bit, especially the barn; it was a faded gray, with a roof once red faded almost white; pale pink might be the best color.

muddy; the driveway was a constant problem in the spring. We got stuck in the mud at least once a week.

a yard where the geese lived— noisy, but better than any watchdog; they cackled at anything that came up.

a pen where the lambs lived, just beside the barn.

a small creek running at the bottom of the sloping yard. The animals drank there. When I was very young, I used to swim there.

Now write a paragraph that tries to capture the way that place looked.

> We lived just off the county road about three miles from town. You turned off into the driveway and saw the old farmhouse right away, sitting there on the left. It was maybe 150 years old, and a little weather-beaten. Faded might be a good way to describe it. Across the yard there was an old barn, and it was really faded and run-down. Nobody put much into barns when they didn't farm seriously, and my family just kind of played at it when I was a kid. We kept geese, and a few lambs. The geese made great watchdogs; they made a lot of noise when anyone came in the drive. The lambs stayed in a little pen beside the barn and went inside it through a hole in the wall when the weather was really bad. A little creek ran through the yard down at the bottom of the slope. When we were little kids, we swam in it during the summer.

The next step is to move outward gradually from that home base to the rest of the area or neighborhood. Start with the location of your home in relation to the other houses and the whole neighborhood. Was the house in the center of the area? Was it far out on the edge of activity? A location three miles outside of town, such as the farm this student describes, must have been a real problem in some ways to the people who grew up there, especially when they were too young to drive and had to wait for adults to drive them, or if they relied on the school bus. Social life was probably hard to maintain if you lived outside of town and didn't have transportation. All these factors could have an important effect on the people involved. You need to consider these facts about your neighborhood:

1. What were its boundaries?
2. Where was your house located?
3. What did the area look like?
4. Who lived near you?
5. Where were the schools, churches, businesses and other important institutions located?
6. Did you venture out of the area very much? Or did you and your family do most of your business and your living inside the boundaries of the neighborhood?

Write approximately two pages about your neighborhood, trying to answer these questions and in general discussing the physical aspects of the place.

> I remember the road into town very well. When I was a little kid it seemed to stretch forever, and going to town was a big event. When I got older, the road got a little shorter, but it was still a real pain to live so far out of town. Trying to catch a ride home from school, or having to leave right after school on the bus was really hard on my social life and on my attempts to be an athlete.

The two pages you just produced are not really an essay or paper in the finished sense. They are background writing for a paper about a place. The process involved is exactly the same as the process you used for collecting visual details of the place on the campus (Assignment 1). The difference in the two techniques of recording is simply that the first uses direct observation, and the second uses recollection and observation of a place remembered rather than observed firsthand.

But a meaningful discussion of the place where you spent those important years will include much more than a simple physical description of that place. An important work on that place will tell about your experiences there, the people who lived there with you, and the important ideas and attitudes that influenced you during those years. Begin now to write down any memories from that time that might serve to illustrate what it was like to live there. Describe the influences that the place and its people had on you.

Here are some brief samples of the sort of writing you should be doing. A good paper will require more material than you will see here, but all the techniques of reporting the material should resemble what you see here.

I remember making hay. Oh, do I remember. My father was a school teacher, but he was really a farmer at heart. Every year we cut two, maybe three crops of hay off the field across the road. Dad would wait for the right weather—it had to be dry—no rain for several days ahead or the hay would get ruined as it lay in the field. This meant just one thing to me—making hay was the hottest, driest, dustiest work anybody can imagine. First we ran the mower to cut the hay, not bad work because you ran the tractor—a sit-down job. Then we drove the hay rake to work the hay into rows so the baler could put it up. Raking wasn't bad either, although it took a little planning and thought to get the hay raked up into rows that allowed the baler to work most efficiently. I guess baling was the real terrible part of the job. The tractor pulled the baler through the field and it gobbled up one row of the hay at a time—Dad always drove then, said I didn't have the skill yet, called me an apprentice hay-maker. My job, and my brother and sister helped, was to take the bale of hay as it came out of the baler and pile it up on the wagon. The baler gobbled the hay and clanked and groaned and finally out of the chute came a bale of hay all wrapped and tied with twine. Clank. Bam. Clank, clankety, clank and out would pop another bale—weighed between seventy-five and 125 pounds—and before it fell on the ground and got run over by the wagon, I had to swing it off the chute and up to the wagon so my brother and sister could stack it with the rest of the bales. Hot, dusty backbreaking work. Grab the bale by the twine, slide it to the end of the chute, swing it, trying to use its weight as it came off the chute to give a little OOMPH to it and heave it up onto the wagon. Grab—swing—heave. Grab—swing—heave. Grab—swing—heave. The twine cut into my hands, the dust washed over me—in my eyes down my shirt into my nose and throat until the whole inside of my mouth was coated with it grab—swing—heave, grabswing-heave GRABSWINGHEAVE until I could hardly bear to lift another bale. Only two things stopped us for a rest—a full wagon—then we rode over to the barn and stacked the hay inside, much easier than stacking it on the wagon, or a jammed baler. We spent a lot of time wishing that old baler would jam itself or run out of twine so we could sit for a few minutes and rest.

Try to record several experiences. You might wish to write about things you did regularly, just as the apprentice hay-maker describes how he had to work every time the hay was cut. Other experiences, however, take place just once. Some suggestions include your high school graduation, the first meeting with a special person, and the first day on the first job. Any experience, as long as you think it was important, is good raw material for these essays.

If you kept your journal carefully, you can probably find materials in those pages that will serve as raw material for the essays. Read through the pages and separate anything that seems useful. You will also get another benefit from reading the journal—you will gain a recollection of other important people, places, and events. Spend a few minutes looking over the journal, and then begin to write again. Try to record several experiences as they come to mind.

Descriptions of the neighborhood and narrations of incidents that somehow illustrate your life in that place provide good raw material for essays. Another ingredient that went into your experiences is the people who lived there and influenced you in one way or another. Start by making a list of people you remember. Include friends, teachers, coaches, people you worked for, and anyone else who comes to mind as a person who played a significant role in your life. Write down your recollections of these people—who they were, what they did, what you did with them, how they influenced you. Almost any memory is good for this exercise. The following recollections of a particular teacher might help you to remember people who were important to you.

My first impression of Miss Carlin almost made me drop the class. She was tall and slender, and she wore her graying hair pulled back into a bun at the back of her head. Her face seemed to be chiseled out of granite: high cheek bones and a nose longer than needed gave her the look of an aging hawk. She dressed simply, plain dresses and no jewelry, and those shoes that my grandmother used to call Red Cross Shoes, low heels with laces. This picture of stern severity was reinforced by her voice; it was low and not unpleasant, but it had a kind of clipped sharpness about it that made perfectly clear that the lady was strictly business when she was in the classroom.

"Who'd ya get? Carlin? Tooo bad." The seniors always delighted in this ritual, rolling their eyes toward the ceiling and stretching out the words on the end. "Toooo BAAAAAD." A fresh, green sophomore, I had no idea what they meant, or if what they suggested was anywhere near the truth. All I knew for certain was that my schedule said "Plane Geo. V. Carlin. Room 203." Killer Carlin. Miss Kindness of Central High. How little I knew. And how soon I would find out the truth about Miss Carlin, the terror in room 203.

"Good morning, students," she said. "Welcome to Plane Geometry. My name is Miss Carlin." That much I already knew, thanks to my buddies in the senior class. Her reputation too for that matter, but even the stories didn't really do her justice. "You are about to enter upon the study of a very difficult but very important subject, for it is the foundation for other mathematical studies and it will also serve to sharpen your mind for other studies." I was so scared I thought I'd faint.

Remember that the samples you read here are just samples. They show the sort of materials you ought to be recording, but they represent only a portion of the writing needed for you to do the assignments in this unit. You ought to have about ten to twelve, or at most fifteen, pages of random writing before you try to move into the actual work on the essays.

ASSIGNMENT 5.

Writing About an Event

When you have a good selection of background writing completed, you are ready to begin work on the first formal paper for Unit Two. The assignment is to write an essay of three paragraphs recounting an important event out of your past.

The first step in writing this assignment, or any other project, is to pick a subject. In this case you have one limitation: you must choose an event or experience out of your past. Beyond that, you are free to choose any event that you wish. As you begin to make a selection, use the following important guidelines:

1. You ought to choose an event that is fairly fresh in your memory. The more details you can remember about the event, the stronger your essay will be. Don't select an event that happened so long ago that you can't remember much about it.
2. Select an event that interests you for some reason. What doesn't interest you is almost certain not to interest your reader. Select an event for this project because it is important, or life-changing, or humorous, or frightening, or embarrassing, but don't choose one that sparks no reaction at all.

   INTEREST IN A SUBJECT AND KNOWLEDGE OF THE SUBJECT ARE THE TWO MOST IMPORTANT INGREDIENTS IN A GOOD SELECTION OF SUBJECT MATTER.

Next, you should work up an identifying tag or phrase for this event. Call it *The Great Train Robbery*, or *The Day I Lost My Shirt*, or simply, *My First Car*, but call it something so as to focus your attention on that single subject. Write that identifying phrase at the top of a sheet of paper.

Now that you have identified the event, you need to record some important information about the event. You will need to write about

the location.
the people involved.
background materials, such as why you were involved, and what sort of situation you were in at the time.
the exact details of the event, listed in chronological order.
any changes that came over you because of the event.

It is probably useful to do some fairly random writing about the event.

- Imagine that the event had never happened, and describe how you would be different.
- Imagine that someone else had had this experience instead of you, and describe the other person's responses to the experience.
- Think of this event as a possible television drama. Identify the actors and actresses you would select to play the important parts. Explain your choices.

After you have completed several pages of this kind of focused writing, take a sheet of paper and write about the event until you have filled two sides of the paper. Write about the event; don't tell the story yet. Simply cover two pages, or as close as you can come to two pages, with random thoughts about the incident.

You have now completed two steps in the process of writing an essay.

You identified a subject
    and
You recorded background information about the subject.

The third step is to decide on a meaning for the essay, a statement the paper can make about the event and its meaning for you. Some writers try to avoid this step, and they try to write without knowing in advance what the paper expects to accomplish. Don't fall into this trap. Writing without a fixed purpose in mind will almost always result in a loose, purposeless paper that does nothing for you or for the reader. The best kind of statement for a paper is a single sentence in which you express the idea you intend to get across to your reader.

Read the following paragraph, a paragraph that fits the third assignment in Unit I, in which the instructions were to write a brief narrative:

The big day had finally arrived. I had been waiting for several weeks for my new car to arrive and today was the day. The time since my father had gone to work after telling me that the car would be ready today and he'd bring it home seemed like another two or three weeks. I came home from school and worked out in the yard, raking leaves. After that I washed the dog. I even pulled all the weeds out of the tomato plants, a job I hate, just to keep myself busy. I had almost given up when I heard the gate squeak at the far end of the drive. The gravel on the road up to the house crunched and I raced around to the front of the house just as Dad pulled to a stop by the front steps. Oh, it was beautiful. A deep metallic blue with special alloy wheels. The interior was different shades of light blue with the thickest carpets you can imagine on the floor. Dad handed me the key and I slid into the seat. The soft vinyl upholstery was cool to the touch. The steering wheel felt just right in my hands. I turned the key and listened to the engine purr. Then I slipped it into gear and drove around the yard for a minute. I was almost in heaven. I thought nothing could be better than getting my hands on that new car for the first time. It's been about two months now, and I've learned something about the importance of the car. It stays a little dirty now from the dust on the roads and it even has a little dent on the door where someone opened a door too hard in a parking lot. I still enjoy it, but it's become more of a tool than a fantasy trip for me. I use it because I need it, but it hasn't changed my life the way I thought it would. I guess the real event can never match our expectations.

Think for a moment about the circumstances surrounding this brief experience. The writer shows us the anticipation, the excitement, and the terrific satisfaction that the arrival of that car brought her. But she continues her comments to show that after a few weeks car ownership had lost its excitement and thrill, and had, in fact, become a responsibility without much reward as compensation. The writer of this piece attempts to get across all of these feelings: the excitement and the loss of the thrill, the wonderful sense of knowing a great thing was about to happen, the joy of actually experiencing that great thing, and the cooling off of that excitement as the car became a common part of her life.

The writer might have expressed her feelings in a sentence such as this one:

Waiting for my new car, actually receiving it, and driving it for the first time thrilled me beyond belief, but the car didn't actually change my life as much as I had expected, and, in fact, it became a commonplace part of my life and even a heavy responsibility after a short time.

This is a good sentence in that it expresses the whole idea she attempts to give the reader, but it is a bit long. It might read

> My new car was tremendously exciting at first, but it soon became just another tool and a responsibility for me.

The second version omits a little of the feeling, but it is easy to control and is therefore useful as a guide to writing the paper. You need to write the same sort of sentence to control your paper.

When you have written the controlling statement, you must then begin to select materials to explain—or as writers say, "to support"—the idea. The purpose of the materials in the essay is to provide information about the event and to make observations on the event so that readers will understand the two important aspects of the event. The essay must tell what happened (the event itself) and what happened to you during and because of the event (the outcome or result of the event).

Answer these questions about the event you have chosen:

> What sort of background information will the readers need to understand your essay?
> Date? Time? Location? Description of place? People involved? Your relationship to them? Your own situation?
>
> What specific details of the event itself will the readers need?
> Check your chronological listing of the narrative details and select those that are important to the reader's understanding. Each detail included should say something important.
>
> What sort of explanation and discussion of the event is necessary to clarify the event for your readers?
> Provide here your reaction to the event. Include changes, new ideas, or attitudes caused by the experience.

If you worked reasonably hard on background writing at the beginning of this unit, you should have already written some of these materials, the answers to the questions, the details of the event, and the observations on it. Look in those materials for passages that can be rewritten for use in the essay.

We looked earlier at a single paragraph of narration, the story of the arrival of a young woman's first car. That version focused primarily on the action involved in watching the car drive up, on her getting into the car, and on her driving it for the first time. That same piece of action can be expanded into a longer, more meaningful essay if the writer added a few items of background and a more thorough discussion of the results in her life.

The background needs to show more information about the reason for the purchase of the car. The writer should also tell how she would use the car. Remember her situation.

> She lived with her parents on a farm about eight miles from town. She needed to drive herself to school and to other activities. When her mother and father were busy on the farm, she often did errands for them on the way home from school, such as picking up medicine for the animals. She had worked for two years to save money to buy a new car rather than a used one, which her father had agreed to pay for. She paid the difference between the new car and a used car.

The details of the event itself are probably sufficient to get across her delight, excitement, and happiness with the new car.

Read again the narrative paragraph on page 66.

The concluding discussion is almost complete enough to make the results clear. The point of the writing would be completely carried off if she included more discussion of her feelings about the car and a brief explanation of her present attitude. She also needs a general observation on the way actual events seldom live up to expectations.

The only step necessary for completing the expansion of that one-paragraph description of an action into a full scaled narrative essay is to write up the background, the narration, and the concluding remarks in three separate paragraphs, one for each section. If expanded to a three-paragraph essay, the paragraph on the arrival of the new car would read like this:

> The day my new car arrived may have been the biggest day of my life. I had been waiting for three weeks since we ordered it, but I had actually been waiting all my life. I live out on a farm, five or six miles out of town, and up till the day I got my license and my car I had spent more time waiting than anyone on earth. I waited for the school bus, for my parents or brother to pick me up; I mean, I waited a lot. And while I waited, I dreamed, and I worked, so that I could get a new car as soon as I got my driver's license.
>
> The big day had finally arrived. The time since my father had gone to work after telling me that the car would be ready today and he'd bring it home seemed like another two or three weeks. I came home from school and worked out in the yard, raking leaves. After that I washed the dog. I even pulled all the weeds out of the tomato plants, a job I hate, just to keep myself busy. I had almost given up when I heard the gate squeak at

the far end of the drive. The gravel on the road up to the house crunched and I raced around to the front of the house just as Dad pulled to a stop by the front steps. Oh, it was beautiful. A deep metallic blue with special alloy wheels. The interior was different shades of light blue with the thickest carpets you can imagine on the floor. Dad handed me the key and I slid into the seat. The soft vinyl upholstery was cool to the touch. The steering wheel felt just right in my hands. I turned the key and listened to the engine purr. Then I slipped it into gear and drove around the yard for a minute. I was almost in heaven. I thought nothing could be better than getting my hands on that new car for the first time.

It's been about two months now since I got the car. I've used it constantly, put about 2500 miles on it, and I think it is a fine car. But I'm not in love with it now the way I was at first; I even let it get dusty sometimes, and it has a couple of little dents in it. Having transportation is a great thing in my life. I no longer spend time waiting for rides. But the car didn't cure all my problems. Those not related to transportation are still there, big as ever. The car did not transform my life; it merely made part of it more convenient. I still enjoy it, but it's more of a tool than a fantasy trip now. I guess reality never can match our expectations.

You are almost ready now to write your own essay. But before you do, read the following essay, an excerpt from an article in the magazine *Car and Driver*. It describes very graphically a single event and what it came to mean in the life of the writer.

A DRIVE IN THE OUTBACK, WITH SECOND CHANCES

by David Abrahamson

[1] It took less than two seconds. The stab of oncoming headlights, a blur of looming sheetmetal in the center of the windshield, a jabbing reaction at the steering wheel and then that awful, indelible noise. And then an unearthly silence, as if nature itself knew that something irrevocable had happened and that a moment—maybe much more—was needed for the reality to be dealt with.

[2] I had been driving fast most of the afternoon. Not really at the car's limit, but well above the posted speed. I enjoy fast driving for its own sake, and this new and isolated environment seemed to urge me on. After all, Australia's wide open spaces are exactly that, and we'd encountered less than one car an hour in either direction of the towns. And besides, Baker, my passenger, didn't seem to mind. We were in the middle of a long, sweeping righthander when suddenly the windshield was filled with another set of headlights. Coming at us, in the middle of the road, was a monstrous truck. The left front corner of the truck cab buried itself in the left front door of our car. The sound was absolutely deafening. Bits of metal and glass were everywhere. The impact ripped the watch off my wrist and the lenses out of

my glasses. But I was lucky. Because it was righthand-drive car, as the driver I was at least three feet away from the point of impact. Passenger Baker, however, was not. The true violence of the crash took place almost in his lap. Part of his seat was torn up and out of its mount. The door and a section of the roof were battered in toward his head and left shoulder. We were both wearing lap-and-shoulder seat belts at the time. Mine saved my life. Baker's did too, but in the process broke his collarbone and badly bruised a few essential internal organs. A grisly tradeoff.

[3] How and why had the accident happened? What exactly had been my mistake? Long after I'd returned to the United States, long after Baker had recovered from his injuries, I was still asking myself those questions. Now, almost a year later, the answers are clear. And they go far beyond any chance encounter on a strange road in a strange land, even beyond the crushing sense of remorse I felt at the time. And they tell me something about who I was and what I might be. I enjoyed driving, and a big part of that enjoyment came from taking a number of risks—risks I thought were calculated, but in truth were not. Rather they were part of a glorious game, imbued with notions of independence, willful mobility and a heavy dose of virility. I'd had more than my share of near misses, but they merely served to prove the range of my skills at the wheel—my ability to judge relative speed and distance, the speed of my reflexes, the correctness of my kinesthetic-instincts. In my car at speed, there was never any hint of my own mortality. Or anyone else's. So the accident had to happen. Maybe not with that truck on that blind curve on the far side of the Earth, but somewhere. It has less to do with the law of averages than the laws of physics. Roads are a decidedly hostile environment, peopled with an unknown number of other drivers who are certain to do the wrong thing at the wrong time. And no amount of skill, real or imagined, can save you. Sweet reason is the only defense. Prudence, moderation and caution are not the stuff of grand illusions, unbridled exuberance and youthful panache. But they are great for survival.

[4] And that in the end, is what my experience boils down to. I now see, as I did not before, that my survival (and that of others who choose to ride with me) is at stake. I've never seen myself as a particularly courageous person, but I've always enjoyed sports containing an element of risk: parachuting, scuba-diving, alpine skiing and the like. Strange that something as mundane as an auto accident should, at age 30, give me my first glimpse of my own mortality. Thinking back to that evening south of Bombala, I am certain I never want to hear that awful sound again. But I also never want to forget it.

COMMENTARY

This brief narrative recounts an event that actually took no more than a second or two, the time it takes two vehicles to round a curve and run almost head-on into each other. The impact and meaning of the event obviously went far beyond the time limits of the event, for the writer is still sorting out his responses to the event months after it occurred.

As a writing project, the narrative can demonstrate two important considerations you will face in writing this and other assignments. First, the essay offers a clear illustration of a story told not simply for the telling, but to make a point, to make clear the importance of the event. The essay answers the first question narratives need to answer:

What happened? I had a terrible, frightening auto accident.

But is also answers the second, perhaps more important question:

What happened to the writer, the person who experienced the event? The writer learned something important about driving and about himself.

Near misses had confirmed his skill . . .
There was never any hint of his own mortality . . .
The accident had to happen . . .
His survival was at stake . . .
Sweet reason, prudence, moderation are the only defense . . .

In a sentence, the writer says that he had trusted his own skills to protect him when he drove, but he now understands that the skills do not count when other drivers make mistakes. Caution alone will allow him to avoid accidents.

The second problem handled in the essay deals with the length or the amount of material needed to make the point of the essay clear to the reader. Specifically in this essay, the question is, "How far back shall I go in telling the story?"

The story begins, in one sense, when the writer is assigned to go to Australia to write an article. This narrative might have started right there. Or it might have started when the writer arrived in Australia, or early in the morning of the day the accident occurred.

The writer had several possible starting points, but the choice of a starting point depends on two things:

How long is essay supposed to be?

How much does the reader need to know to understand what the essay is saying?

Clearly the writer had to balance these two considerations. Recounting the entire trip was a task for a book, not for a short article. Too much introductory material might confuse or bore the reader. Too little information might leave the reader uncertain about the point of the article. A compromise was necessary. The writer chose to feed in facts about the event—location, for example—as he told the story. The real action of the story is simply the crash itself.

"Coming at us, in the middle of the road, was a monstrous truck." There was no need to tell about the plane ride to Australia, or breakfast that morning; the focus of the article is on the accident, and that focus provides a clue about where to start and where to stop the story.

There is one more important point about the essay. The writer tells us that he was still searching for the meaning of the event "long after I'd returned to the United States, long after Baker had recovered from his injuries." The meaning did not dawn on him a few minutes after the event; it took time for him to develop that meaning; time and writing about the event brought the meaning out very clearly. You ought to allow yourself these two things—time and an opportunity to write about the subject— before you should expect to find a statement for your essay. Writing is an act of learning and discovery. Before you begin to write the essay itself, give yourself time to write your way through to the discovery about the meaning of your assignment. Only considerable background writing will bring out the ideas hidden in your subject.

ASSIGNMENT 6.

Writing About a Person

For the second essay in this section you are to write a character sketch of a person who was important to you in some way. Perhaps the person had a great influence on you, or was a help to you in some situation, or perhaps the person is interesting just because of character, intelligence, or personal philosophy. Look through your journal to see if you have mentioned anyone who might fit the bill for this essay, or run through a list of people out of your past to see if you can find someone. The person you select should meet the two basic tests for selection as a subject for an essay: interest and knowledge. Find a person who interests you, and who therefore might interest your readers, and a person whom you remember quite clearly, so that it will be an easy task to write down a great many recollections.

A high school teacher, especially one who makes a very vivid impression on his or her students, might make an interesting subject for a profile. Viola Carlin was just such a teacher. Read again the journal entries and free writing materials from a typical student:

> My first impression of Miss Carlin almost made me drop the class. She was tall and slender, and she wore her graying hair pulled back into a bun at the back of her head. Her face seemed to be chiseled out of granite; high cheek bones and a nose longer than needed gave her the look of an aging hawk. She dressed simply, plain dresses and no jewelry, and those shoes that my grandmother used to call Red Cross Shoes, low heels with laces. This picture of stern severity was reinforced by her voice; it was low and not unpleasant, but it had a kind of clipped sharpness about it that made perfectly clear that the lady was strictly business when she was in the classroom.

The first day in one of her classes was equally impressive:

1. "Who'd ya get? Carlin? Tooo bad." The seniors always delighted in this ritual, rolling their eyes toward the ceiling and stretching out the words on the end. "Toooo BAAAAAD." A fresh, green sophomore, I had no idea what they meant, or if what they suggested was any where near the truth. All I knew for certain was that my schedule said "Plane Geo. V. Carlin. Room 203." Killer Carlin. Miss Kindness of Central High. How little I knew. And how soon I would find out the truth about Miss Carlin, the terror in room 203.
2. "Good morning, students," she said. "Welcome to Plane Geometry. My name is Miss Carlin." That much I already knew, thanks to my buddies in the senior class. Her reputation too for that matter, but even the stories didn't really do her justice. "You are about to enter upon the study of a very difficult but very important subject, for it is the foundation for other mathematical studies and it will also serve to sharpen your mind for other studies." I was so scared I thought I'd faint.

The way she conducted each and every class was designed to make the students do their very best work:

3. She ran her classroom with a precision that the military would have envied. The homework for the previous night was always checked at the beginning of class; she called the roll by asking for a report of the number of problems wrong on the homework. Next in the carefully ordered plan was the presentation of the new concept for the day, usually a theorem or a new corollary that had to be memorized and written out word for word in a little quiz. The last ten minutes of each class were given to homework for the next day. The assignment was written on the

board before school and each student copied it on a sheet of paper. While the students worked on the assignment, she walked around the room trying to help those who were in difficulty.

Stories told by students and legends that surrounded her all served to create one impression of Miss Carlin:

4. All of the students, and many of the teachers feared and respected Miss Carlin. She was a bit like the president of the United States or a foreign dignitary. We didn't always like her or what she did, but we were always afraid to say anything that went contrary to her wishes. Years ago at the high point of the football season she had a fearsome run-in with the football coach over his star running back. He simply stopped doing his work and she of course gave him the grade he earned, an F. He was immediately suspended from the team. The coach was enraged; she couldn't do that, spoilt the season for the whole team for the whole school ruin the boys's chances of getting a scholarship. He ranted and raved, went to the principal threatened everything but a lawsuit. But it did no good. "After all, Mr. Jackson," she said softly, "the young man will have no need for football when he leaves school. He will need geometry and the work habits he develops here for the rest of his life."

5. Her words came out slowly, with emphasis. Short and clipped. "No homework again, Cynthia? Report to this room at 3:15. You and I need to discuss your situation." "But, Miss Carlin, I have cheerlead ..." The word died in her throat as she realized her mistake. To suggest that cheerleading, or baseball, or anything for that matter, was more important than studies, especially study of plane geometry, was to incite Viola Carlin to riot. "3:15, Cynthia. No excuses." She was as tough and demanding as any teacher I ever knew, but in the end she gained a kind of grudging respect from her classes, and the undying devotion of her students who went on to study math after taking her course, and found the math, no matter what level. a breeze because of the thorough grounding in fundamentals they had received in Miss Carlin's class.

6. Outside of school she kept herself active in garden clubs and an organization devoted to the preservation of the city's historic landmarks. She had lived, years ago, with her parents in a beautiful Victorian house on Central Avenue; her first work in the preservation society had been to have that house declared a historical site so that it had to be maintained in its original condition by anyone who bought it. She lived at that time in a small but well kept house in a neighborhood near the school; she had no car and walked the two blocks to school in all but the worst winter weather. In the spring her gardens were the most beautiful, the best cared for in all the town. She grew day lilies and roses outside and had about a hundred pots of African violets on her sun porch.

7. In my hometown, she was famous. At least as famous as a teacher could be. Every college bound sophomore at Central High had taken plane geometry from her ever since she had joined the faculty twenty-seven years ago. The mayor, the baseball coach, several of the lawyers

downtown: they had all had Miss Carlin and they all had stories to tell, stories full of hard work and terror, out-and-out terror, but stories full of affection and respect for the toughest, most demanding teacher they had every known.

8. No one seemed to enjoy her classes; they were difficult and time-consuming. Few of the students visited her after class, at least not voluntarily. Everyone who passed her class was immensely relieved to be finished with the experience. But it was Viola Carlin the former students returned to visit. When the state university dismissed for Christmas and the end of the year, a steady stream of students dropped by to see her. "Just came back, Miss Carlin, to show you I remember and to say thanks for everything you did for me." When she retired five years ago, three hundred people came to a reception in her honor. They all seemed to be saying pretty much the same thing: It was really tough, getting through her class, but it made everything else after that seem a little easier.

9. Late in my sophomore year, I asked a senior a question that had been on my mind for some time. "Jack," I asked, "what's the story here? I see the people in my class almost despise Viola Carlin, but lots of people come back just to see her and talk to her. Is she different now? Did she used to be much nicer?" "Young man," he said, when you get older and wiser (I think he meant as old and wise as he was) "you will understand. Miss Carlin may not be a very pleasant experience while it is happening, but when you go on and realize how much she taught you, you'll appreciate her as much as we all do."

You should notice certain things about the free writing entries you have just read. First, they are not neat, not edited, not corrected. They stand as they were written, hurriedly and without attention to form. Your journal entries and free-writing efforts probably look pretty much the same, and that is just fine. You wrote these for your own use, not for submission to an editor or teacher or employer. They are simply recordings of information, not a finished product.

Second, there might not be enough notes for a long essay, but there are enough for a start. If more material is needed, the writer will simply go back and write down more until there is enough to supply the materials necessary for the paper.

There is enough material recorded for you to begin to work on the next step in the process. For this step, you must establish a central idea or impression about the subject. The writer is dealing with a teacher, one remembered with some fondness now that a few years have passed. That fondness, however, came only after this student left the teacher's class. The memories of that class and the stories told about the teacher create a different impression, an impression established by words such as *serious, businesslike, difficult, demanding, hard*. Watch as the writer works toward establishing that idea about the teacher:

> Miss Carlin was a hard teacher. She scared people in her classes. She demanded awful amounts of work. She never accepted excuses. But I learned from her. I learned how to study. And that hard work never killed anyone. And I'm just like the seniors who talked to me about her class. I see now how valuable that experience was.

The goal here is to work those thoughts down into a single sentence that can control the paper.

> Miss Carlin was difficult and demanding, but I learned much in her class and I'm glad I had the experience.

That is a pretty good statement. A great deal of work, trial and error substitution of various words and phrases occurred between the first, long version of this controlling sentence and the final short, direct statement. It takes time and effort to work your way to a good controlling sentence, but it is the only way to be certain that you include in the paper the materials necessary to make your point. This is the only route to success.

When you complete a trial version of the controlling idea, move to the next step. You may need to work more on that idea later in order to make it more precise, but it is good enough for now. Read the sentence again and look back into your collection of materials for discussion and illustrations of that idea.

As an example, examine the materials about Miss Carlin.

Certainly Paragraph 5 contains a good illustration of her attitude about the importance of school work and outside activities.

Paragraph 4 creates a very similar impression.

Paragraphs 2 and 3 together illustrate how hard and demanding she was in her classroom.

Paragraphs 7, 8, and 9 all comment on the appreciation students felt after they had left her class.

The other materials, with one exception, serve to develop the same impression of the teacher. Paragraph 6 comments on her outside interests in gardening and local history. Those aspects of her life don't add to the picture of a tough, demanding teacher, and they don't help to explain the devotion of her students. It would therefore be better to leave them out of the paper. A short paper can make only a limited statement, not a total exploration of every area of the subject. It is better to stick to one limited idea and explain it fully than to take on too much and leave your reader without a complete explanation of your idea.

The next step is to decide on an order for presenting the materials chosen to develop the idea. There are no hard and fast rules for order of presentation; probably the only rule is that several orders will work for any paper, but the key to success is to pick some order that will help the reader and stick to the method you choose. You can help your reader if you present the materials in an order that is easily recognized. Recall that when you wrote paragraphs of narration and description there was a sort of natural order built into the work; narration runs in time order from start to finish of the event, and description moves through space in some direction such as left to right, or right to left. Look for a natural order for this paper.

One possible order for this essay is a loosely connected kind of time order. After a paragraph of introduction, you could introduce an early, even a first, impression of the person.

Paragraph 2 from the illustration gives a picture of the very first day in Miss Carlin's class.

"Good morning, students . . ."

Next in order of time, considering the average student's experiences with Miss Carlin, might be Paragraph 3, which describes the way she ran the class.

She ran her classroom with a precision . . .

Then it is probably a good time to put in specific incidents in the classroom, such as is described in Paragraph 5.

Her words came out slowly, with emphasis . . .

Next, moving out of the classroom, use the paragraph about her problems with the coach. The second half of Paragraph 4 is good here.

> Years ago at the high point of the football season . . .

Finally, a rewritten version of Paragraph 8 and Paragraph 9 would provide observations of those who had studied under Miss Carlin earlier and had thus digested the experience and understood its meaning.

> Students in her classes didn't enjoy the experience, and they were glad to get out of the class, but it was Miss Carlin that they visited after they had graduated.
>
> Late in my sophomore year, I asked a senior . . .

The suggested order above is not the only order that will work for this paper; it is one of several orders that will work. It starts by providing a first impression of the subject, moves through early experiences, especially those within the classroom, and then it goes on in time and outward from the classroom to a story about a coach, and finally offers the thoughts of people who had taken Miss Carlin's class earlier.

Two steps remain in the process of producing a draft of this paper. First, write out a version of the paragraphs of development you selected, and put them in the best order of presentation. Finally, write an introduction and conclusion to the paper.

Notice that we have left the introduction for almost the last step in the rough draft. You can write the introduction any time you wish in the course of putting the paper together, but don't wait until you have a workable introduction before you go on to write the other paragraphs. Any number of papers never get written at all because their writer waited for a good opening line or paragraph. Instead of waiting, just pick any paragraph that seems an easy place to begin. Write that paragraph and then move to the next one that seems easy to write, and continue in that fashion. When you have written everything, you can move the paragraphs into the order you selected earlier.

There are several ways to introduce an essay, but an introduction serves only two purposes. First, an introduction must catch the attention and arouse the curiosity of the reader. The first line of any written work should have in it some attractive statement, some sort of hook to catch the reader and lead further into the essay. Second, an introduction should tell the reader where the essay is going. It does so by telling what subject the essay explores and what idea the essay is going to express.

One workable way to catch the reader's interest is to tell a very brief story. A good one for the piece on Miss Carlin would be to tell what happened just before the writer went into her class on the very first day of the school year:

> I stood across the hall outside her door and looked at her for just a moment before going into the room. The butterflies were flying formations in my stomach, and my knees must have been shaking just a little. I had heard too many stories about her class in geometry, too many scary stories, too many pointed remarks wishing me, "Good luck, you'll sure need it," to feel anything but nervous as I waited to start class under the hardest, most demanding teacher at Central High, Viola Carlin.

Using a description is also a good method for catching the reader's interest.

> She looked just exactly the way I expected. She was known to be the hardest teacher in school, and her appearance surely matched her reputation. She was rather tall and slender, and she wore her hair drawn back into a severe bun at the back of her head. Sometimes she seemed to have drawn her face and her personality tight along with her hair. She seldom smiled, and her eyes were piercing gray. She wore plain, tailored dresses, mostly grays and blues. Mostly, she was . . . businesslike. Every student knew her classes were serious, difficult, and very, very demanding.

Notice that both versions of the introduction try to give the reader a sense of direction by using key words:

> . . . good luck . . . feel nervous . . . Miss Carlin, the hardest, most demanding teacher at Central High.

> . . . she was . . . businesslike . . . classes serious, difficult, and . . . demanding.

Both tell the subject's name, Miss Carlin. Both use a few words to establish her personality, and both thus suggest that the paper will try to explain the nature of this person and the nature of the experience students had in her classes. Neither introduction tells everything there is to tell, and neither states the controlling idea in its exact words, but each supplies the reader with the subject area and with a very clear suggestion as to what the paper will say on the subject. Other methods would also work, and a careful revision of these efforts will improve them, but for a rough draft version of the introduction either one will be good enough.

The paragraphs of development, arranged in the suggested order and reworked just a little, read like this:

When the bell rang that first day, everybody was sitting quietly, waiting to hear the worst. "Good morning, students," she smiled. "My name is Miss Carlin, and this is Plane Geometry." That much we already knew from our schedules and from her reputation around the school. She spoke with precision, her words clipped and very carefully chosen. "We are about to undertake the study of a very important subject, one of the foundations for all your mathematical studies. You will need to work very hard and very carefully if you intend to make a good grade in this class." And that was the good news. The bad news came next: homework, quizzes, tests, neatness counts on every paper, a daily grade for class participation. I didn't know whether I could survive or not.

She ran her classroom with a precision a general would have envied. The homework for the previous night was always checked at the beginning of class; then she called the roll by asking for the number of problems wrong on the homework. Next in the plan was the new concept for the day, a theorem or a new corollary to be memorized in class. The last ten minutes of the classes were spent beginning the homework for the next day. While we worked on the assignment, she walked around to help those who were in difficulty.

"No homework, Cynthia? Again today? That's the second time this week you have failed to do your assignments. Report to me at 3:15 today. We need to talk about your situation." "But, Miss Carlin, I have cheerlead . . ." The words died in her throat as she realized her mistake. Nothing made Miss Carlin more angry than a suggestion that some outside activity, cheerleading or sports, took priority over an important subject such as geometry. "That can wait. Be here at 3:15." We began to understand her values and priorities. It was a new idea for most of us, that studying was more important than playing. But she gradually worked it into our heads.

She held to these values even when it caused her big problems. Years ago at the height of the football season the team's star running back simply stopped doing his work in her class. And just as surely as the sun comes up in the east, Miss Carlin failed him and he was suspended from the team. The coach almost went crazy. Ranted and raved all over school, threatened her with everything but a lawsuit. She wouldn't budge. "After all, Mr. Jackson," she said softly, "the boy needs to understand what is truly important. He will need the skills and study habits he develops in my class long after he stops playing football."

She stuck by her guns then, and she stuck by them all the time I was in her class. She kept a steady pressure for hard work and careful preparation, and probably didn't crack a smile the entire year. She pushed me to work hard, and I thought it was terrible. But I passed the course, and I learned a lot about math. I didn't know what that meant till I went to college and found that I already knew how to study and knew much about math that others were only beginning to learn. I had hated that class, and from time to time, hated her. But at the end of my freshman year, she was the only teacher I went to see, just because I wanted to say, "I now appreciate what you did back in that geometry class."

Before you work further on your own essay, read the following character sketch of Tom Seaver, the major-league pitcher:

TOM SEAVER'S FAREWELL

by A. B. Giamatti

Shea stadium is not Eden, and the picture of Tom and Nancy Seaver leaving its graceless precincts in tears did not immediately remind me of the *Expulsion of Adam and Eve in the Brancacci Chapel.* And yet, absorbing the feelings generated by Seaver's departure from New York led me to the kind of inflated cogitation that links Masaccio and the Mets, if only because the feelings were so outsized and anguished and intense. After all, Brad Parks had gone to Boston, and Namath to Los Angeles, and Julius Erving to, if you will, Philadelphia. Clearly evil had entered the world, and mortality had fixed us with its sting. If Seaver is different, and evidently he is, the reasons must be sought somewhere other than in the columns of the daily press. In fact, the reasons for Seaver's effect on us have to do with the nature of baseball, a sport that touches on what is most important in American life. Where Parks, Namath, and Erving are only superb at playing their sports, Seaver seems to embody his.

George Thomas Seaver almost did not become a Met. In February of 1966, the Atlanta Braves signed the University of Southern California undergraduate to a contract and assigned him to Richmond. At that point, Commissioner William Eckert stated that the signing violated the college rule. The contract was scrapped. USC, however, declared Seaver ineligible. The commissioner announced that any team, except Atlanta, matching the Richmond contract could enter a drawing for rights to negotiate. The Indians, the Phillies, and the Mets were favored, and Seaver, signed in early April, went to Jacksonville of the International League. He was twenty-one and would spend one year in the minor leagues.

Seaver pitched .500 ball for Jacksonville, 12–12, with an earned-run average of 3.13. He would not have as weak a season again until 1974, when he would go 11–11, with an ERA of 3.20. Yet even at Jacksonville he struck out 188 batters, thus foreshadowing his extraordinary performance with the Mets, with whom, from 1968 to 1976 he would never strike out fewer than 200 batters a season—a major-league record. And from the beginning Seaver pitched as much with his head as with his legs and right arm, a remarkably compact, concentrated pitcher, brilliantly blending control and speed, those twin capacities for restraint and release that are the indispensable possessions of the great artist. There is no need to rehearse the achievements of Seaver with the Mets: three Cy Young awards; Rookie of the Year with a lastplace ball club in 1967; the leading pitcher in the league at 25–7 (ERA 2.21) in 1969, the same year he took the Mets to their first World Series (and, in the process, reelected John Lindsay as mayor of New York—a cause for the trade no one has yet explored). In 1970 and 1971 he led the league in strikeouts (283; 289—a league season record for right-handers) and in ERA (2.81; 1.76— which is like having an IQ of 175, though the ERA is easier to document and vastly more useful.) One April day in 1970, Seaver struck out ten Padres in a row, nineteen in all—an auto-de-fé that has never been bettered. One could go on.

The late Sixties and early Seventies were celebrated or execrated for many things besides someone being able to throw a baseball consistently at ninety-five miles per hour. These were the days of the Movement, the Counter-culture, the Student "unrest." Yippies yipped, flower children blossomed and withered, America was being greened, by grass and by rock and by people who peddled them. This was a pastoral time, and it would, like all pastorals, turn sere, but for three or four years, while Seaver was gaining control over a block of space approximately three feet high, eighteen inches wide, and sixty feet six inches long, many other of America's "young" were break-ing loose. That great wave against structure and restraint—whatever its legiti-macy—begun publicly by people like Mario Savio at Berkeley in 1964, was now rolling East, catching up in its powerful eddies and its froth everyone in the country. In 1964 Tom Seaver, Californian, was moving on from Fresno City College to USC, his move East to come two years later. Here are, I think, the origins of the Seaver mystique in New York, in the young Californian who brought control, in the "youth" who came East bearing—indeed, em-bodying—tradition.

Most Americans do not distinguish among Californians at all, and if they do, it is certainly not with the passionate self-absorption of the natives. Yet we should, for there are real differences among them, differences far more interesting than those implied by the contrast most favored by Californians themselves, the one between the self-conscious sophisticates of San Francisco and the self-conscious zanies of Los Angeles. There are, for instance, all those Californians, North and South, who are not self-conscious at all. Such is Seaver, who is from Fresno.

Fresno—the name means "ash tree," that is, something tangible, durable; not the name of a difficult saint, with all its implications about egotism and insecurity, not a mass of heavenly spirits, with its notions of indistinct sprawl, but "ash tree"—Fresno is inland, about the middle of the state, the dominant city in the San Joaquin Valley, that fertile scar that runs parallel to the ocean between the Coastal Ranges and the Sierra Nevada. Fresno is the kingdom sung by Saroyan—flat, green, hot, and fertile; the land of hardworking Armenians, Chicanos, Germans; the cradle of cotton, alfalfa, raisin grapes, melons, peaches, figs, wine. Fresno is not chic, but it is secure. You do not work that hard and reap so much of the earth's good without knowing who you are and how you got that way. This is the California Seaver came from, and in many ways it accounts for his balance as a man as well as a pitcher, for his sense of self-worth and for his conviction that you work by the rules and that you are rewarded, therefore, according to the rule of merit.

All this Seaver brought East, along with his fastball and his luminous wife, Nancy. They were perceived as a couple long before this became a journalistic convenience or public-relations necessity. They were Golden West, but not Gilded, nor long-haired, nor "political," nor opinionated. They were attractive, articulate, photogenic. He was Tom Terrific, the nickname a tribute to his all-American quality, a recognition, ironic but affectionate, that only in comic strips and myth did characters like Seaver exist. I have no idea what opinions Seaver held on race, politics, war, marijuana, and the other ERA, but whatever they were, or are, they are beside the point. The point is the way Seaver was perceived—as clean-cut, larger than life, a fastballer, "straight," all at a time when many young people, getting lots of newspaper coverage, were none of the above. And then there was something else, a quality he exuded.

I encountered this quality the only time I ever met Seaver. One evening in the winter of 1971 I spent several hours with the Seavers and their friends and neighbors the Schaaps (he is the NBC-TV broadcaster) in the apartment of Erich Segal, then at the height of his fame as the author of *Love Story*. The talk was light, easy, and bright, and was produced almost entirely by the Schapps, Nancy Seaver and Segal. Because I was about the only member of the gathering who was a household name only in my own household, I was content to listen, and to watch Seaver. He sat somewhat apart, not, I thought, by design, not surely, because he was aloof, but because it seemed natural to him. He was watchful, though in no sense wary, and had that attitude I have seen in the finest athletes and actors (similar breeds), of being relaxed but not in repose, the body being completely at ease, but, because of thousands of hours of practice, always poised, ready at any instant to gather itself together and move. Candid in his gaze, there was a formality in his manner, a gravity, something autumnal in the man who played hard all summer. He sat as other men who work with their hands sit, the hands clasped chest high or folded in front of him, often in motion, omnipresent hands that, like favored children, are the objects of constant if unconscious attention and repositories of complete confidence.

Seaver had, to be brief, *dignitas,* all the more for never thinking for a moment that he had it all. A dignity that manifested itself in an air of utter self-possession without any self-regard, it was a quality born of a radical equilibrium. Seaver could never be off balance because he knew what he was doing and why it was valuable. He contrasted completely with the part of the country he was known to come from and with the larger society that he was seen as surrounded by. With consummate effortlessness, his was the talent that summed up baseball tradition; his was the respect for the rules that embodied baseball's craving for law; his was the personality, intensely competitive, basically decent, with the artisan's dignity, that amidst the brave but feckless Mets, in a boom time of leisure soured by divisions and drugs, seemed to recall a cluster of virtues seemingly no longer valued.

And Seaver held up. His character proved as durable and strong as his arm. He was authentic; neither a goody two-shoes nor a flash in the pan, he matured into the best pitcher in baseball. Character and talent on this scale equaled a unique charisma. He was a national symbol, nowhere more honored than in New York, and in New York never more loved than by the guy who seemed in every other respect Seaver's antithesis, the guy who would never give a sucker an even break, who knew how corrupt they all were, who knew it was who you knew that counted, who knew how rotten it all really was—this guy loved Seaver because Seaver was a beautiful pitcher, a working guy who got rewarded; Seaver was someone who went by the rules and made it; Seaver carried the whole lousy team, God love 'em, on his back, and never shot his mouth off, and never gave in, and did it right. The guy loved Seaver because Seaver did not have to be street-wise.

In bars in Queens, in clubs in the Bronx, in living rooms in front of Channel Nine in Suffolk and Nassau, out on Staten Island, everywhere, but particularly in the tattered reaches of Shea Stadium, they loved him for many things, but above all because he never thought he had to throw at anybody's head. From the Columbia riots to the brink of fiscal disaster, there was someone in New York who did not throw at anybody. They loved it in him, and in that act sought for it in themselves.

None of this reasoning, if such it is, would appeal to the dominant New York baseball writers, who have used the Seaver trade as a *casus belli;* nor to M. (for, I think, Moralistic) Donald Grant, chairman of the board of the Mets, who would quickly tell us that Seaver wanted too much money, meaning by that something he would never say aloud but would certainly formulate within himself—that Tom wanted too much. Tom wanted, somehow, to cross the line between employee and equal, hired hand and golf partner, "boy" and man. What M. Donald Grant could not abide—after all, could he, Grant, ever become a Payson? Of course not. Everything is ordered. Doesn't anyone understand anything anymore?—Tom Seaver thought was his due. He believed in the rules, in this game governed by law; if you were the best pitcher in baseball, you ought to get the best salary of any pitcher in baseball; and money

—yes, money—ought to be spent so baseball's best pitcher would not have to work on baseball's worst-hitting team.

Of course Tom Seaver wanted money, and wanted money spent; he wanted it for itself, but he wanted it because, finally, Tom Seaver felt about the Mets the way the guy from Astoria felt about Seaver—he loved them for what they stood for and he wanted merit rewarded and quality improved. The irony is that Tom Seaver had in abundance precisely the quality that M. Donald Grant thinks he values most—institutional loyalty, the capacity to be faithful to an idea as well as to individuals. Grant ought to have seen that in Seaver; after all, the man worked for the Mets for eleven years. Grant ought to have had the wit to see a more spacious, generous version of what he prizes so highly in himself. Certainly the guy who had watched Seaver all those years knew it, knew Seaver was holding out for something, a principle that made sense in one who played baseball but that grew from somewhere within him untouched by baseball, from a conviction about what a man has earned and what is due him and what is right. The fan understood this and was devastated when his understanding, and Seaver's principle, were not honored. The anguish surrounding Seaver's departure stemmed from the realization that the chairman of the board and certain newspaper columnists thought money was more important than loyalty, and the fury stemmed from the realization that the chairman and certain writers thought everybody else agreed with them, or ought to agree with them.

On June 16, the day after Seaver was exiled to Cincinnati by way of Montreal, a sheet was hung from a railing at Shea bearing the following legend:

> I WAS A
> BELIEVER
> BUT NOW WE'VE
> LOST
> SEAVER

I construe that text, and particularly its telling rhyme, to mean not that the author has lost faith in Seaver but that the author has lost faith in the Mets' ability to understand a simple, crucial fact: that among all the men who play baseball there is, very occasionally, a man of such qualities of heart and mind and body that he transcends even the great and glorious game, and that such a man is to be cherished, not sold.

COMMENTARY

This article may seem to be difficult at first glance. A second, longer look will still not make it seem easy. Please don't let that

difficulty throw you off or keep you from reading the article. If
you find it a bit hard to read, this is a good sign. You cannot
spend your life doing what is easy; Dick and Jane first-grade readers
will not keep you happy forever, and they certainly will not help
you to develop college-level reading skills.

The introduction to the article uses an interesting technique and
makes a neat connection to the concluding paragraph. First the introduction compares to a work of art the departure of the Seavers
from Shea stadium. This work of art is probably vaguely familiar
to a small group of the readers of the magazine in which this piece
was published. Those who recognize it feel some pride, while the
readers unfamiliar with the work feel they should be acquainted
with it. The introduction thus serves to catch the attention. The
introduction mentions a physical location, Shea Stadium. This
place is familiar to most baseball fans, and it calls up a picture that
many people are able to see in their minds.

The introduction also makes a preliminary statement about the
content and direction of the article:

> Where Parks, Namath, and Erving are only superb at playing their sports,
> Seaver seems to embody his.

This idea suggests that Tom Seaver is the living, breathing example
of all that an athlete in his sport should be. This idea is repeated,
in the concluding paragraph, by a slightly longer and more detailed
expression. This repetition of idea is tied to a repetition of the
physical location, Shea Stadium:

> On June 16 . . . a sheet was hung from a railing at *Shea Stadium* . . .

The return to the location mentioned in the opening paragraph,
joined with the restatement of the core idea of the article, provides
a sense of completeness, of "finishedness" about the article, and
offers us a good example for constructing openings and closings.

Next the author proves he has an awareness of his audience. The
article first appeared in *Harper's*, a magazine aimed at college-
educated, fairly affluent people. Not all of the magazine's readers
are baseball fans, and many would be attracted to this article by
the author's name (Giamatti is the president of Yale University)
rather than by its subject. Giamatti gives the readers not familiar
with baseball a factual account of Seaver's accomplishments, and

he provides for those who need it an explanation of the man's importance to his sport. We also need to consider our readers and give them all the help we possibly can.

Then, in an effort to explain the nature of the man Seaver, Giamatti moves into a series of comparisons. He selects two fairly well-known ideas and uses them to highlight aspects of Seaver's personality. First he uses the Student Revolution, The Counterculture of the late Sixties and early Seventies, and the Hippies. He says, in effect, "You all remember what that movement, those people were like. Seaver was almost exactly the opposite." Second, he does exactly the same thing with two stereotypes of California, the image of Los Angeles and of San Francisco, and shows that those two images are not like the area where Seaver was born, Fresno. Comparison or contrast is a useful way of clarifying an idea for your reader.

A second useful device is illustrated in the middle of the article in the paragraph that opens with, "I encountered this quality . . ." The device makes use of a combination of narration and description in which Giamatti recounts a very common, very brief incident. He met Seaver at a small party, and listened to him talk, watched him in a social situation, and drew a certain conclusion about him. He uses words such as *watchful, at ease, candid,* and *poised* to describe Seaver. These words and the report of Seaver's actions and conversation add up to the character trait—dignity. Giamatti establishes this impression for us by telling the brief story of the party and describing the person.

The following qualities add up to a successful article:

a. An introduction designed to catch the reader's interest. The introduction should also state the main idea of the article.
b. Carefully established comparisons between known quantities—the Student Revolution and two cities in California—and the subject of the article, Tom Seaver.
c. Narrative and descriptions that present traits of character. From these traits, it is possible to draw a conclusion about the person.

Try to reproduce these qualities in your writing. They will serve as aids for you to develop your subject.

The following newspaper article offers a brief sketch of a single person. The description is much like the one you are developing.

MEMORIES OF GRANDFATHER

by Roger Simon

Mostly, I remember his hands. How large they were, how the big, blunted fingers would wrap around my own. When I was little, I would hold my palms up against his, feeling his hard callouses and measuring how far up his hands my own reached.

My grandfather's hands were a working man's hands, a carpenter's hands. He would tell me how when he was very young, it was decreed that he should become a blacksmith because that was what his village needed. He would work over the forge, the heat and smoke blackening his young features, until one day he could stand it no longer and ran away. It was an act of unheard-of rebellion, shocking the entire community. But he won in the end and was allowed to become what he wanted to become, a carpenter. "But why did they try to make you do something you didn't want to?" I would ask him. He would laugh, knowing the hopelessness of explaining 19th Century village life in Russia to a child of America.

He came over by boat to Canada with his young bride. This, too, is something that can barely be understood now. It was an arranged marriage. I think my grandfather once told me he had never seen my grandmother before their wedding day. And yet he loved and cared for her with a single-minded devotion that lasted beyond her own death a few years ago. They settled in the ghetto of Montreal and he built wooden railway cars for the Canadian Pacific. They paid him 13 cents an hour. He reared two sons and a daughter, my mother, and then came south to the land of unlimited promise, where he became an American citizen. In Chicago he built homes and stores. Nothing fancy, nothing famous, no landmarks. Just places where people lived and worked. He would carry his toolbox from job to job, from contractor to contractor, going wherever there was work.

For years I think he harbored the hope that one of his grandsons would become a carpenter, too. It was something he used to joke about, and I do not really know if there was seriousness behind the joking. I remembered as a child begging him to show me his tools. And how he would go into the bedroom, carefully lift up the bedspread and reach beneath the bed to drag out his huge, wooden tool box. He would lift it with one hand and give it to me. I would grab it with two hands and stagger around the room like a drunk, trying to keep it from crashing onto the floor. Inside the box, carefully oiled against rust, there would be his hammers and saws and planes and awls. He would let me hold them, let me breathe the sharp oil-smell and run my hands over the smooth blueness of the steel. When it became clear that none of us would follow him in his trade, that none of us would work with our hands for a living, he put the tools away for a final time. I do not know where they are today.

When I first became a reporter, he sat me down and asked me to explain just what I did for a living. "I talk to people, Grampa," I said. "Then I take what they say and I put it in the paper." He just looked at me for awhile, "Tell me something," he said, with the beginning of a smile, "for this they pay you?" Two weeks ago at age 91 my grandfather had a heart attack. He recovered well, drawing his strength from a life of hard, physical labor. When I visited him in the hospital, he was sitting up and eating a large lunch. I showed him the picture of him and me, which he had not yet seen. "I would say very handsome," he said, holding it. "Very handsome." I told him that he looked handsome, too. "I was talking about me," he said, smiling.

My grandfather does not need these words for his memorial. His memorial is to be found in the homes of this city, homes that still stand, homes in which people still live. When I was 10, my family decided to move to California for a while. We broke the news to my grandfather, who sat weeping at our kitchen table, sure that he would never see us again. I still remember seeing him wipe his eyes with the backs of those huge hands. I tugged at his jacket and asked him why he was crying. "Your grampa will miss you," he said, wrapping me in his arms. "He will miss you."

Today, I miss him.

COMMENTARY

Two aspects of this essay are worth noting. First, the writing contains a warm, loving statement about the affection and admiration of a grandson for his grandfather. It expresses the kind of sentiment we all hope someone will express about us. The core idea of the essay is that the writer deeply loved his grandfather, who was a proud, independent craftsman who loved his family and approached life with a sense of humor. The interesting thing about the development of the essay, however, is that the writer gives us a picture of this man without ever even identifying by name the characteristics he wishes us to see. Instead we learn of those character traits by a more indirect means. We learn, for example, that the grandfather is

Very independent, perhaps even stubborn
 when we learn of his refusal to become a blacksmith.

A loving family man
 when we see how he treated his wife and how he took the separation from his grandchild.

A person who approaches life with a sense of humor
 when we hear his words
 "Tell me something, for this they pay you?"

"Very handsome." I told him that he looked handsome, too. "I was talking about me," he said, smiling.

A craftsman who wanted to pass on his trade and his pride of workmanship to his grandchildren
    when we read the anecdote about the tools.

Notice that statements such as *he was proud*, and *he was loving* are relatively meaningless when they stand alone. They come to mean something only when we see the facts, the words, and the actions that support and explain these statements. Writers call these specific pieces of information

CONCRETE SUPPORTING DETAILS

The facts of the grandfather's life, the appearance of his hands, his actions, and his words are the details that make the picture of the man come alive and have meaning for us. It is of little value for a writer to make a statement unless that statement is supported and explained by concrete information of some kind.

If you learn only one thing from writing this assignment, let it be this idea:

ALWAYS USE CONCRETE SUPPORTING DETAILS TO CLARIFY AND EXPLAIN THE IDEAS YOU WISH TO GET ACROSS TO YOUR READER.

Think of it this way:

If you tell your readers that a person is brave, show how she saves someone from drowning.

If you claim that the person is humorous, let your readers hear the jokes.

If you maintain that the weather has been extremely hot, reveal what the temperature has been, and let the readers feel the heat through your choice of descriptive words.

SUPPORT EVERY STATEMENT WITH CONCRETE EXPLANATION AND ILLUSTRATIONS. UNSUPPORTED STATEMENTS MEAN LITTLE OR NOTHING TO YOUR READER.

Finally, give the paper a brief conclusion. Sometimes in a short paper one sentence at the end of the last paragraph is long enough.

> But as I look back I see how much I learned about geometry, and about other more important things too.

Occasionally a single sentence doesn't seem to be sufficient. You may need to write a short paragraph of conclusion.

> I passed the class, and graduated from Central High. Last June I went back to visit the school, and I found myself in the doorway of Miss Carlin's room. She smiled at me, more brightly than I remember her smile when I was in the class. "Come in, Carl," she said. "Miss Carlin, I just came by to tell you how. . ." Then I understood how much I had learned in her class.

Now write the draft of the paper in which you portray a person. Remember to check the draft carefully and copy it over neatly before you submit it to your teacher.

ASSIGNMENT 7.

Writing About a Place

You have now completed two longer essays: the first, three paragraphs long, narrated an event; the second, four or five paragraphs long, described an individual who was in some way important to you. The third, and last, assignment in this series of projects based on recollection asks that you examine the place where you "grew up," that is, the place where you spent a large portion of the past few years.

Possibly you moved around a good bit during the past few years. If this is true, choose one of the places where you lived, one where important events and important people influenced you as you became the person you are today. It is also possible that you have been an adult for a number of years. In that case, you should look at the last few years, for they are the years in which people and events in your life moved you to come to college. Think of the community—the people, places, events, and even the institutions such as schools, churches, and businesses—that influenced you as you made your important decisions.

The purpose of the project is to get you to take a look into your background, the place where you made some important decisions, developed important attitudes, and met important people.

That community helped to form you, and so it should be an interesting subject for writing. The material is readily available in your memory, and perhaps it is already recorded somewhere in your journal. You need to read that journal and mark the sections in which you have written about this community. Then you should begin to write about the events and people in the journal. Expand on the people, events, and ideas until you have a good-sized block of writing that somehow relates to your hometown. Eventually, as you write, you will discover something meaningful to say about that place and about its influence on you.

People make two statements about this assignment, both related to their perceptions of the place. First they say, "I grew up in a dull place; I'll never find anything interesting to write about." Joe Clark, a professional photographer who specializes in photographic studies of people living in the southern mountains, tells a story about a beginning photographer who complained that he could never make progress in his field because he was stuck in a small town where "nothing interesting ever happened." Joe Clark responded to the story by taking a series of photographs of places and people in the town. His photographic essay was then featured in *Life* Magazine.

The second comment is similar to the first. A student once said, "I don't think this place has influenced me. Nothing important has ever happened to me. It's all very dull." She began to write about the place, not expecting anything good at all from the writing. As she wrote, recording at random whatever she could remember, a pattern began to emerge. "All we ever did when I was younger was play. We came home from school, and our mothers gave us a snack. Then we went out to play, down the street, in the park, at someone's house. We played until our mothers called us for supper. Then we stayed home and watched TV or did a little homework. I can't ever remember working, having anything I was responsible for, helping my mother. We just played." The next day the student declared, "I think I see something. I grew up in that neighborhood without ever learning to take responsibility, or discipline myself, or work at anything. Maybe that's the reason I'm having difficulty in school, always late with assignments, never really working, always being a little dissatisfied with myself and my progress. I never learned to work because in that neighborhood kids didn't work; they just played. Now I see."

That was an important insight for the student. It is noteworthy, though, that she came to this insight because she was willing to write about that very dull place. Many subjects seem unexciting at first glance. It is the second and third looks, and in this case a look accomplished through writing, that provides insight into the nature of the place. Every community seems dull on the surface. Don't let the surface dullness keep you from writing, however, for writing will allow you to discover things of importance about your community and about yourself. Writing can become an act of discovery if only you will let it.

To begin your look at your hometown, focus on the place where you lived. Think about the house, apartment building, or farm. Write a description of that place. Remember to use the technique for gathering details that you learned in Unit 1. You can refer to the beginning of this unit (p. 59) and use the exercise you wrote then as a beginning for this work. Start by writing the two key sentences, and then record as many details as you can remember.

The house has ———————————— The house is————————————

When you have a fairly complete list of details, practice free-writing about the impression that the place created. Then shape a paragraph of description for that place.

The paragraph you wrote as a journal entry at the beginning of this unit is a close approximation of that kind of description. The example reads this way:

> We lived just off the country road about three miles from town. You turned off into the driveway and saw the old farmhouse right away, sitting there on the left. It was maybe one hundred and fifty years old, and a little weatherbeaten. Faded might be a good way to describe it. Across the yard there was an old barn, and it was really faded and run-down. Nobody put much into barns when they didn't farm seriously, and my family just kind of played at it when I was a kid. We kept geese, and a few lambs. The geese made great watchdogs; they made a lot of noise when anyone came in the drive. The lambs stayed in a little pen beside the barn and went inside it through a hole in the wall when the weather was really bad. A little creek ran through the yard down at the bottom of the slope. When we were little kids, we swam in it during the summer.

You might have written a description of this place in the background writing at the beginning of this unit. Don't let that earlier effort stop you from doing the same thing again. By doing the work again, you can improve the description and learn more about the place.

Next, imagine yourself standing in front of the place, looking down the street. Write a brief description of the street.

Next, think of schools, stores, churches, and other institutions that were part of that area. Write a brief description of each one.

> The local high school was the only really important institution in the whole neighborhood. It had been built years ago, beautifully done, with great decorations on the outside—those lions and other stuff like that. The halls were arched and had high ceilings. The doors to the classrooms were solid looking. And the teachers were incredible. You know, the kind of people who liked kids and enjoyed teaching, who wanted to help, they loved the school, reminded us all the time of how lucky we were to go there. They didn't make things easy for us. They made us work but they helped. Lots of people in town had graduated from that school, lots of them were successful people who had made a good life for themselves. We never talked about it then, and we laughed at the teachers when they preached about the school but when I look back I think we knew—it occurs to me now that we knew then that we had something special going for us, that we were making it through a good school. I think the notion was that going there, getting through with the help of the teachers, finally graduating, gave us a kind of assurance that we had a good chance to succeed in life. I guess we figured we could pretty well handle whatever came along because we had been through that school.

Now turn your attention to the people who lived in that neighborhood. List the names of some of your friends or acquaintances, people your own age, and some of the adults in the community. Select two from each list, and write a half page about each one. Tell who they were, what sort of people they were—as you did in the previous assignment—and try to reach some conclusions about the ways they influenced you. Remember that this writing will not be judged for its quality or correctness. Rather, it is probably better for this purpose if your writing is messy, jumbled and rambling. Good ideas get discovered in such writing. You will have time after you write the rough draft to improve and revise anything you choose for inclusion in the paper.

> I remember old coach Worthington. The meanest nastiest guy I've ever known yelled screamed cursed kicked guys threw his golf cap down and stamped on it. I mean he made the meanest professional coach you can think of look like a salvation army worker. I really hated him spoiled my

whole football experience. the only good memories I have of him were when he made a fool of himself. One day he lost his temper at Johnson our right end, "Blocked like your grandmother," he said. "Teach you how to do a downfield block," he said. Threw his cigar down, stomped it. threw his golf cap down cut it to ribbons with his golf shoes cleats—he must have bought those hats by the case, he ruined at least one a week. Started off running at Johnson "block like this you sissy," he screamed. Ran about ten yards down the field at Johnson, hurled himself into a perfectly executed downfield block, hit Johnson square on, bounced off, and fell flat on his back. Johnson never moved, just set his feet and bent his knees a little, and Worthington bounced off him like a tennis ball off a block wall—flat on his back. It was dead quiet for a minute—everybody was too scared to laugh. The coach looked at the team, and at Johnson and back at the team and commenced to roar laughing hugged Johnson slapped him on the back. Just for a minute I though he was really human, but it didn't last long. I still can't really abide football.

Next, you should recall several incidents that happened while you were living in the place you are describing. Look for two kinds of events. First, try to set down some things you did that were typical of life in that place. Then look for two or three incidents that had some sort of influence on you.

To be worth looking at in writing, these events don't need to be earthshaking, life-changing-experiences. Much of the movement of life is made up of seemingly small, unimportant events. These opening lines from various students' free-writing should give you the idea.

The day I met Jeremy was just an ordinary day in school.

The phone rang. "Jim, it's for you," my brother said. "Jim, this is Marlene," the voice on the other end said. "I'm going sailing with my parents Saturday, and I thought you might enjoy going with us."

Do you know what it's like to discover a whole new interest? I was down at the newstand the other day and picked up a magazine on radio-controlled gliders.

The cops came this morning and hauled away old Mr. Sessions, the guy down the hall. Nothing new about cops on my hall or in my neighborhood. They camp out around here waiting for trouble. What was different this morning was that I suddenly got fed up with the whole scene—the drunks, the stink, the dopers—all of them. So I took my last five bucks and went downtown and joined the Air Force. I figure anything has to be better than this lousy place.

I went down to Jack's, you know, the used car place on Second. I could afford about 1200 bucks for a car. Thought maybe I'd find something I could drive for a while till I got some more bread together to get a decent set of wheels. Well, I'm nosing around the back of the lot—a guy with 1200 bucks doesn't look on the front line at anybody's car lot—and I walk around the back of this shed where they store paint and other stuff that blows up, and almost fall over a '68, maybe '69 Cougar convertible. Horrible looking, dirt and stuff piled on it like it had been stored and forgotten. But the interior isn't destroyed, and the body, under all that dirt and junk, doesn't have much rust. So I begin to talk to Jack, hoping he doesn't know what he's got there, I'm lucky it isn't a Mustang, or I'll never touch it with my money. And he says, Oh, yeah. That old crate. Took that in trade a year or so ago. Some woman took it out for a test and the engine threw a rod. Never seemed worth fixing. You want it, it's yours for what I gave in trade 550 bucks." "But I got a friend with an old Merc engine that will probably fit it. Yeah, I'll take it." So I began one of the great car restoration projects of all time.

All those seemingly small incidents, and all the circumstances that surround them, are the things that shaped your attitudes and directions. It was a coincidence that the last writer grew up in a community where everybody, male and female, over twelve, lusted after cars, and where cars were an absolute necessity for getting around. Coincidence, but the man who wrote that last piece is well out of high school and is still interested in cars, still working on them, and still getting genuine pleasure from his hobby. It was just a little thing, finding a seemingly worthless car under some junk, but an event that played an important part in his life.

It would also be useful, and would add to your understanding of that place, if you would explore for a few minutes the expectations people in the community had for those growing up there. The question is:

What did the adults, your parents and others who influenced you, expect of you while you were growing up, and what did they expect your occupational goals and directions would be?

Some neighborhoods expect that every kid will go to college, some even specify a certain kind of school—Ivy League, perhaps. Others don't seem so optimistic about the future. They harbor faint hopes that the kids in the neighborhood will stay out of jail and get a job, any job. Between these two extremes, where most of us find ourselves, are a whole host of hopes and dreams that parents, relatives, teachers, coaches, and others have for those growing up around them. Those hopes and dreams, the fears also, direct you, push you, help you and even pressure you to move in certain directions.

Careers, hobbies, mates, even choices of places to live after college, all these things are influenced by the expectations of those around you. Consider them, for they may give you some insight into your own attitudes and directions.

As always, you should be looking for two things from this background writing. First, you should find materials to develop the body of the essay: illustrations, discussions, stories, people. All these are the raw material of the essay. Record everything you can remember; some of it will be useful, some will not, but you won't know what will be useful and what won't until you begin to select materials to use in the essay. Don't edit this free writing. Record whatever comes to mind, and select later what is useful.

Second, while you are engaged in free writing, you should be looking for the development of a statement for the essay. If writing is an act of discovery, then the writing will lead you to an idea, to a statement answering the questions:

> What sort of place was this, and what effect did it have on me, on my attitudes, my goals, my dreams?

There is a parallel here to doing reading for a research or library paper. An assignment on a topic completely new, for which you know little or nothing, requires that you go to written sources—books and magazines—and, if necessary, people, to get information. Ordinarily you would go to the library and find some sources, and then you would take notes on cards, putting down a good deal of information as you find it. Eventually, as you did this reading and recording, you would begin to see that there is a direction and an outline to the materials, and you would find an idea important enough to be developed.

The process for writing about your community is quite similar to library research, with one major difference. The materials you need for this paper are usually not in books; they are in your memory. Your job in researching this topic is to record all the information stored in your memories of your community, and to continue writing until you develop a statement about the place.

The sample free-writing materials at the beginning of this unit are preliminary materials jotted down in preparation for the three essays in this unit. They need to be developed in length and in scope before the writer can discover an idea for the essay. Read these additional materials on the subject of growing up in a farming community in the Upper Midwest.

What did we do for entertainment? On Saturday nights we'd get in our cars or trucks, usually they weren't really ours, they belonged to our parents or older brothers, and we'd go down to the parking lot in the shopping center and hang around. Sometimes we'd have a beer, or a Coke. Mostly we just talked, or fooled with the cars. Once or twice a night a little money would go down on whose car was the fastest anyway, and then we'd all whiz over to that flat stretch on Powerline Road and watch the people race. Actually it was a little silly. Nobody in that town had a really decent car for driving around, much less having something that would race. Mostly we just sat around in the cars, or on the fenders listening to music. Pretty soon after sitting there awhile, we'd get bored, so we'd crank up and drive downtown and go slowly down Main Street—draggin' Main Street, my old man used to call it, to see if anything was happening. But nothing ever did, so we'd go back and sit in the parking lot. It was really boring.

In the winter we went skiing, mostly cross-country skiing because it's really flat around here. I liked it—I like to be out of doors, and to get some exercise and get all tired out. The best part of all that messing around in the cold was getting back to the house and drinking some of my Mom's good hot cider. Warmed me up all over, in about two seconds.

Mary Jane and I broke up last week. She's worked for a while and leaves for State in a few days. But I don't feel like writing about that right now. Maybe I won't ever.

Worked a couple of days last week making hay. Hot and horrible as ever. I saw a couple of guys I played ball with in high school. They're just bumming around from job to job hating it all, bored, looking for something, anything to do. I told them to join the army. They laughed and threw me off the hay wagon. Oh, well.

First snow last night. It was beautiful this morning, all clean and white. Covered up all the mud and junk along the road. But I just don't know if I can bear another winter cold, snow, ice on the roads. Feeding the cows at 5:30 in the morning when the water is frozen and the feed stiff and cold and cuts your hands. Jim slid his car off the road this morning into a ditch. Thought he could make one more day before putting on snow tires. In a few days, if it warms up a little, we'll help him dig the car out and get it up on the road. What a dumb trick.

This whole place is beginning to get me. Nothing to do. No jobs. No prospects of any jobs. Sometimes I think there must be some place else where it isn't so cold and nasty and so boring.

The last entry in that free-writing session has the possibility of becoming an idea. Any number of people in this country have been inspired by the lack of opportunity, or the unpleasantness, or by some set of negative ideas about their community to move to another place, to try another situation, to search for a better climate, to find a better job, or to meet a new set of people. If that observation in the last entry holds up under further writing and thinking, it could become the controlling idea for a paper on life in that little farming community in the middle west.

An essay based on those entries would need a controlling statement similar to this one:

> That little community seemed to offer me no opportunity and very little comfort, so I moved on by joining the Navy.

An essay developing the idea that the whole place was beginning to get to the writer needs to establish the parts or elements that make up what was "getting to him" and finally motivated him to enlist in the navy. The collections of materials written about the place provide a few clues:

1. The weather—beautiful at first, as the new snow falls, but troublesome and hard to take over the long term.
2. The hard work of making hay, coupled perhaps with the realization that not many other, better jobs were available.
3. The social life or entertainment available, the answer to the question, "What do you do for fun?" which may have looked like not much fun at all, dragging Main Street, sitting in the park-lots, a little drag racing, all those may not add up to much to a person who has been doing them for years.
4. The loss of Mary Jane, his girl friend, true love, and light-of-his-life.

All these observations, when added together and examined, answer the question, "What kind of place is this?" The answer might be expressed as follows:

> It is the kind of place where the winters are long and hard, where the work available to me is extremely hard manual labor, where there is precious little to do for excitement, and where a guy can lose his girl because she is going off to the university hundreds of miles away. It is the kind of place, in other words, that offers me so little that I just don't want to stay there any more.

A set of writings about a place has led to a statement of some importance, and that same set of materials collected by both free- and directed-writings has provided development—illustrations, ideas, and observations—for an essay. Now the problem is to arrange that collection of material in a way that will best get the statement across to the reader.

> It seems logical to provide the reader with the location of the town and a general description of the place: a small town in the northern Midwest. It is a very quiet place, and the writer lives on a farm out of town.
>
> Next should come a description of the weather, both winter and summer. Discuss the extremes of cold and heat.

Then comes a choice. Should the writer next discuss the opportunities for work, or the lack of social life, or the loss of Mary Jane? Part of the answer depends on the importance of each of these three factors. The presentation ought to work up to the most important of the three. Two possibilities are obvious. If we start the paper with a general description of the place and a discussion of the weather, we then have two options:

1. General description of the town
2. Description of the winter weather

Option I	*Option II*
3. The dull social life	3. Dull social life
4. Limited opportunities for work	4. The loss of Mary Jane
5. The loss of Mary Jane	5. Limited opportunities for work

The choice between the two options depends on the importance of the items. If the loss of the girl is most important, it occurs last in the outline. If the lack of opportunity is the most important influence, it occurs last in the outline. The order of presentation runs from least important to most important.

Both of these orders of presentation will work; they have logic and a clear order of importance. When the writer has selected an order, the next step is to write a draft version of each of the paragraphs, keeping in mind the formula for writing effective paragraphs which was discussed in Assignment 4, Unit One. (See page 33.)

Write a topic sentence.	The weather in my home town was, at best, terrible.
Provide discussion and explanation.	In the winter the first snow came in November or December, and by January the ground was covered with four feet of snow.

| Provide illustrations. | There were fifty days last winter when the thermometer didn't go above zero. |

Each of those factors that motivated the writer to leave should be discussed in a thoroughly developed paragraph joined to an interesting introduction, and concluded with a sentence to wrap up the whole idea. That set of five or six paragraphs can add up to a successful first draft.

The following essay was written by a young woman who moved on by joining the Air Force. She has found better circumstances through marriage and further education, but she has also discovered that her community possessed some wonderful qualities which she did not recognize earlier. Now that she has moved on, she feels that she cannot recapture these qualities.

SMITH CREEK

by Mary Acevedo

[1] Smith Creek, a drab community hidden in the folds of the Appalachian mountains, is a depressing sight. Its dingy little grey houses are pressed against the mountain sides, their tired frames retreating as far as possible from the creek which divides the valley in half. Dry gritty cone dust covers the trees, houses and even the people with a thin grey film. The natural beauty of the mountains is the village's only saving grace. Heavily forested slopes tower above the valley. In summer, their dark green sides appear almost black. A grey mist surrounds their flanks in fall, the brilliant foliage creating the illusion of a forest fire as far as the eye can see. I loved growing up in this peaceful village, but as I matured I began to see my hometown in a new light. To me Smith Creek was barren, and totally devoid of excitement and possibility. It took me many years to fully realize the true value of my community.

[2] Our village was poor. The men worked in the coal mines, supplementing their incomes with livestock and kitchen gardens. Every family owned a truck of some obscure vintage, but there wasn't a television antenna for miles. Ten extended families comprised our village, all of them working and sharing together. The women commonly gathered together to share the chores of canning, babysitting, and ironing. When they weren't at the mines, the men puttered together, swarming like flies over the carcass of some ailing truck or tractor. Their leisure time was spent hunting or lolling across a convenient front porch sipping beer and discussing crops and politics. Socially and economically we were all equals, status never became a dividing factor in our lives. Money, the lack of it, was a major factor that hindered everyone.

[3] My family attempted to earn extra money by peddling to the tourists, my father's brainstorm. "Come on kids, grab your buckets! no work, no eat!" he would bellow. Depending on the season, we picked persimmons, blackberries, papaws, or gathered black walnuts to sell down at the highway. It was eleven bumpy dusty miles of dirt road to our market stall. We passed the time merrily singing, and joking about the new quality produced in our voices by the bouncing truckbed. At first peddling was embarrassing, but after awhile it didn't bother us.

[4] "Hey folks, how about some blackberries, only thirty cents." "Come on lady, we been picking all day," we pleaded. People were interested in our unusual produce, and we usually sold everything. Sometimes they posed us for pictures, and they were always asking silly questions. "Do you kids go to school?" "Is it true Hillbillies have one leg shorter than the other?" Men always asked the last question and then laughed at their own joke. We learned to laugh too, they bought more that way. Later fall was usually our busiest peddling season, we always tried to have some extra money saved for the winter.

[5] Usually by November, the small local mines where my father and our neighbors worked were closed. The shafts became too icy to work in safely. My father and the others would try to get work at the big "Diamond," a union mine. I can remember being instructed to pray for a strike, just so our local men could work as scabs. My parents were always extra cheerful during the bad times to avoid frightening us; but we always knew, the gas truck stopped coming around, and we ate beans and potatoes almost every meal.

[6] Warm weather always improved our financial situation. The mines reopened in the Spring, and odd jobs became plentiful. We eagerly shed our heavy winter garments and began to look forward to summer vacation.

[7] Summertime was my favorite. The majority of our free time was spent swimming and fishing in the creek. We had a marvelous swing, made from rope and an old truck tire, and spent hours swinging and leaping into the water. Hunting crawdaddies in the creek shallows was a rewarding sport. Pinched fingers produced painful squeals of success, but their wonderful flavor was well worth the discomfort. The mountains were also an excellent playground. We climbed trees, explored caves, and built tree houses. Although we had many enjoyable play experiences our favorite summer activity was the annual community picnic.

[8] On the fourth of July our entire community gathered in a large field next to the creek to celebrate. My mother and the neighbor women began baking days ahead, and the scent of cooling pies produced stomach rumbles of anticipation. We children loved to help set up the saw horse tables and build the fire, but we had only one thought on our minds. "When do we eat, Mommy?" "I am starving to death!" Just when you thought it wasn't possible to last a moment longer, dinner was ready. Massive amounts of barbecued chicken, fish, baked beans, and fresh ear corn were consumed, followed by berry, apple,

and peach pies. After dinner sides were chosen for softball, the losing team always ended the evening in the creek.

[9] Looking back on my childhood I realize that what I thought were difficult times are actually my fondest memories. The mutual cooperation and goodwill shared by my community was a rare experience. The fast modern world I live in now, filled with congested highways, supermarkets and giant shopping centers, seems more like a bad dream. My friendly village has been replaced by a frightened neighborhood fearful of riots and crime. The "Neon World" of fancy stores, restaurants and discos has its place, but the privilege of living within it's glow isn't worth the price.

Revising and Editing

Every car manufacturer builds into the process of constructing the car a process known as Quality Control. This procedure insures that cars finally sold to the public meet certain standards of performance and workmanship. This process enables the manufacturer to evaluate the engineering and design, the construction of the basic components, the fit and finish of the body and interior, and most important, the actual performance of the vehicle.

Every writer who hopes to produce a quality piece of writing uses the same type of process. Every component of the paper must be examined to insure that all the parts fit together and that the fit and finish of the final product is up to high specifications. Writers call that process of quality control *revising and editing*, and they apply the process before they present their work to the reader.

You have written several papers this term, but your work on each project stopped before you revised and edited your assignment. You have written what are known as first draft versions of your projects. Now it is time to learn to apply quality-control techniques to your writing projects. When you have learned to revise and to edit, you will hand over to your reader only projects that are up to high specifications.

The first step in the revision process must occur in the mind of the writer rather than on paper. When a draft copy is finished, most writers feel a certain amount of affection for the product.

They have invested time and hard work in the production of the draft copy, and they are reluctant to make any changes in it. Overcoming this reluctance is the first step in the process of revision.

You will find that two steps will help you to develop good attitudes about revision. First, set the project aside for a day or two and let your affection and your recollections of the project cool off just a bit. Then take the draft copy into a quiet place, and read it aloud twice. Try to see the copy as a reader would see it. Look for flaws, errors, and for weaknesses that reduce the effectiveness of the work.

Read slowly, and read aloud, remembering that your mind has a tendency to correct problems in the draft by supplying missing words and endings, by adding omitted pieces of information, and by providing emphasis where you know it is needed even when the corrections and emphasis may not be present in the written version. Convince yourself through this reading that the paper is not as strong as it might be, and that it can use improvements. Remember, no first draft is ever genuinely successful; the only good writing is rewriting.

When you have read the paper through completely the second time, write a simple outline of the draft. First, write out the thesis statement of the paper as you just read it. Then write a topic sentence for each of the paragraphs in the paper. Do this work without reference to notes or earlier versions of the outline. It is important, at this point, to work on what you wrote in the draft, not on what you thought you would write. Often, the plans for a paper or essay get changed in the writing of the draft; the draft version rarely follows the early plans for the paper.

WITH THIS OUTLINE OF THE DRAFT OF THE PAPER COMPLETED, YOU ARE NOW READY TO BEGIN WORK ON THE PROCESS OF REVISING AND EDITING.

Step 1.   Thesis Statement/Background Writing.

Read through the notes and background writing for the paper. Be sure that what you wrote in the draft is true to the information you collected. Ask yourself these questions:

Are you comfortable with the thesis statement?

Does it rise naturally from the notes and background writing?

Is the thesis statement clear and carefully framed?

Is it exactly what you wish to say on this subject?

When you have done this work on your paper, read the following student's paper. Note the ways in which this step or the revision process changes the organization of the paper.

[1]   When we first moved to Logan Square, a long time ago, it was a predominately Polish-Italian neighborhood, located on the northwest side of Chicago. The last few years, though, saw it change to a Puerto Rican, Mexican, Indian and Black neighborhood. It also changed from a once beautiful neighborhood to a very ugly and depressing one. Growing up there helped me very much because it taught me to be independent and that the only way to get somewhere in life was through a great deal of hard work. It prepared me for life as it is not for a fairy tale version of it where everyone lives happily ever after with no problems.

[2]   My neighborhood was really no different from most inner city neighborhoods. We had our share of drunks, prostitutes and pimps. We also had a few lunatics that made life difficult. When I was younger there was a couple that lived in our building and everyone thought they were happily married until one night they got home from a party and he was drunk, they got in a fight and he slashed her face up with a butcher knife then left her in the apartment building. The whole building was out in the courtyard watching her being taken away by the police ambulance. My brother and sister and I were the envy of all the neighborhood kids because it happened in our building. For weeks after that we used to sneak upstairs to see the blood on the kitchen floor.

[3]   My neighborhood was mostly made up of three or four-floor buildings. The buildings were very ornate but obviously about one hundred years old. They were falling apart piece by piece and the landlords didn't do too much about it because it was considered a bad risk neighborhood and they figured it wasn't worth fixing up. The outsides of the buildings had spray paint all over them from gang propaganda. The gangways were always dark and dirty. Once in a while you'd find a little pile in the corner of the gangway where the local bum had gone to the bathroom. The sidewalks were cracked and uneven. The trees were all dying because of the smoke from the cookie factory in the alley behind our apartment building. The few places where there was any grass left were full of dog doo-doo and broken glass from gang fights.

[4]   Growing up in Logan Square was a hassle very much of the time but I'm glad that's where I did grow up. I learned many things about myself that I might not have otherwise. I learned to be self sufficient and that if I wanted something the only way I would get it was by working for it. I didn't expect someone to lead me by the hand and show me what to do. When I got into ninth grade and started going to a private high school, I knew my mother couldn't afford it so I started working

as soon as I could find someone who would hire me. I paid for my first three years of high school until we moved and I started going to a public school but even then I paid $20.00 a week room and board. I didn't mind though because I considered a good education worth it.

[5] I found out that the only way I could get out of that kind of neighborhood and stay out would be by using my time constructively and getting an education. I saw many of my friends get in trouble with the police and get records. They ruined their lives because they didn't care enough about themselves to do something about it. I saw people lose all respect for themselves and just become leeches on society and I promised myself I would do something better with my life. I thought it was sad to see people I had respected dwindle into nothing until they couldn't get any lower. Seeing people in that state convinced me to finish school, I would get an education and I would make a career for myself.

A brief outline for this essay contains the following points:

Thesis:

Logan Square was a rough neighborhood that taught me the realities of life and the value of hard work. (This is the statement as it occurs in the introduction. See the note on page 108 for necessary changes.)

Topic Statements:

P1. Introduction using recollection of early days in Logan Square as a device to catch reader's interest.

P2. My neighborhood contained typical inner city inhabitants, including a couple who got in a knife fight with each other.

P3. The appearance of the neighborhood was typical ghetto: dirty and run down.

P4. I learned self-sufficiency and the value of hard work.

P5. I saw my friends ruin their lives, but learned that education could be a way out for me.

The controlling statement for the project occurs in very loose form at the end of the first paragraph, where the writer says that the neighborhood taught her to be independent and to appreciate the importance of hard work in the struggle to get somewhere in life. This loose statement is not complete, for the materials in the remaining later paragraphs indicate that she learned something else: the value of education in that struggle. Therefore, as often happens, the writer needed to make a minor revision, in this case an addition, to the statement. With the addition, the statement probably should read:

> Logan Square, a pretty rough neighborhood, taught me to be independent and to appreciate the value of hard work and education as a way to a better life.

Step 2. Thesis/Support.

The next step is to check the materials in the essay, beginning with the introduction, to be sure that the materials support the statement and that they are presented in the most effective place in the essay.

The introduction presents a problem in that it emphasizes an idea that is never developed in the paper, the idea of change in the neighborhood. The young woman who wrote the paper was born in Canada and moved to Logan Square when she was about eight. As part of the background writing, she compares her first impressions of the place with her most recent recollections. The changes in the neighborhood, both in its population and its appearance, were important in that piece of writing. In her effort to catch the reader's interest in the introduction, she picked up the idea of *change*. In fact, however, she never discusses these changes anywhere in the paper, and they seem to have been completed by the time of the incidents she uses in the paper. Some change needs to be made in the introduction so that it does not cause the reader to look for a discussion that never occurs in the paper. Expectations that are not fulfilled distract the reader and weaken the paper.

One possibility that should be readily available to serve as an opening device is a story or an account of an incident that occurred regularly in the neighborhood:

> When I was ten years old, I ran home every day from school and locked myself in our apartment. . .

If this incident were joined to a statement of the thesis the two items would produce a satisfactory introduction.

With the introduction rewritten, the next step is to examine each of the paragraphs of development to be sure that they support the main statement of the paper.

In Paragraph 2 the writer discusses the people in the neighborhood. She describes drunks, prostitutes, pimps, and lunatics. The writing employs a specific incident as a concrete example, and certainly seems to illustrate the part of the statement that says, "Logan Square, a pretty rough neighborhood. . ." Paragraph 3 uses vivid imagery—dying trees, broken glass, and dirt. All of these images serve to emphasize and illustrate very concretely the rough nature of the place. One change would probably improve the presentation of this material: it would be logical to reverse the order of the second and third paragraphs, so that Paragraph 3, which provides physical description, comes first and sets the scene for the story of the people which occurs in Paragraph 2. Thus the introduction would begin

> When I was ten years old. . .

and the next paragraph would move immediately to a description of the place:

> My neighborhood was made up three- and four-story buildings. . .

Then with the scene properly set, the next paragraph would describe the people:

> The neighborhood was really no different from any inner city neighborhood.

Paragraphs 4 and 5 both seem to address the statement of the paper. They discuss the circumstances and the people that made up the neighborhood. But the paragraphs seem to come in the wrong order: Paragraph 3, in the new order, mentions a specific incident in which residents of the neighborhood played a part, Paragraph 4 shifts to observations about the writer herself, and Paragraph 5 shifts back to members of the neighborhood. Changing the order would increase the consistency of the paragraphs arrangement.

Paragraph 3—subject—the couple who had the fight.
Paragraph 4—subject—friends in school.
Paragraph 5—subject—the writer and her attitudes.

The beginning stages of the revision process evaluate the largest elements of the essay. The following chart lists the four areas which need to be examined in this first stage of the revision process. Each section has with it a question to focus your examination.

1. The fit of the core idea with the background writing
    Is the core idea a true reflection of your knowledge of the subject?
2. The effectiveness of the introduction
    Does the introduction catch the reader's interest and provide either a thesis statement or a direction for the paper?
3. The support provided to the core idea by the content of each paragraph of the development
    Does the content of each paragraph in the development offer valid support of the core idea?
4. The order in which the paragraphs of development are presented
    Is the order of the paragraphs of support the most logical, the most easily followed of all the possible orders of presentation?

The next step in the process of revision is to apply to the paragraphs of this essay the rules for good paragraphs discussed in Unit I. As an example of this sort of work on paragraphs, look briefly at Paragraph 5 from the essay about Chicago.

[5] I found out that the only way I could get out of that kind of neighborhood and stay out would be by using my time constructively and getting an education. I saw many of my friends get in trouble with the police and get records. They ruined their lives because they didn't care enough about themselves to do something about it. I saw people lose all respect for themselves and just become leeches on society and I promised myself I would do something better with my life. I thought it was sad to see people I had respected dwindle into nothing until they couldn't get any lower. Seeing people in that state convinced me to finish school, I would get an education and I would make a career for myself.

Remember that a good paragraph has three important qualities clearly present:

1. A strong topic sentence.
2. Unity—the discussion of one, and only one idea.
3. Completeness—sufficient information and detail to give the reader everything needed to grasp the point of the paragraph.

This paragraph has a topic

Constructive use of time was the only way out of that neighborhood.

and the topic is stated in the opening sentence. The paragraph stresses one idea and does not seem to move into any new topic. The problem in the paragraph is lack of specifics to illustrate its statements. After the first sentence begins, "I found out. . ." the reader naturally expects to read how the writer "found out." The second sentence takes up the answer.

> I saw many of my friends get in trouble with the police and get records.

The third and fourth sentences also provide development for that answer.

> They ruined their lives. . .
> I saw people lose all respect for themselves. . .

The problem with this discussion is that it stops at a rather general level, as it deals with "My friends," "they," and "people." What is needed is a specific reference to a single person. This will give the paragraph weight and impact.

> Susan's bother Tom is a perfect example. He was a bright kid, but he ran with the wrong people. One day he got caught trying to hold up a liquor store, and now he's doing five years in the state prison.

This statement is a useful, powerful example. Without specific, concrete examples, generalities are weak.

In summary, then remember to check the following points as you revise a paper:

1. Check the fit of the thesis statement or core idea with the background writing.
2. Test the effectiveness of the introduction.
3. Test the support provided to the core idea by the content of each paragraph of development.
4. Check the order of the paragraphs in the essay.
5. Test each paragraph for a strong topic sentence, unity, and completeness.

The remaining steps in the revision process occur at the end of Unit Three.

WRITING EXERCISE 14

Sentence Combining

The woman was tall and slender.
She wore a gray coat.   (who was. .)
She met a man.
She met him in the lobby of the hotel.

The man was extremely young.
He was not handsome.   (who was. . . and . . .)
He was poorly dressed.
He had no important information to give the woman.

The man told the woman his sad story.
She was disappointed.
Her disappointment was extreme.
She told him   something.   (that)
He was fired.
He would never work in industrial espionage again.

The man told her something.   (that)
He had just landed a job with IBM.
The job was in their security department.

Journal Entry

Discuss, in about a page, the most important things you learned
in high school; concentrate on things outside of academic matters.

WRITING EXERCISE 15

Sentence Combining.

The boys were short.
They were handsome.
They drove to the farmers' market.
They bought some vegetables.
The vegetables were fresh.

The boys were extremely hungry.   (who)
They drove home.
They drove quickly.
One of them cooked the vegetables.

Autumn has finally arrived.
The air is cooler.   (with)
The skies are clear and blue.

My friends enjoy hiking.
They hike through the mountains.
They look at the beautiful leaves.
The leaves are red and gold.

Journal Entry

Discuss your plans for the future, both occupational and personal.
Compare your current plans with the plans you had five years ago.

WRITING EXERCISE 16

Sentence Combining

The rain <u>fell</u> softly.   (while)
The boys and girls <u>walked</u> quickly to the shelter.

The old men <u>jogged</u> slowly down the street.
The young women <u>ran</u> very fast.   (but)

The hornet <u>buzzed</u> menacingly at the door of the cabin.   (although)
We <u>got</u> out safely anyhow.

The president <u>bought</u> new dishes.
The old ones <u>were</u> very ugly.   (because)

The girls <u>were</u> tired   (since)
They went home early.

We <u>opened</u> the door slowly.
Then we <u>threw</u> the water down the stairs.   (and)

Note: In each pair of sentences, the two clauses are joined by a comma.

As a second exercise, change the tense of each of the underlined
words to present. In the first pair, the changes would be from

fell   to   *falls*   and   *walked*   to   *walk*.

WRITING EXERCISE 17

Sentence Combining

The man <u>picked</u> up his golf clubs.
He <u>walked</u> out to the first tee.

He hit his first shot straight down the fairway.
It only traveled about ninety-five yards.

He dug his spikes into the ground.   (ing)
He waggled the club.
He took two practice swings.

Finally he swung at the ball.
He swung with all his might.
He shanked the ball into the rough.

It was a perfect day for golf.   (but)
The man did not enjoy himself very much.   (because)
The entire round went pretty much like the first two shots.

Again, change the tense of the verbs from past to present. It is important to note that in the present tense with a singular noun the present tense verb form ends in -s.

The man   picked   picks
It traveled   travels

WRITING EXERCISE 18

Combine the short sentences in each group into a single longer sentence by following the suggested forms.

The hurricane headed toward land.   (with)   or   (since)
The forecasters issued a warning.
We all put up the storm shutters.

The girls helped with the shutters.
We finished the job very quickly.

The hurricane never grew very large.   (which)
It turned north.
It turned at the last moment.
It missed Miami.

The storm went off into the North Atlantic.   (After)   (with)
We went out to take down the shutters.
The girls had left for college.
The job took a very long time.

As a second exercise, underline the verb in each sentence twice and the subject in the sentence once. If you have difficulty with the exercise, follow these simple directions.

Ask for each sentence, "What happens? What is the action?"
In the first group of uncombined sentences the answers are

headed
issued
put up

This answer, in each case, provides the verb for the sentence. Then ask, "Who or what" and fill in the verb.

Who or what headed?   hurricane headed
          issued   forecasters issued
          put up   We put up

The answer to the question formed by joining *Who* or *what* to the verb always provides the subject of the verb.

WRITING EXERCISE 19

Sentence Combining

Tom Mix was an early movie star.
He protected women and children from the outlaws.   (who)

Gene Autrey now owns a baseball team.   (who)
He was a singing cowboy in the early movies.

Roy Rogers was another early movie cowboy.   (use appositive)*
He had a beautiful horse named Trigger.
Trigger was actually better known than Roy Rogers.   (who)

All the early movies had similar plots.
The heroic cowboy saved the women and children.   (in which)
He saved them from the bad guys.

Afterward, the beautiful girl tried to thank the hero.
She tried to thank him with a kiss.
The hero always blushed and rode away.   (but)
He mumbled, "Aw, shucks, ma'am, It wasn't nothin' at all."

*An appositive is a phrase which renames a noun; it is set off by commas from the rest of the sentence.

Roy Rogers, another early movie cowboy, had a beautiful horse. . .

WRITING EXERCISE 20

Sentence Combining

Registration at our school is a fairly easy process.
Sometimes there are minro difficulties.

A student first discusses next semester's courses.
The student discusses the courses with an advisor.
Then the advisor signs the course selection card.

The student goes next to the computer terminal.
The operator gives the student a schedule of classes.
The scheduling process takes only a few moments.

If you believe that story, I've got a beautiful bridge I'd like to sell you.

In the first three groups, change the underlined words in the un-combined sentences from singular to plural or plural to singular. Since the verbs are present tense, each of them will need to be changed to match the number of the subject.

student discusses changes to *students discuss*
difficulties are changes to *difficulty is*

WRITING EXERCISE 21

Sentence Combining

The boy and the girl walked slowly down the street.   (and)
They turned left at the first corner.

Punctuation rule: If you create a compound sentence, use a comma before the word *and*.

The boy and the girl walked . . .,
and they turned . . . .

But do not use a comma if the sentence reads

The boy and the girl walked . . . and turned . . . .

We walked across the campus.   (and)
We passed the gym and the soccer field.

We walked . . . and passed . . . .   (no comma)

Columbus sailed across the Atlantic Ocean.
He finally landed on a tiny island.

    Columbus sailed . . ., and he . . . landed . . . .

Joan and Sally wanted to go sailing.   (but)
They did not have the time.

    Joan and Sally wanted . . ., but they did not have . . . .
      (comma plus conjunction in a compound sentence)

Two tall boys stood on the basketball court.   (and)
They waited for more boys to come play ball.

    Two tall boys stood . . . and waited . . . .
      (no comma)

They will send the paper to you by mail.   (or)
Tom will bring it to school with him next week.

    They will send . . ., or Tom will bring it . . . .
      (comma plus conjunction in a compound sentence)

Read through one page of your current writing and check the punctuation of compound sentences to be sure you have joined them with a comma and a conjunction.

WRITING EXERCISE 22

Sentence Combining

The men drove the truck to town.   (After)
One of them bought a new saw.

Punctuation rule: If you join one clause to a second clause by using words such as *when, since, after, although,* (and others), join the two clauses with a comma.

    After the men drove . . ., one of them bought . . . .

We saw John in the gym.   (when)
We called to him to wait for us.

    When we saw John . . ., we called . . . .

The children played stick ball all morning.   (because)
They were extremely tired.

    Because the children played . . ., they were . . . .

> The boys were extremely tired that afternoon.   (although)
> They wanted to visit the new zoo.
>
>   Although the boys were . . ., they wanted . . . .
>
> They come to our meeting tonight.   (If)
> We will ask them to join the club.
>
>   If they come . . ., we will ask . . . .

Read through one page of your current writing and check the punctuation of any sentences opened with *when, since, after, although, because,* and so on. Be sure to join with a comma such opening elements to the remainder of the sentence.

WRITING EXERCISE 23

Sentence Combining

> The three women rigged the sailboat.   (having rigged)
> They sailed to the small island.
>
>   Having rigged . . ., the two women sailed.

Punctuation rule: Elements using *-ing* or *-ed* forms of the verb to open a sentence are joined to the main clause with a comma.

> I found two rare shells on the beach yesterday.
> I sold them to a collector this morning.
>
>   Having found . . ., I sold . . . .
>
> The man hoped to see a South American oriole.
> He went to the field early in the morning.
>
>   Hoping to see . . ., the man went . . . .
>
> The women were defeated in the semi-final match.
> They decided to watch the finals on television.
>
>   Defeated in the semifinal match, the women decided . . . .
>
> The hiker clung precariously to the slippery tree trunk.
> He called desperately for help.
>
>   Clinging precariously . . ., the hiker called . . . .

Select five sentences from Exercises 21 or 22. Convert the opening element of each sentence to an *-ing* or *-ed* phrase, and punctuate the new sentence correctly.

UNIT THREE

Writing Based on Reading

INTRODUCTORY READING EXERCISES

In this section, you will begin to use written materials as the basis for writing essays. In the two previous sections, you used both observation and recollection as the basis or source for written projects. Now you will move into a type of writing much more closely related to classroom assignments required in most college courses. This change to a different source of material should not alarm you, for it does not call for changes in any other steps of the writing process you used in earlier projects.

The only new skills you need to master in this unit involve reading and controlling written materials. To help you refresh your memory about the reading skills you learned earlier in school, we will first cover a few pieces of material and work on those skills. Two skills are especially important for this work:

1. Restating a difficult passage. This process is called paraphrasing.
2. Reducing the size of a passage. This process is called summarizing.

If you develop these skills and strengthen your ability to establish a thesis and outline for an article, passage, or chapter, you will be able to write the assignments in this unit and in most of your college classes.

Before you work to sharpen your skills, be sure that you understand the purpose of each of these processes.

Paraphrasing is much like translation. We can take a Spanish sentence and convert it to English by translating it. In paraphrasing we don't convert from one language to another; we convert from a difficult English version to a more simple statement of the idea. The purpose of a paraphrase is to simplify and to clarify, but not to shorten.

Summarizing shortens a passage to its essential elements by rephrasing and eliminating illustrations and explanations.

Read the short paragraph below two times and follow the steps as we establish a paraphrase.

NUCLEAR POWER IN PERSPECTIVE

by R. K. Bennett

Sensitive detection systems are built into the plant to pick up abnormal increases in radiation and humidity changes, a possible precursor of a radiation leak. There are elaborate systems to control or completely stop the nuclear chain reaction when necessary (by inserting control rods in among the fuel rods). Finally, an Emergency Core Cooling System (ECCS) ensures sufficient water in the event of an accident to draw off the reactor's residual heat.

From *Readers' Digest*, June, 1981.

The first step in paraphrasing is to establish the meaning of key words and phrases. In the first sentence three phrases must be defined:

1. Sensitive detection systems—
   A system is a collection of devices. In this case, the devices detect abnormal increases.
2. Abnormal increases—
   These are increases that are out of the ordinary; they are beyond what is safe or acceptable.
3. Precursor—
   This is a person or thing that goes before to indicate the approach of something else.

The first sentence thus says

There are systems to detect increases or changes in radiation or humidity. They detect changes that often come before a radiation leak and may indicate that one is approaching.

Note that a simplified version of a sentence is sometimes longer than the orginal. This is because several shorter words replace a single longer word. In the second sentence, the writer continues to list the systems that protect the plant. The author uses the expression *nuclear chain reaction*. A chain reaction is a "series of events where one event causes the next event and so on and so on." The word *nuclear* refers to atomic energy, the process in which the nucleus of an atom, or really a series of atoms splits, releasing energy.

The second sentence thus says

> There are other systems to slow down or stop the production of the atomic energy (by chain reaction splitting of the nucleus of the atoms) which is done by putting control rods among the fuel rods.

Although the scientific processes may be beyond your understanding, it is important that in the second sentence you learn that there is a way to stop the production of atomic energy.

The third sentence simply mentions one more system.

> There is a system to provide sufficient water to cool, really, to flush away the reactor's heat in case of an accident.

Although this work doesn't seem too difficult, it is necessary to outline the process to be sure you understand what to do when you are faced with a sentence or sentences you don't understand:

1. Read the sentence twice.
2. Mark out words or phrases that are not clear.
3. Look up all the words you don't know in a dictionary.
4. Substitute portions of the dictionary definition or some simple synonyms for the difficult phrases.
5. Write a new, simplified sentence.

Now read this longer passage, a selection from the magazine *Road and Track*. The passage deals with the selection of a sound system for a car.

BONUS FEATURE: STEREOS

by Gary Stock

You'll obviously be looking for a front-end unit whose radio and cassette performance capabilities are both excellent, but you should also take the time

From Bonus Feature: Stereos, *Road & Track*, July 1981, p. 84–5.

to evaluate the ergonomics or human engineering of competing units when pondering your choices. There are a great many high-performance front-end units available today, but some are far more difficult to use in a car environment than others because of poor control layouts, tiny knobs and switches, or poorly marked dial scales. A few minutes of "hands-on" experimentation with competing units, especially when tested in a dimly lighted room, could save you from nagging dissatisfaction later. Other points to consider at this stage concern automated features. Some front-end units hunt stations by themselves, reverse at the end of the tape, eject when the ignition key is turned off, or seek out particular musical selections on the tape by listening for brief pauses. Many digital tuners also function part-time as digital clocks. If any of these "trick" features appeal to you—or conversely, strike you as irritating, now is the time to think about them.

A third consideration while you're talking with different dealers is the question of anti-theft provisions. If you currently have an alarm system in your car, the cost of wiring the sound system into it should be small. If you don't have a system, remember that high-quality sound equipment seems to significantly raise the likelihood of break-ins in most urban areas. An electronic alarm system is not cheap, but it may be worthwhile if you live or park in a high crime area, and it may well cost less to put in while a sound system is being installed than it would on its own. At the very least, you should discuss means of camouflaging the speakers and electronic elements so as not to draw attention to your new acquisitions. One other option, made by Burbank Enterprises, is an inexpensive gizmo called Audio Safe that offers protection of the electronic components in a car: It's a cast aluminum cover that locks around the front-end unit using a cylindrical lock, protecting the front-end unit's faceplate and its mounting nuts.

Most material of any difficulty requires three readings for complete understanding and control. The first reading ought to be rather rapid, an overview in which you find the general subject matter of the article and develop a sense of where the author is taking the subject. That first reading is also the time for picking up and paraphrasing sentences that don't seem clear in the reading. Part of the first sentence in the passage on sound systems does indeed need paraphrasing:

> ... you should also take the time to evaluate the ergonomics or human engineering of competing units when pondering your choices.

The first and most difficult problem is the word

ergonomics

which is defined in the dictionary by a single synonym:

> biotechnology.

A quick look at that word gives us the following definition:

> the study of relationships between humans and machines, especially in terms of physiological, psychological, and technological requirements.

Yet we still do not know much more at all about the word. We are told to evaluate the relationship between the user of the electronic unit and the unit itself. Exactly how we are to evaluate the unit is not quite clear but the idea begins to take shape when we read the next few lines. Helpful phrases include

> far more difficult to use
> poor control layouts
> tiny knobs and switches
> poorly marked dial scales

and in the next sentence, "hands-on experimentation."

The idea we came up with is something like this:

> While you are considering, trying to decide among the units (the word was "pondering"), check to see how easy they are for you to use.

The rewritten version is clear, but it's a far cry from "evaluating the ergonomics." There is one more sentence that might need a bit of work.

> If any of these "trick" features appeal to you—or conversely, strike you as irritating, now is the time to think about them.

"Trick features" means, of course, the special automated features the author lists immediately above this sentence in the text. "Conversely" means "on the other hand." Now the sentence is clear:

> If any of these features seem worthwhile, or on the other hand, seem irritating, make a decision about them now.

With this additional practice in paraphrasing, you can now move on to the next important reading skill, *summarization*. The summary is supposed to shorten a passage without taking away any essential parts of the idea. The passage quite often gives signals as to what its important parts are. The first sentence in the passage on sound systems contains the words

"but you should also . . . "

In the fourth sentence, the author says,

"Other points to consider . . . "

and then at the beginning of the second paragraph, he writes,

"A third consideration . . . "

These three word groups signal important points in this passage. Some authors do not provide the reader with such helpful key words to divide a passage into its parts. In that case, the reader must find the divisions without help.

The first step in preparing a summary is to express each of these three parts in a brief phrase or sentence.

In addition to selecting a front-end unit that gives excellent performance,

a. Consider the convenience of operating the various buttons and dials.
b. Decide which automated features you want and which you do not want.
c. Select some sort of theft protection and have it installed along with the unit.

Then you should try to express the sense of the passage in a single sentence or perhaps, in the case of a long passage, two or three sentences. Here the writer suggests certain points by which one can judge a given stereo unit for a car. Therefore, any summary ought to suggest that idea.

Besides excellent performance, consider the ease of operating the buttons and dials, which automated features you want, and some method for protecting the unit from theft.

You could also try another version, one which contains more sophisticated use of sentence-combining techniques.

> When you select a stereo unit for your car, select one that gives excellent performance, but consider also ease of operating the dials and buttons, selection of any automated features you want (or don't want), and the possibility of installing some sort of anti-theft device.

This a fairly smooth version of a single-sentence summary for the passage on auto stereos.

The two skills of paraphrasing and summarizing will help you as you work on the next important reading skill to be covered, which is learning to establish a thesis and outline for a passage.

You need to be able to read an article or section of written material and find the thesis and supporting points. The thesis of a piece of reading material is exactly the same as the thesis or core idea of an essay or article you are writing. Remember in the narrative essay you wrote in Assignment 5 that one of the first requirements was to make a point, to make a statement through the telling of that story. When you worked on that essay, you read a short article called "A Drive in the Outback," in which the writer, David Abrahamson, states quite clearly that he learned something very important through an auto accident. He learned that his safety, and that of those with him, depended on prudent, defensive driving. That statement, whether quoted directly from the article or phrased in your own words, is the thesis of the article. When you wrote your own essay, one of the important steps in the writing process was to establish a statement for the essay and to write that statement out in a single sentence. That statement is the thesis of your essay. Now we will look for the same kind of statement in the work of another writer.

The exercise here is to read an article and determine exactly the point the writer wishes to make. If you do not have a strategy for reading and analyzing written materials, here is a method that has helped many people.

First, read the article from start to finish rather rapidly, and look for:

a. Words and phrases, even whole passages you don't understand.
b. The general subject matter of the article.
c. Some sense of direction or purpose for the article.

Read the following article, a kind of editorial or statement of position on the subject of energy.

THE CASE AGAINST ABUNDANT, CHEAP ENERGY

by Noel Perrin

[1] If there's one thing Americans agree on, it is that we need abundant and cheap energy. If we can no longer get it from oil, then we have to find other means—and fast.

[2] Some experts insist that nuclear energy is our only hope; others believe we can keep the Btus pouring out with a clever mix of solar energy, coal, wind power, and drill-holes for geothermal energy. All theories share one assumption: the more power we have, the better human life will be.

[3] But is this true? I doubt it. In my prophecy, the present energy shortage figures as just a temporary problem. Maybe breeder reactors will not just work, but turn out to be safe, practical, and cheap. Or maybe there will be a major breakthrough in collection techniques for solar energy. In any case, imagine that in 20 years electricity is absurdly cheap. Then imagine a breakthrough in storage techniques, so that electricity is also absurdly portable. Airplanes are using batteries not much larger than those in today's cars, peasants in Bangladesh are acquiring electric tractors that run six weeks on a single charge, and so forth.

[4] Would people like the world that resulted? Not for long, I think.

[5] If power became plentiful, a host of changes would occur, mostly bad. For one, transportation costs would cease to be significant in the economy, whether for carrot growing or tourism. The advocates of cheap power think this would be good. They see the whole global supply of carrots as grown in the half-dozen places best suited for carrot culture, and they see a tourist from the average American city as able to buy a roundtrip ticket to Paris for a mere $50.00.

[6] I also foresee these things, but as almost totally bad. On the one hand, goodbye to the home vegetable garden except as an act of eccentricity; hello, more TV watching. On the other hand, what keeps Paris a pleasure for Americans to visit is that it is protected by distance. Take that shield away, and the world will lose its variety. We will go farther to see less, until our planet will be a single mass-franchise culture. Boring.

[7] A more serious change that unlimited cheap power would bring about is an enormous increase in human passivity. Even the relative cheapness of power in the U.S. between 1940 and 1973 produced the electric knife for people who couldn't slice their own roast beef. Also the ski lift, the vibrator bed, and the all-terrain vehicle for people who won't bother to walk. Really cheap power would turn us into what Rene Dubos has called human tapeworms. The literal tapeworm has found itself a perfect environment, where the temperature never changes and the food comes by ready-chewed; it has lost the no-longer-needed power of locomotion, its eyes, and its ears.

From *Quest*, October 1981.

[8] I don't claim that a monthly electric bill of say, $10, would cause us to go blind and have atrophied legs. But I do believe it would produce such a spate of labor-saving devices that few of us would do much. We would just lie down and be vibrated, fed, and amused. The process of living would be abolished, and the process is the living. That is what most problem solvers don't realize.

[9] Most serious of all, unlimited power would enable the human population to keep expanding until Paris, Chicago, and Buenos Aires could be part of the same world-city. By then, almost all adventure or accomplishment would be impossible. And there would be no turning back, except by catastrophe or by enduring many generations of rigorous, even brutal, control.

[10] I don't want nuclear technology (or solar, or any other kind) to work—at least not too well—because the blessings of abundant energy are even more to be feared than the undoubted risks. Those who agree with me are probably moved by similar feelings, just as the advocates are moved by their vision of a super technology future.

[11] Such feelings are tricky for a middle-class American to express, because it is easy to sound selfish, like the fat person who says the world ought to grow less food so that he won't be tempted to eat so much—although a billion or so people are undernourished at the present level of food supply.

[12] In many countries people lead lives of appalling toil; for them more energy could only be good. But those of us who live in developed countries need to be aware that it is possible to be overdeveloped. In the end we Americans are going to have to argue not just about how to reprocess spent fuel rods, or how much sulfur to allow in the air from coal-fired power plants, but about what cheap power means to human life.

Definitions and Explanations

There are four items in the article that might need explanation:

1. Case, as in a legal case, here simply means the arguments or reasons against.
2. Btu, sometimes written B.T.U., stands for British Thermal Unit, a way of measuring energy production.
3. Mass-franchise culture suggests that just as all MacDonald's restaurants are identical, this type of world would look pretty much the same whether in America or New Guinea.
4. Passivity means lack of action or reaction.

You may need to refresh your memory on some other words. Look them up in the dictionary at this time, and write some kind of short note to fix the definition in your mind.

Subject Matter of the Article

The article is identified as a "commentary," or a kind of editorial that states an opinion or position on a subject. If we begin with the broadest kind of subject, we would say the article is about energy, such as electricity and gasoline. More specifically, the subject deals with the results of having a great abundance of cheap energy resulting from an overflowing supply of inexpensive energy.

In overall appearance and structure, the article contains twelve paragraphs and provides in that stucture some hints about the direction the author intends to take this subject. Notice that at the end of the second paragraph, the writer states a position held pretty generally by people working in the field of energy production and by those who comment on our problems in that area:

> The more power we have, the better human life will be.

In the third paragraph, the author immediately tells us his own views when he asks and answers the question

> Is this true? I doubt it.

He then begins to set out his own position. In the third paragraph, he sets up a hypothetical situation, a kind of imaginary setting twenty years in the future, a time in which he imagines energy is plentiful and inexpensive. Then in the fourth paragraph he states his position again:

> Would people like the world that resulted?
> Not for long, I think.

Notice the size of Paragraph 4; it is only two lines long. It consists of one question and one short answer. Writers use this type of paragraph to set off important statements or to show a marked and important change in idea. In Paragraph 5, then, he moves to state and explain his position. He says in the first sentence that a host of changes, mostly bad, would occur. Notice the use of the word *changes*, for it is repeated later on to introduce points following this first one.

First. A host of changes would occur . . . (Paragraph 5)
Second. A more serious change . . . (Paragraph 7)
Third. Most serious of all . . . (Paragraph 9)

The key here is to learn to look for words or phrases that serve to tie the article together and establish parts of the essay. Here the writer uses repetition of a word or an expression very close to that word. Sometimes writers use words such as

First . . . Next . . . And then . . . Finally.
Thus . . . Therefore . . . And so . . . .

Learn to look for such connecting expressions.

After the ninth paragraph, in which the author reviews the most serious of all changes, he moves into three paragraphs of discussion and then closes the essay. The last section, paragraphs 10-12, states the writer's position once again and provides a discussion of that position. Read these sections again.

In the tenth paragraph, "I don't want nuclear technology . . . " is the restatement and summary.
Such feelings are tricky . . . (Para. 11)

and in Paragraph 12 he reminds us of the careful balance needed to make our position on energy development realistic for ourselves and yet helpful to other nations.

So the general structure of the article looks like this:

1. Introduction and thesis (Paragraphs 1-3).
2. Three main points of his position (Paragraphs 4-9).
3. Further discussion of a complex factor in the argument (Paragraphs 10-12).
4. A final sentence concluding the article (Paragraph 12).

At the end of this first reading, your control of the article is not complete and so the work is not complete either. Read the article again, and write an outline by summarizing the points listed in the general outline.

Introduction and Thesis.
All Americans and all the experts in the field agree that America needs abundant, cheap energy. I see a time when energy will be abundant and cheap, but I do not believe people will like the world that results. The changes brought about by cheaper, more abundant energy will be mostly bad.

Change number one.

Transportation costs would no longer be important. Travel would
be remarkably cheap.

The bad result would be a kind of specialization (all carrots grown
in a single location) and a loss of mystery and thrill in traveling
to places now quite exciting.

Change number two.

Cheap power brings on an increase in human inactivity.

The bad result would be that people would rely more and more on
labor-saving devices and might eventually become just like tapeworms, who have lost sight and mobility because of lack of use.

Change number three.

Unlimited power would allow unlimited growth in population.

The bad result would be a loss of room and opportunity for adventure and accomplishment.

The Conclusion.

The blessings of unlimited power are not really benefits at all, but
will cause problems greater than the problems created by short
energy supplies.

Further discussion.

It is tricky for Americans to be opposed to the development of
abundant supplies of energy because such a position seems to
make us opposed to the development of abundant energy in
other countries where more power is clearly needed. We need to
promote development of cheap energy sources for those who
have little now, but we need to be very careful about assuming
that abundant energy is an unqualified blessing for everyone.
We will have to argue about the meaning of cheap power for
human life.

The process of finding an outline, and writing out the major
points in that outline, will use the skills of summarizing and paraphrasing that you began to develop in the earlier exercises in this
unit. Refer to those sections and follow the same instructions as
you work on the sections of this article.

We now have an overall structure for the article, and a summary
of each major point to fill in the outline. We are still not quite
finished. We don't have control of this article until we can express

the idea in a single sentence or in two or three short sentences. The third phase of the close-reading process is the development of that brief summarizing statement. This next step is very similar to the method you used to write a controlling statement or thesis in your own papers.

> Contrary to what many believe, I think that cheap, abundant energy will produce some bad effects: such as over-specialization in industry and farming, a loss of variety in the world, an increase in labor-saving devices which would increase inactivity, and a loss of adventure and opportunity for new accomplishments. We need to be careful to limit our own use of such power and yet make it available for underdeveloped nations.

Writing a thesis statement such as this may seem an impossible task at this point, but it looks difficult only when you look at the whole sentence in its completed form. Such sentences don't jump fully-developed onto the page; they are developed section by section and then made into a single sentence. Notice that the divisions in the sentence above reflect a sense of introduction, development, and conclusion. The shortest possible thesis statement for the article is found toward the end of the introduction in the three words that answer a question posed in the opening sentence of the third paragraph. The question is: But is this (the idea that "the more power we have, the better human life will be") true? The answer provides the thesis for the paper:

> I doubt it. I doubt that the idea is true.

This statement contains the basic idea, but the form doesn't produce a good thesis statement: it does not state what the author doubts. To get that idea into the sentence you need to supply a clear statement of what it is the author doubts. The idea, in another form of the idea stated above, says that abundant, inexpensive energy may not be entirely beneficial to the people of our country. Stated in a positive, rather than in a negative phrasing, the sentence says

> Abundant, inexpensive energy will cause problems for the people of our country.

A further look at the content of the article allows us to develop the thesis statement. This occurs when we add a list of the problems that would be caused by an abundant, inexpensive supply of energy. In other words, if we replace the word "problems" with the names of those problems—in this case, three problems—we come up with a more complete statement of the thesis.

The problems discussed are:

Problem 1. Overspecialization in agriculture and industry, and loss of variety in world's cultures caused by cheap transportation.
Problem 2. Increased passivity.
Problem 3. Expanded population, enormous cities.

An extended version of the thesis statement reads:

Abundant, inexpensive energy will cause problems: overspecialization and loss of variety in culture, increased passivity among people, and an expanded population gathered together in enormous cities.

For most purposes, that last version of the thesis is too long and too complicated to be used easily. We should cut it by saying

Abundant, inexpensive energy will cause serious problems in the world.

With this thesis sentence completed, it is fairly easy to move on to an outline of the entire article by working through the article one more time and dividing it into large units. Notice that we have done most of this by establishing what the "serious problems" mentioned in the thesis are. Now we should set out these main points and add a summary of the introduction and conclusion of the article. One possible format for this type of outline takes this form:

Title: The Case Against Abundant, Cheap Energy
Introduction: Contrary to what most experts believe, that more, cheaper energy is desirable, the author takes a different position. (The introduction establishes a commonly held position and then contradicts it in order to catch the reader's interest.)
Thesis: Cheap, abundant energy will cause serious problems.

  Outline: 1. Overspecialization and loss of variety in the cultures of the world.
      2. Increased passivity caused by labor-saving devices.
      3. Expanded population, enormous cities.
 Conclusion: Americans must be careful to avoid seeming to be opposed to cheap power for underdeveloped countries, but they must consider possible negative impact of cheap power on their own lives.

This format for a presentation of thesis and outline attempts to establish both the method of introduction and the thesis, the main points of support and explanation for that thesis, and the method of concluding the article. There are other formats for outlining written materials, but use this one if you do not already have a form to which you are accustomed. It would be useful to attach to this outline the definitions of words, paraphrases of difficult sections, and important notes taken during the work on the article. All of these materials would be useful if you had to take a test on the material.

ASSIGNMENT 8.

Restating an Idea and its Support

For the first writing assignment based on written material, take a one-paragraph project based on the editorial called "The Case Against Abundant, Cheap Energy." The goal of the assignment is to write a paragraph expressing the thesis of the article and its major points in your own words. Where possible, add examples from your life and circumstances. The length ought to be about three-quarters of a page.

  The first step in writing this paragraph has already occurred: you know that the assignment asks that you state in your own words the idea and supporting materials of a certain article. The next step, after you select or identify the subject, is to establish what you know about the subject. What you know in this case is summed up in the reading exercise you did earlier on this article. Go back to those notes and review the thesis,

> The changes brought about by cheaper, more abundant energy will be mostly bad.

and then review the three points that explain the thesis:

> Cheap transportation will produce a world that is much the same everywhere we go.
>
> Human beings will become more and more inactive.
>
> Unlimited power will not produce genuine benefits but will lead to problems greater than the problems caused by energy shortages.

Those points make up the content of the second step, the answer to the question

> What do we know about this subject?

It's important to note that what we know is exactly what the author told us, and does not include any other items of information. What we know for this assignment does not include other bad points or problems rising from abundant energy, nor any criticism or commentary on the author's statement, nor our own opinions, if they run counter to or in addition to the statement made in the article. Up to this point we have only been asked to state the writer's idea. We can't add anything to the article, because these additions would go beyond the scope of the assignment.

This kind of work on an article—a limited project asking only that we restate an idea—provides an important kind of exercise for reading. In becoming a good reader, it is important for you to deal only with the written words before you try to add new points, reactions, or criticisms. The first step is to control the idea of the writer. After you gain that control, you can then do many things with a piece of written material.

With control of the writer's idea established and the second step completed, move to the next step, which is to establish a thesis for your paragraph. Spend a few minutes on trial versions of a thesis. It ought to include the general idea about bad results from cheap energy, and it should mention very briefly the three specific results cited in the article.

The thesis should begin with the central idea

> Abundant energy will produce bad results; it will result in sameness in all societies, inactivity, and a loss of opportunity caused by growth of population.

and should mention the three supporting points

monotony.

inactivity.

restricted opportunity.

Now try to write these ideas in a single sentence.
One possible version reads like this:

> Abundant supplies of energy will produce not benefits, but harmful results in our country and the world as cheap transportation brings on sameness in all cultures, labor-saving devices produce inactivity among our citizens, and population growth restricts opportunity and room for adventure.

Step 4 and Step 5 follow automatically from this thesis sentence. The materials included in the paragraph will certainly be the three points mentioned in the editorial: monotony, inactivity, and restricted opportunity. The order of presentation will also follow naturally; the paragraph will move in the same order as in the editorial.

Finally, we reach Step 6, writing the draft or trial version of the paragraph. Start at any point that is easy for you, but remember that a good paragraph contains certain basic components.

1. An introductory statement leading to or containing the topic which will express the thesis of the article.
2. The topic sentence.
3. A sentence explaining and illustrating each point of the article.

Begin with an introductory remark, perhaps one similar to the remarks in the article:

> Almost everyone, whether an expert or a private citizen, who comments about the energy problems facing our country, assumes that we need as as much energy as we can possibly produce, and that we need it as cheaply as we can manage to produce it.

From this introductory remark the reader learns

the subject matter for the article
the standard opinion on the subject, or what might be called the "conventional wisdom."

Next you need a topic sentence to express the thesis:

> The author of this article (provide the name here) disagrees, stating that an abundant supply of cheap energy will produce not benefits, but harmful effects.

Now write a sentence expressing the ideas in each of the three supporting points and provide an example for each one:

monotony
> Cheap travel will probably make the whole world pretty much the same. Fast food shops like MacDonald's or Burger King are pretty much the same everywhere.

inactivity

restricted opporturnity

When you complete this preliminary part of Step 6, combine the parts so that you produce a single paragraph.

ASSIGNMENT 9.

Combining Two Articles

Now that you have practiced some important reading skills, you are ready to move on to the next writing assignment.

> Read the following two articles and write a three-page paper reporting on the evaluation of the car.

As you read, be sure to use the three-stage reading process presented in the previous section:

1. Read for general overview and for understanding of difficult passages.
2. Read for thesis and outline.
3. Read for general impression.

The steps in writing this paper are exactly the same as the steps used in the earlier assignments.

Step 1. Selecting a topic. In this assignment the topic of the paper is specified. When you do not have a choice of topics, your task is to be certain that you understand the nature of the assignment.

Step 2. Collecting materials. Since the materials for the paper come from two articles rather than from recollection, the task in this step is to read and outline the articles.

Step 3. Establishing the thesis. The thesis for your paper will be a combination of the statement made by each of the articles you read.

Step 4. Selecting content for your paper. These materials will come directly from the two articles, not from any other source.

Step 5. Selecting an order. The same principles used in earlier as-assignments will direct your work in this step.

Step 6. Writing the first draft. Use the same techniques you used with earlier papers.

TOYOTA STARLET

Might this be the ideal commuter car for the Eighties?

[1] Some carmakers believe they are in sole possession of the truth; if you dislike some facet of their cars, it's your failing, not theirs. Others attempt to read the mass market through extensive research, but get it wrong; how else to explain Edsels, Volkswagon 412s and GM intermediate aero couples? And then there's Toyota. One of the world's largest automakers. Toyota evidently got there by carefully gauging the mass market and responding with great accuracy.

[2] Not that every Toyota we've seen is, in our eyes, a winner. Take the 1977 Corolla 1200 (please . . .). Toyota called it The Answer, suggesting that the car's robust mechanicals and $2788 base price (1977 dollars) would make it just the thing for minimal-cost new-car motoring. We tested it in March of that year, though, and we felt otherwise; this 2-door sedan was simply a bit too stripped for our tastes. It had loose rubber floor mats, a passenger seat devoid of release latch (it tilted inward to fold its seatback forward) and an instrument panel with fewer displays than your average digital watch. "The answer is really no answer at all," we concluded. On the other hand, it was to many people; indeed, recently a mint 1979 version became the answer for a staff member's niece asking whether a bulletproof used car was a realizable proposition.

[3] So this brings us, round about, perhaps, to the subject of this road test, the Toyota Starlet. Although new to the U.S. market, the Starlet already

From *Road & Track*, February, 1981, pp. 41–43.

has plenty of fans in Europe and Japan, where it has been around for a couple of years. As for the U.S., think of the Starlet as a second-generation Answer, one that profits from what Toyota does best—listening and responding to the needs and desires of the market. Think of it as well as a means of experiencing minimal-cost motoring without being positively embarrassed about it all.

[4] Much of what comes with the Starlet's $4798 base price is unabashedly conventional. A front engine driving, of all things, the rear wheels. MacPherson struts and rack-and-pinion steering up front and a coil-sprung live axle located by four trailing links at the rear. In between, there's adequate space for four people and their belongings. And it's all boxed in a package that one staff member likened to a Renault Le Car; another said no, it's more like a Honda Civic; and a third said "it tiptoes that thin line between looking like all the others and looking potato-dumpy." But an interesting point is that the Starlet fits rights in with the front-wheel-drive crowd, despite its less than fashionable drive-train layout. Another point on this choice of layout: Should anything untoward ever happen to the Starlet's motive components, the costs of bringing things right again would be well below those of fussing underhood with super-compact fwds.

[5] The Starlet comes in precisely one model and trim level, a well equipped 3-door hatchback. Its wheelbase of 90.6 in. coincides with that of the Plymouth Champ; its 152.2 in. overall length is 3.1 in. shorter than the VW Rabbit's. But its curb weight, 1810 lb. is considerably lighter than those of competing cars, most of which run 200–300 lb. heavier. We'd guess some of this weight saving comes from omitted sound insulation, because the Starlet's doors and rear hatch hardly close with a Mercedesesque thunk. Nevertheless, quality of materials and the level of fit and finish are up to the usual Toyota standard—this is commendably high.

[6] The Starlet's passenger compartment is fully carpeted, its seats are not miniature parodies of real seats, and the interior side and door panels are covered in tasteful monochromatic vinyl. There's no plush here, mind; instead, a starkness that looks pleasantly European. The front seats provide very good lateral and thigh support, and there's adequate head and leg room. In the rear, the only compromise is fairly low seating that gives acceptable, if not gobs of, head room only to trade adequate thigh support despite its full-length cushion. In any case, two adults would not consider it a hardship to crawl back there and sit for a fairly short ride.

[7] And wonder of wonders in an economy sedan, the Starlet's driver faces a clearly labeled instrument panel containing such niceties as a tach, coolant temperature gauge and trip odometer. Steering wheel, pedals, shift lever and other controls are all well located; the steering wheel and shift knob are even vinyl padded. All this, as standard equipment at less than $5000 base.

[8] Other elements of the Starlet's interior are also well done. Its ventilation system is an excellent one, with two adjustable vents on dash extremes

and two more center vents that are part of the system whether you opt for air conditioning or not (are you listening, penny-pinching Detroit?). Our Starlet was equipped with the optional a/c ($550), and we've only a minor complaint about it. Its thermostat control is concentric with the 3-speed fan control; handy enough, but the a/c needs a more positive off detent. As it is, it's too easy to turn on the a/c inadvertently when adjusting fan boost.

[9] In typical hatchback fashion, the Starlet's rear seat folds forward to increase its 11.0 cu.ft. cargo volume by another 11.8 cu.ft. The cargo area displays one of the Starlet's few tradeoffs in front-engine/rear-drive space efficiency, in that it's relatively shallow, what with a live rear axle lurking beneath. The only other outward sign of non-fwd, by the way, is the drive-train tunnel splitting the passenger compartment, but this is less noticeable than the rather high-floored cargo area. Overall, Toyota has done a commendable job of packaging a great deal of space within the Starlet's traditional layout.

[10] The car's 1290-cc ohv 4-banger fires readily enough with the aid of its manual choke, followed by a ticketa-ticketa of pushrods and valves in this 15-year-old design. The engine produces 58 bhp at 5200 rpm and 67 lb-ft of torque at 3600, and if you dislike mechanical resonances you'd best keep the revs closer to the latter than the former. And it's easy to do with one of the nicest 5-speed gearboxes aaround (also standard equipment, we can note). The first three ratios are ideal for city driving; 5th quite tall at 2.74: 1 overall, gives long legs for freeway cruising (2700 rpm at an actual 60 mph, for example); and 4th fills in for those situations when 5th's lack of pulling power becomes evident.

[11] The engine doesn't feel overwhelmingly powerful at any rpm. "There's one giant flat spot across the rev range," noted one staff member. Another staff member disagreed, saying, "For a carbureted engine in this emission-controlled world, it's completely acceptable. And, what's more, it feels positively indestructible." Everyone agreed that intelligent use of the excellent 5-speed would allow one to keep up with the pack. In fact, one is likely to pass most of them when they stop to refuel, what with the Starlet exhibiting an almost diesel-like 37.0 mpg in our ordinary driving. Fuel economy was in the high 20's for the tank reflecting our day of full-throttle performance testing, and we'd guess high 40's would not be impossible in 5th-gear cruising.

[12] In our acceleration testing, the Starlet places toward the slower end of the gasoline-fueled spectrum, but a lot quicker than any diesel competitors. We recorded a 0-60 mph time of 14.2 seconds and quarter-mile figures of 19.5 sec at 68.0 mph. Not enough to get your adrenaline pumping? Maybe not, but the resonances that arise as redline approaches may do the trick. It's evident that Toyota did its homework for ordinary driving, but there are two modes in which the Starlet's lack of sound insulation makes itself evident. One is going to the car's 6000-rpm redline, a practice, by the way, that

gave the quickest acceleration times. At around 4500 rpm, there are some minor vibrations; beyond 5000, much of the structure picks these up; and by the time redline is reached, you begin resonating as well. At the other extreme, there's an annoying rumble in the low-rpm range in 5th gear. Neither of these characteristics need be a bother in normal driving, however. It's simply a matter of shifting up or down a gear to bring the engine back into its comfortable 2000–4000 rpm range.

[13] In truth, there's a bit of every kind of automotive noise about the Starlet, but none is especially grating and the total is part of its personality. A crucial aspect that makes the car appealing is its cruising ability. "You can drive all day," one staff member observed, "without feeling buzzed to death."

[14] In the handling department, the word "predictability" sums up the Starlet very well. Its cornering limits are not terribly high, but there is benign understeer, moderate roll and a typical Toyota sedan feeling of tippiness yet stability in just about any cornering mode. The Starlet is agile as can be in traffic, helped in part by excellent outward visibility, and it feels quite stable even at its 93 mph top speed. It posted a slalom speed of 57.2 mph and rolled its way on skinny little 145SR-13 tires to a fairly low 0.684g on our skidpad. Our tester found the car liked a tight line weaving around the slalom pylons, with any attempt at tail wagging just scrubbing off speed. Around the skidpad, the Starlet was limited by front tires that wanted to leave the line and a rear end that would break loose as the inside rear tire unloaded.

[15] The Starlet's ride belied its 90.6-in. wheelbase, taking culvert dips and other road irregularities with rather less pitch than expected. It's evident that Toyota has done an excellent job of balancing this straightforward suspension fore and aft. Botts dots raise a racket of thumpiness, but it's tire noise and not body structure. We did note a bit of freeway hop, though, and the Toyota radials exhibited some nibble on rain-groove surfaces.

[16] The braking system, a usual disc/drum combination, was well up to the rest of the Starlet's performance. An ease of modulation was its definite long suit; a tendency toward rear locking, its only untoward characteristic. The latter, and tires that felt somewhat hard-compounded were limiting factors in our panic-stop tests. Despite excellent fore/aft balance and easy modulation ability, the car recorded only an average 168 ft stopping from 60 mph, and this grew to 293 ft from 80 mph, where rear-lock sensitivity became more apparent. In ordinary use, particularly around town, the brakes were rather impressive, retarding the car's forward progress in short order.

[17] Noise levels for the Starlet confirmed our subjective impressions. At constant speeds of 30, 50, and 70 mph, we recorded levels of 66, 73, and 77 dBA, respectively, each a couple of dB above the general small-car average. And the Starlet's 90 dBA at redline in 1st gear was considerably higher than any competitor's; apparently our sound meter picks up resonances as well as the human body does.

Nevertheless, as a group the R & T humans came away most impressed by the Starlet. It displays Toyota quality through and through. Although compromises have evidently been made in the interest of weight and cost, these haven't drastically affected the utility and pleasure of a car whose as-tested price of $5721 is actually below the base price of several competitors' stripped models. Perhaps the biggest coup of all is that the Starlet has an engaging personality. As one staff member put it, "This Starlet is a little sweetheart." "In spirit, " said another, "it reminds me of the VW Beetle—simple, honest, but entertaining." A third staff member wondered how the Starlet would have done, had we stretched the criteria of last month's fwd comparison test. We all agreed that the Starlet could well become the benchmark for commuter cars of the Eighties.

TOYOTA STARLET

by Jean Lindamood

[1] Bushido—"the way of the warrior"—the enduring, 800-year-old samurai code of personal conduct that emphasizes respect and responsibility. Bushido is what makes Japan tick. Bushido is the reason Japanese autoworkers work so diligently to turn out high-quality automobiles. Bushido is what possesses Japanese auto companies to take such remarkably complete care of their workers, offering them jobs for life and benefits the UAW can only dream of in its wildest utopian reveries.

[2] When Toyota politely offered Japan's most popular car, the stodgy little Toyopet, or "Tokyo Taxi" to the United States market in 1958, it had the right idea of the kind of car America was backing—a small, solidly built, high-mileage (roughly 24 to 33 mpg) economy sedan. But behind that meek introduction was an ambitious aspiration: squashing the VW Bug.

[3] By 1961, each Toyota dealer had sold an average of 1.3 Toyopet Crowns and Tiaras per month; it was obvious that these cars weren't about to deflate VW's sales curve. Toyota withdrew from the U.S. car market and went home to get its Bushido together.

[4] After a deep breath, Toyota returned in 1964 and began a phenomenal rise in U.S. sales that culminated in supplanting the Ford Motor Company as the world's number-two auto manufacturer. This marketplace magic came from a simple conviction to build a fleet of solid, high-mileage, desirably appointed econoboxes. The latest addition to Toyota's staggering, 39-model 1981 lineup, the Starlet three-door hatchback, offers no unpleasant variations on the company's highly successful theme; build 'em small, deck 'em out, and sell 'em at attractive prices.

Car and Driver, February, 1981, pp. 90-92.

[5] The Starlet is the tiny tot of the Toyota family—eight inches shorter and about 200 pounds lighter than the Tercel. Its Rabbit-like lines are typical of Japan's latest shift toward European styling, and Toyota accentuates the Starlet's fresh, sporty image with lots of black: on the grille, the urethane-clad bumpers, the window moldings, the side mirror, and the body striping. It's a very eye-appealing package. Furthermore, the Starlet will be one of the few cars in America vailable for under $5000. (The bottom-of-the-line Tercel is a bit cheaper.) But its greatest distinction is an EPA city-rated mileage of 39 mpg—the absolute tops in gas-powered autos for 1981.

[6] A look under the Starlet's hood reveals no hydro-catalysts or marvel-mystery motor to explain this remarkable efficiency. Nestled way over in one corner is the second-tiniest engine available in any car on sale in the U.S. (Datsun sells a 1237 cc engine as base 210 equipment). This fifteen-year-old, 1290 cc pushrod four-cylinder is so compact that you could easily squeeze another one in there beside it.

[7] To help such a small engine manage our big country, Toyota sends Starlets to America with but one transmission, a slick-shifting five-speed. Wave that wand properly and the Starlet turns in above-average econocar performance. If you're willing to wind out the revs, you can rush to 60 miles per hour in less than fourteen seconds—quicker than you can in an Escort or a Chevette. But unfortunately, that's all the rush there is. It will take you an additional five-plus seconds to complete the standing quarter-mile after you hit 60 mph. And once you've completed the shift progression into fifth gear, you'll just have to resign yourself to following, not leading, the flow of traffic.

[8] While this may not be a samurai-enthusiast's car, regular civilians should be more satisfied—even pleased—with what the Starlet delivers in mileage-for-money. It comes with a wide array of big-car luxuries—all standard—including steel-belted radials; rack-and-pinion steering; power-assisted front disc brakes; back-, side-, and thigh-supportive, reclining front buckets; carpeting; a tachometer; and a trip odometer. The only essential left out is a day/night rearview mirror.

[9] In fact, the only options for a Starlet are an AM/FM-radio/cassette deck (and you can buy a better one for your $395 in the aftermarket), a rear-window wiper (worth the $80 sticker), and air conditioning ($550). Actually, the excellent ventilation system does nicely without the A/C option; it could even be called excessive. In our test car, arctic air blew from the air vents at force ten, and the ball diffusers only served to cut the chill factor a bit. At the other extreme, the heater pumps out a furnace-strength blast that could easily melt pantyhose on the "low" setting.

[10] The heating-and-ventilation system could use a little fine tuning, but otherwise the interior of the Starlet is a lesson in craftsmanship, functionality, and simply good, clean design. Visibility is excellent. All the moldings and trim fit flush and tight. The carpet lies flat. The ashtray fits in its slot. The doors latch quietly and securely the first time, every time. The view

of the tach and the speedo is unobstructed by the steering wheel, and the idiot lights (as well as the gas and temp gauges) are neatly positioned between the two. The light and the wiper-washer controls are on the steering column. The only discordant note we found in this harmonious layout was a temperature-control decal that was so short on stickum, it had bulged up around the heater switches.

[11] Shunning the mad rush to front-wheel drive hasn't helped the Starlet's compact interior, but then again, no real harm has been done. This is strictly a four-seater, so the driveshaft tunnel running through the center of the car never infringes on anyone's personal space. There's a reasonable amount of room for two in the back seat—enough leg space to feel comfortable for short distances and plenty of headroom for a 55th-percentile female wearing a cow-girl hat.

[12] The Starlet isn't sound-deadened quite thoroughly enough to prevent wind noise and engine drone from assaulting your senses—but this is hardly a surprising discovery in an econocar. What is suprising is the absence of rattles and jiggles and groans and squeaks from the dash, the doors, the body, the seats, and the windshield.

[13] Don't look for an air suspension under the car to explain the Starlet's ride integrity. At the front there's the most rudimentary MacPherson-strut arrangement possible. In the old days you'd get cart springs to match in back, but now that Toyota is an all-coil company (except for trucks), the Starlet has a modern, four-link rear suspension. The whole system works well enough to keep you off the ceiling, but your buns pick up the majority of blemishes in the road surface. So where are the rattles? It may just be another manifestation of Bushido. Or it may just take a few thousand miles to shake a couple loose.

[14] One other unexpected facet of the Starlet's friendly nature is its good conduct on the highway at speeds beyond the law-abiding limit. Directional stability is solid; the rack-and-pinion steering is one of the better guidance systems sent over from Japan to date.

[15] The Starlet is less well behaved, however, when the cornering gets tight and pavement roughness increases. Scratching around switchbacks is just not this car's forte. And the teeth-gnashing thrills received from such maneuvers don't justify the energy necessary to keep four tortured tires on the pavement, not to mention between the lines. The front end also has an annoying habit of jerking indiscriminately left or right over chatter bumps and similar road rudeness.

[16] Toyota has never aggressively gone after a reputation for roadholding, and the biggest importer won't with the Starlet, either. That's not its role. The Starlet is what you might call more civic-minded: a chance to meet or exceed the competition in the biggest game in town at the moment, mpg. So even though the Starlet's not state of the art in packaging, handling, or even ventilation, it's the perfect made-to-order gift for that huge group of

people out there who are anticipating their first car and insisting on two features above all else: high mileage and low cost. If you've raised Junior and the Princess right, they'll thank you for kicking them out of the nest in a Starlet. That would only be good Bushido.

Step 2

Your first glance at the article from *Road and Track* shows that the article is a road test and evaluation of a car, the Toyota Starlet. In such an article you should expect to find information about the car and opinions about the car's general construction, quality, and usefulness. Most of the article is not extremely technical, and it offers only minor problems in understanding. These difficulties can probably be resolved when you look up the definitions of a few words in your dictionary. One passage does present some problems, and it might be useful to work out a paraphrase of it before we go on. In Paragraph 16 the first three sentences read:

> The braking system, a usual disc/drum combination, was well up to the rest of the Starlet's performance. An ease of modulation was its definite long suit; a tendency toward rear locking its only untoward characteristic. The latter, and tires that felt somewhat hard-compounded, were limiting factors in our panic-stop tests.

The difficulties lie mostly in the technical terms. A few definitions will be useful:

1. Disc/drum combination—a brake system employing disc brakes on the front wheels and drum brakes on the rear.
2. Ease of modulation—easy regulation or change of pressure used in braking.
3. Rear locking—a tendency for rear wheels to lock up causing loss of braking effectiveness and possible skidding.
4. Untoward—unfavorable or unfortunate.
5. Hard-compounded—made of a hard rubber, increasing tire life, but reducing stopping traction.

With these definitions, it is possible to write a simplified version of these three sentences of Paragraph 16.

> The brakes, discs in front and drums in the rear, are good enough for the performance of the car. It is easy to regulate braking pressure, but the rear

brakes have a tendency to lock up. That tendency, and tires that were a little too hard to provide good grip, kept performances on panic stop tests in the "average" range.

You may find other passages that are not clear to you. If so, consult your dictionary and write paraphrases of the passages. If you wish to expand your knowledge of automotive technology and find out what a disc brake really is , ask your librarian to show you a reference work or encyclopedia that deals with such matters.

Now that you have completed the first reading of the article, move quickly into the second step: discovering the thesis and outline. There is no magic, no special way of discovering the outline and the thesis of an article. These concepts develop as you read the article slowly and carefully. You are to establish the content of each paragraph and to group these paragraphs into sections. From those contents you can then establish the thesis of the article.

Read the article one paragraph at a time and note the subject matter covered in each paragraph.

Paragraph 1.
General introductory remarks.
Paragraph 2.
Additional introductory remarks.
Paragraph 3.
Establishes the subject matter of this article to be the Starlet. Suggests that the author's opnion of the car is rather high, and that the car provides minimal-cost motoring in a satisfactory fashion.
Paragraph 4.
Discusses the general makeup and arrangement of the car.
Paragraph 5.
Description, size, shape, and other factual information.
Paragraphs 6, 7, 8, 9.
The interior: size, shape, equipment, quality.
Paragraphs 10, 11, 12.
Engine, drive train, performance.
Paragraph 13.
Noise levels.
Paragraphs 14, 15.
Handling and ride.

Paragraph 16.
  Brakes.
Paragraph 17.
  Noise levels.
Paragraph 18.
  General summary.

This outline does not lead directly to a thesis statement, but a look at each section will help you to move to a thesis. In the third paragraph, the writer concludes with this statement:

> The Starlet is "a means of experiencing minimal-cost motoring without being positively embarrassed about it all."

The section on the general description compares the car favorably to the Honda Civic and the Renault Le Car, two very good automobiles. The discussion on the construction uses words such as

> fit and finish up to the Toyota standard . . . commendably high.
>
> elements . . . well done.

and makes many additional complimentary remarks. The section on engine, drive train and performance makes very positive statements also. The balance of the article continues in a positive vein and concludes with several generally good reactions:

> The *Road and Track* humans came away most impressed by the Starlet.
> This Starlet is a sweetheart.
> The Starlet could well become the benchmark (standard) for commuter cars of the Eighties.

Those observations and opinions can lead us to a thesis statement:

> The Starlet is a car of excellent quality, outstanding economy, and good performance.

Read the article one more time to fix the ideas in your mind. The next step in this process is to read the article on the same car from *Car and Driver*. Here the author, Jean Lindamood, takes pretty much the same direction as is taken in the article in *Road and Track*. Be sure to follow the three-step reading process. The second reading ought to produce an outline somewhat like this one:

Paragraphs 1, 2, 3, 4.
Provide a general introduction and the direction for the paper, an evaluation of the Starlet.
Paragraph 5.
Deals with the overall description.
Paragraph 6.
Deals with the engine.
Paragraph 7.
Deals with the transmission and performance.
Paragraphs 8, 9, 10, 11, 12.
Deal with the interior and its equipment, and provide observations on room, noise level, and the absence of rattles.
Paragraphs 13, 14, 15.
Discuss and evaluate the suspension, handling, and the ride.
Paragraph 16.
Offers a conclusion: The Starlet is a fine car for those who need reasonable performance, high economy, and low initial cost.

Now you have a sketchy outline for each article. Next you need to take notes on each section of the outlines for both articles. *Taking notes* is a specific skill, not a loose jotting of randomly selected items from an article. Be sure to follow these guidelines as you take notes on these articles:

1. Write a separate, specific note for each section in the outline of an article.
2. Write a sentence summarizing each section. This sentence is very similar to the topic sentence of a paragraph.
3. Write two or three sentences discussing and explaining the summary sentence. Define any terms and clarify the ideas used in the summary sentence.
4. Provide illustrations and examples of the ideas in the summary sentence. Record sentences or phrases that are particularly effective expressions from the article, so that you may quote them later on. When you record words, phrases, or sentences directly from the article, put quotation marks around them so that you will remember you have taken them word-for-word from the article.

One section from the article from *Car and Driver* will serve as an example of this type of work. Read Paragraphs 13 and 17, which

comment on noise levels in the car. The summary sentence for the
two paragraphs might read like this:

> The noise levels in the car are a bit high, but they are not unbearably high.

Explanation, discussions, and definitions.

> The car makes all sorts of noise, exceeding the decibel levels in other
> small cars by two points or so at most cruising speeds. At peak RPMs it
> is extremely noisy. Overall the test drivers did not find the noise excessive
> or extremely annoying.

Examples and quotations.

> "... the Starlet's 90 dBA at redline in first gear was considerably higher
> than any competitor's ... "
>
> (Par. 17)

> "... You can drive all day and not feel buzzed to death,' said one staff
> member."
>
> (Par. 13)

You need to note the page of the quotation so that you can give
the writer credit later on, if you use the quotation in your paper.
You need to make similar notes for each section of the outlines of
the articles. You do not need a full note on each paragraph, just
on each section of the outline, whether the section is one paragraph or several paragraphs long.

Now with your notes spread out before you, make a list of the
subject areas covered in the two articles.

Road and Track	Car and Driver
overall appearance and arrangement	evaluation
description	description
size	engine
shape	transmission
interior	performance
equipment	interior-room and noise level
engine	suspension
drive train	handling
performance	ride
noise levels	
handling	
ride	
brakes	

It is easy to see two things about the lists:

1. The articles deal with the same car in almost the same way, by dealing with important aspects of the car.
2. The important aspects of the car can be grouped into rather large units.

Grouping the small items into larger, related groups provides a kind of rough outline of ther materials.

> Overall appearance, arrangement, description.
> The interior and its equipment.
> Engine, transmission, brakes, performance.
> Suspension, ride, handling.
> Evaluation and conclusions about the car.

Step 3

At this point we have finished Step 2 of the writing process; we have selected a subject (The Starlet) as Step 1, and have gathered and organized material as Step 2. Step 3, which is to establish the thesis of the paper, follows easily in this case, since both articles are so positive in their appraisal of the car:

> The Toyota Starlet is an excellent commuter car, high in quality, outstanding in economy, and acceptable in performance. It may be the model for commuter cars of the eighties.

Step 4

Step 4, selecting materials for inclusion in the paper, is also quite easily accomplished because the articles cover very much the same areas of information. The rough outline produced by matching the areas covered in the two articles will service as an outline for the paper.

Step 5

Looking back at the end of Step 2, we see that the logical first point in the outline, is

> The general description and layout of the car.

Now we see two areas very closely related

Engine, transmission, brakes, performance.
Suspension, ride, handling.

These areas can be treated in either order, but should not be separated by the section on the interior of the car.

The paper probably ought to end with a general summary and evaluation of the car. We thus have two possible orders for presenting the materials:

General description
Engine and mechanical aspects
Suspension, ride, and so on
Interior
Summary and evaluation

OR, by interchanging the three middle sections

General description
Interior
Engine
Suspension
Summary

When you have made a choice between these two orders, you are ready to write the draft or trial version of the paper.

Step 6

Writing the Draft or Trial Version of the Paper.

Remember that this paper, like any other, must have an introduction to catch the interest of the reader and to state the direction or the thesis of the paper. Remember also that it is not necessary to write the introduction first, even though it will appear first in the paper. Start to write the draft version of the paper at any point in the outline at which starting to write will be easy for you.

The best method for starting to write successfully is to select one section of the outline and begin to work on it as though it were a paper all by itself. If you select the section on the interior as the first one to write, move immediately to Step 2, in which you ask yourself

What do I know about the subject—the interior of the car?

Move to your notes from both articles on that section, and review the materials. You will find that the interior is fully carpeted and roomy, the seats quite comfortable, and their support adequate. The interior is finished in vinyl and is tastefully done. The instrument panel is easily read, provides temperature gauge, tachometer, and odometer. The pedals, steering wheel, shift lever and other controls are well-located, and the ventilation system is excellent. Taken as a whole, both articles say that the interior is roomy, well-designed, comfortable, and very well-equipped.

The following is an effective topic sentence:

For a small car, the interior of the Starlet is well-designed and equipped, roomy and comfortable.

Then for the topic sentence, write several sentences of explanation and discussion.

It provides adequate room for four people, two quite comfortably seated in front and two a bit less comfortably in the back seat. The front seats are comfortable; they give good lateral support. The passenger compartment is lined in tasteful vinyl and is fully carpeted. The instrument panel is clearly labeled, well equipped with dials and gauges, and easily read. All the controls, the steering wheel, pedals, shift lever, and other gadgets are convenient for the driver. The steering wheel and shift knob are vinyl-padded. The ventilation system is excellent; the optional air conditioning works very well and the heater "pumps out a furnace-strength blast," even when running on the low setting. The rear seat folds to make a cargo space over 22 cubic feet in volume.

Note that this paragraph also includes many specific details to support the general statements. The names of the accessories, the specific mention of the covering of the steering wheel and shift knob, and the quotation used to support the quality of the heater, are all good examples of the kinds of concrete, specific supporting details needed to complete the development of the general statements.

Finally, the paragraph needs a concluding sentence to summarize the whole statement. The last sentence of Paragragh 9 of the article in *Road and Track* can be rewritten to make a good summary statement:

> Overall, Toyota has done a commendable job, providing a roomy, comfortable, and extremely workable compartment for driver and passengers.

One more thing remains if this paragraph is to be complete: you must cite the sources of the two quotations. The easiest way to give credit for this sort of informal article or paper is the mention in an early paragraph the source of the materials:

> In two recent articles on the Toyota Starlet, *Road and Track* (March, 1981) and *Car and Driver* (February, 1981) reported . . .

Give credit for a specific quotation by citing the article and page number. Note these in parentheses, within the text:

> "pumps out a furnace-strength blast" even when running on the low setting. (*Car and Driver*, P. 91.)

> "Overall, Toyota has done a commendable job," providing . . . and passengers. (*Road and Track*, P. 42.)

As a last word of advice, take careful note of the introduction for the paper. It is a great temptation to set up the thesis sentence at the beginning of the paper and to leave it standing alone as the entire introduction. It is useful to provide a short version of the thesis, but it is very important to make some effort to catch the interest of the readers and to inform them of the general direction the paper will take. You will notice that both articles made specific attempts to arouse your interest. The article in *Road and Track* gives a quick history of Toyota's efforts in commuter cars, and the article in *Car and Driver* introduces the Japanese concept called "Bushido" and offers a summary of previous entries from Toyota in the commuter car field. You need to make just as much of an effort to catch your reader's interest. The following opening lines are appealing:

> With the price of gas trying to bump over the $1.50 mark, and the price of even a mid-sized vehicle exceeding $10,000, it might be a good time to survey the commuter car field to find acceptable basic transportation at minimum cost. Toyota has an entry in this field that comes highly recommended by both *Road and Track* and *Car and Driver*, magazines that have written road tests of the Toyota Starlet in recent months.

From this point, tell the reader that you intend to summarize the articles. Then state your thesis.

The assignment for Assignment 9 is to write a paper based on these two articles. Summarize the content and give the reader the judgement of the two magazines. The paper should be at least six paragraphs long, including the introduction and conclusion.

As an alternative assigment, find articles on another consumer item such as a camera or a stereo, and summarize the ideas of the two articles. This paper should be about six paragraphs long. A very interesting paper would compare a report in a specialty magazine for that product with a report on the same product in *Consumer's Report*.

ASSIGNMENT 10

Stating a Personal Position Based on Readings

For the final essay assignment based on readings, you will read five brief essays on the subject of work. These essays discuss the place of work in American society and its place or importance in your life. After reading the essays you will write a three- to four-page essay expressing your ideas on this subject. You may use material from any of the five essays in any way you see fit. You may quote an author to support a point, you may agree or disagree with an idea in one of the essays, or you may ignore any essay entirely. You may bring into your essay any idea or attitude you already hold, and connect it to any you choose to use from the five essays in the book.

You may ask why this topic ought to be important to you. The topic deals with work in the sense of occupation of career. It relates to the job you will pursue after you finish your education. Preparation for this career will occupy most of your time while you are in college, and the work itself will take a major portion of your time for a great number of years. The investment you are making in money, time, and effort to prepare yourself for the career, and the importance of that career to your future well-being suggest that the topic is worth some thought.

Along with the ideas presented in the five essays, you might wish to consider some important questions about the nature of work and its place in your life.

You should do a free-writing response to some of these questions before you begin to work on the essays.

1. How important is success in your career? How important is financial success? What is your definition of success?
2. Do you want meaningful, enjoyable work, or will you be satisfied with a somewhat routine job and find satisfactions outside of work?
3. Which is more important, family or career? What kind of balance will you seek to establish between the two?
4. What occupation or career are you currently considering? Why did you choose it? What is the nature of the day-to-day work in that occupation? How well are your skills and your personality suited to that occupation?

When you finish these exercises, set them aside and read the following five articles. Be sure to use the strategies for reading that you learned earlier in this chapter. Produce a thesis and outline for each article and write a brief reaction or commentary on the idea presented in the article. Also, try to connect the ideas in the articles with your ideas as you recorded them in the free-writing exercises.

IS THERE REALLY SUCH A THING AS TALENT?

A Pulitzer Prize winner's reassuring message to those who feel they'll never be great at anything

by Annie Dillard

[1] There is no such thing as talent. If there are any inborn, God-given gifts, they are in the precocious fields of music, mathematics and chess; if you have such a gift, you know it by now. All the rest of us in all the other fields are not talented. We all start out dull and weary and uninspired. Apart from a few like Mozart, there never have been any great and accomplished little children in the world. Genius is the product of education.

[2] Perhaps it's a cruel thing to insist that there is no such thing as talent. We all want to believe—at least I do—that being selfless was "easy" for Albert Schweitzer, that Faulkner's novels just popped into his head, that Rembrandt painted because he "had to." We want to believe all those nonsensical things in order to get ourselves off the hook. For if these people had no talent, then might the rest of us have painting or writing or great thinking as an option? We, who have no talent? I think the answer is yes, absolutely.

From *Seventeen Magazine*, June 1979.

[3] So I maintain that the people who have made something of their lives—the Pasteurs and Cezannes and Melvilles—were neither more talented nor more disciplined nor more energetic nor more driven than the rest of us. They were simply better educated. Some of them did it the hard way studying all the difficult works of their fields at home on their own. Others studied in school. But they all studied. You won't find a writer who hasn't studied the details of the works of other writers—although occasionally you find an American writer like Hemingway or Whitman who deliberately pretended to be spontaneous and unstudied, probably in order to mislead the competition. And occasionally you find a writer like Thoreau, a very well-educated Harvard man whose reading was in the Greek classics and in whose work most readers overlook the evidences of scholarships and effort simply because they don't want to see them.

[4] It's hard work, doing something with your life. The very thought of hard work makes me queasy. I'd rather die in peace. Here we are all equal and alike and none of us much to write home about—and some people choose to make themselves into physicists or thinkers or major-league pitchers, knowing perfectly well that it will be nothing but hard work. But I want to tell you that it's not as bad as it sounds. Doing something does not require discipline, it creates its own discipline—with a little help from caffeine.

[5] People often ask me if I discipline myself to write, if I work a certain number of hours a day on a schedule. They ask this question with envy in their voices and awe on their faces and a sense of alienation all over them, as if they were addressing an armored tank or talking giraffe or Niagara Falls. We all want to believe that other people are natural wonders, it gets us off the hook.

[6] Now, it happens that when I wrote my first book of prose, I worked an hour or two a day for a while, and then in the last two months, I got excited and worked very hard, for many hours a day. People can lift cars when they want to. People can recite the Koran, too, and run in marathons. These things aren't ways of life; they are merely possibilities for everyone on certain occasions of life. You don't lift cars around the clock or write books every year. But when you do, it's not so hard. It's not super-human. It's very human. You do it for love. You do it for love and respect for your own life; you do it for love and respect for the world; and you do it for love and respect for the task itself.

[7] If I had a little baby, it would be hard for me to rise up and feed that little baby in the middle of the night. It would be hard, but it certainly wouldn't be a discipline. It wouldn't be a regimen I imposed on myself out of masochism, nor would it be the flowering of some extraordinary internal impulse. I would do it, grumbling, for love and because it has to be done.

[8] Of course it has to be done. Any something has to be done with your life too, something specific, something human. But don't wait around to be hit by love. Don't wait for anything. Learn something first. Then while you are getting to know it, you will get to love it, and that love will direct you in

what to do. So many times when I was in college I used to say of a course like Seventeenth-Century Poetry or European History, "I didn't like it at first, but now I like it." All of life is like that—a sort of dreary course which gradually gets interesting if you work at it.

[9] I used to live in perpetual dread that I would one day read all the books that I would ever be interested in and have nothing more to read. I always figured that when that time came I would force myself to learn wild flowers, just to keep awake. I dreaded it, because I was not very interested in wild flowers but thought I should be. But things kept cropping up and one book has led to another and I haven't had to learn wild flowers yet. I don't think there's much danger of coming to the end of the line. The line is endless. I urge you to get in it, to get in line. It's a long line—but it's the only show in town.

CONFESSIONS OF A WORKING STIFF

by Patrick Fenton

[1] The Big Ben is hammering out its 5:45 alarm in the half-dark of another Tuesday morning. If I'm lucky, my car down in the street will kick over for me. I don't want to think about that now; all I want to do is roll over into the warm covers and hug my wife. I can hear the wind as it whistles up and down the sides of the building. Tuesday is always the worst day—it's the day the drudgery, boredom, and fatigue start all over again. I'm off from work on Sunday and Monday, so Tuesday is my blue Monday.

[2] I make my living humping cargo for Seaboard World Airlines, one of the big international airlines at Kennedy Airport. They handle strictly cargo. I was once told that one of the Rockefellers is the major stockholder for the airline, but I don't really think about that too much. I don't get paid to think. The big thing is to beat that race with the time clock every morning of your life so the airline will be happy. The worst thing a man could ever do is to make suggestions about building a better airline. They pay people $40,000 a year to come up with better ideas. It doesn't matter that these ideas never work; it's just that they get nervous when a guy from South Brooklyn or Ozone Park acts like he actually has a brain.

[3] I throw a Myadec high-potency vitamin into my mouth to ward off one of the ten colds I get every year from humping mailbags out in the cold rain at Kennedy. A huge DC-8 stretch jet waits impatiently for the 8,000 pounds of mail that I will soon feed its empty belly. I wash the Myadec down with some orange juice and grab a brown bag filled with bologna and cheese. Inside the lunch bag there is sometimes a silly note from my wife that says, "I Love You—Guess Who?" It is all that keeps me going to a job that I hate.

[4] I've been going there for seven years now and my job is still the same. It's weary work that makes a man feel used up and worn out. You push and

From *New York Magazine*, 1973.

you pull all day long with your back. You tie down pallets loaded with thousands of pounds of freight. You fill igloo-shaped containers with hundreds of boxes that all look the same. If you're assigned to work the warehouse, it's really your hard luck. This is the job all the men hate most. You stack box upon box until the pallet resembles the exact shape of the inside of the plane. You get the same monotomous feeling an adult gets when he plays with a child's blocks. When you finish one pallet, you find another and start the whole dull process over again.

[5] The airline pays me $192 a week for this. After they take out taxes and $5.81 for the pension, I go home with $142. Once a month they take out $10 for term insurance and $5.50 for union dues. The week they take out the life insurance is always the worst: I go home with $132. My job will never change. I will fill up the same igloos with the same boxes for the next 34 years of my life, I will hump the same mailbags into the belly of the plane, and push the same 8,000-pound pallets with my back. I will have to do this until I'm 65 years old. Then I'll be free, if I don't die of a heart attack before that, and the airline will let me retire.

[6] In winter the warehouse is cold and damp. There is no heat. The large steel doors that line the warehouse walls stay open most of the day. In the cold months, wind, rain and snow blow across the floor. In the summer the warehouse becomes an oven. Dust and sand from the runways mix with the toxic fumes of fork lifts, leaving a dry stale taste in your mouth. The high windows above the doors are covered with a thick, black dirt that kills the sun. The men work in shadows with the constant roar of jet engines blowing dangerously in their ears.

[7] Working the warehouse is a tedious job that leaves a man's mind empty. If he's smart he will spend his days wool-gathering. He will think about pretty girls that he once knew, or some other daydream of warm, dry places where you never had a chill. The worst thing he can do is to think about his problems. If he starts to think about how he is going to pay the mortgage on the $30,000 home that he can't afford, it will bring him down. He will wonder why he comes to the cargo airline every morning of his life, and even on Christmas day. He will start to wonder why he has to listen to the deafening sound of the jets as they rev up their engines. He will wonder why he crawls on his hands and knees, breaking his back a little more every day.

DULL WORK
by Eric Hoffer

[1] There seems to be a general assumption that brilliant people cannot stand routine; that they need a varied, exciting life in order to do their best. It is also assumed that dull people are particularly suited for dull work. We are told that the reason the present-day young protest so loudly against the

From *In Our Time*.

dullness of factory jobs is that they are better educated and brighter than the young of the past.

[2]   Actually, there is no evidence that people who achieve much crave for, let alone live, eventful lives. The opposite is nearer the truth. One thinks of Amos the sheepherder, Socrates the stonemason, Omar the tentmaker. Jesus probably had his first revelations while doing humdrum carpentry work. Einstein worked out his theory of relativity while serving as a clerk in a Swiss patent office. Machiavelli wrote *The Prince* and the *Discourses* while immersed in the dull life of a small country town where the only excitement he knew was playing cards with muleteers at the inn. Immanuel Kant's daily life was an unalterable routine. The housewives of Konigsberg set their clocks when they saw him pass on his way to the university. He took the same walk each morning, rain or shine. The greatest distance Kant ever traveled was sixty miles from Konigsberg.

[3]   The outstanding characteristic of man's creativeness is the ability to transmute trivial impulses into momentous consequences. The greatness of man is in what he can do with petty grievances and joys, and with common physiological pressures and hungers. "When I have a little vexation," wrote Keats, "it grows in five minutes into a theme for Sophocles." To a creative individual all experience is seminal—all events are equidistant from new ideas and insights—and his inordinate humanness shows itself in the ability to make the trivial and common reach an enormous way.

[4]   An eventful life exhausts rather than stimulates. Milton, who in 1640 was a poet of great promise, spent twenty sterile years in the eventful atmosphere of the Puritan revolution. He fulfilled his promise when the revolution was dead, and he in solitary disgrace. Cellini's exciting life kept him from becoming the great artist he could have been. It is legitimate to doubt whether Machiavelli would have written his great books had he been allowed to continue in the diplomatic service of Florence and had he gone on interesting missions. It is usually the mediocre poets, writers, etc., who go in search of stimulating events to release their creative flow.

[5]   It may be true that work on the assembly line dulls the faculties and empties the mind, the cure only being fewer hours of work at higher pay. But during fifty years as a workingman, I have found dull routine compatible with an active mind. I can still savor the joy I used to derive from the fact that while doing dull, repetitive work on the waterfront, I could talk with my partners and compose sentences in the back of my mind, all at the same time. Life seemed glorious. Chances are that had my work been of absorbing interest I could not have done any thinking and composing on the company's time or even on my own time after returning from work.

[6]   People who find dull work unendurable are often dull people who do not know what to do with themselves when at leisure. Children and mature people thrive on dull routine, while the adolescent, who has lost the child's capacity for concentration and is without the inner resources of the mature, needs excitement and novelty to stave off boredom.

A NEW ATTITUDE TOWARD WORK

by Sam Keen

[1] Jay, a carpenter who has worked for me on several occasions, is a barrel of a man, stout as an oak log. Though not yet 30 years old, his convictions are well seasoned; he is true to the grain of his own wood. On good days he shows up for work between 9 and 10 A.M. If it is raining, or his dog needs to go to the veterinarian, or he has promised to help a friend, or there is an exhibit of Zen art at the museum, he may not get here at all. As yet he hasn't called to say the day is too beautiful to spend working. But I wouldn't be surprised if he did. When he arrives, he unwraps his bundles of Japanese woodworking tools, removes the fine saws and chisels from their mahogany cases, puts some shakuhachi flute music on his tape deck, and begins methodically to sculpt the elaborate joints in the beams that will form the structure of the studio we are building. He works slowly, pausing to watch a hawk circle overhead, to tell a joke, to savor the smell of the wood. Occasionally I try to hurry him. "That looks close enough, Jay." I say. "May as well take the time to do it right the first time," he replies and goes on working at his own pace. After several days he announces that the beams are ready to be hoisted into place. We lift and tug and push. Notch joins notch. Tongue slips into groove. The puzzle fits together. We sigh with relief. A satisfying day.

[2] Some would say Jay is an underachiever, a dropout, that he lacks ambition. A college graduate with honors in football, he works sporadically, for carpenters' wages. He has no pension, no health insurance, no fringe benefits. He drives an old truck and lives in a funky neighborhood near the industrial district of Oakland. When he doesn't need money, he tends his garden, writes poetry, paints, and studies Japanese and wood joinery. "I get by." he says. "It doesn't make any sense to sell your soul for security and have no time left to do the things you love."

[3] I say Jay is one of a new breed of Americans who are refusing to make work the central value in their lives. These lighthearted rebels have paused to consider the lilies of the field (executive coronaries and the pollution of the Love Canal) and have decided neither to toil nor to spin. They are turning everything upside down, creating what Nietzsche called "a transvaluation of values," and calling into question the traditional, orthodox virtues of the Protestant work ethic and American dream. They are inventing new "life-styles," forging new myths and visions of the good life, new definitions of happiness.

[4] A revolution in cultural values, like a storm front, is difficult to chart. Our values, self-images, myths, heroes, goals, visions of the good life, shift like to weather. The best computers and statistics give us only a fair to middling account of what's happening and why. To have any hope of predicting the emerging trends that will shape tomorrow's climate we need intuition, the latest reports from the barometer, Grandma's rheumatism, and a good

Condensed from an article in *Quest*.

deal of what an irreverent engineer friend of mine calls S.W.A.G. (Scientific Wild Ass Guess). By assembling a collage of statistics, events, ideas, and social movements we may construct a weather map of our times—a profile of a revolution in process.

Items:

[5] • Discontent with the world of work is widespread. Yankelovich surveys report that only 40 percent of all adults now believe that "hard work always pays off." As many as 75 percent of adult Americans are involved in some way in a search for new meanings, for self-fulfillment. More men in their prime working years are dropping out of the work force. Some, tired of the unrewarding jobs and professions for which they were trained, are undergoing the now nearly obligatory "mid-life crisis," retiring early and taking up a second life. Alan, for instance, "retired" from a high-stress, high-paying job in a Silicone Valley computer industry at age 47 and moved to Prescott, Arizona, where he sells real estate, rides his horse, and enjoys the immense silence of the desert.

[6] • The vast majority of Americans endure their work because they see no other way to make a living. But even among those faithful to organized business, there is an increasing demand to make the rules of work more flexible. Businesses are gradually yielding to the pressure for humanizing and personalizing the office and factory. Flex-time and job-sharing are being tried in many progressive industries. The most adventurous are trying to find ways to coordinate changing individual body rhythms and work schedules. It is even rumored that in some far-out establishments—in where else but California—job descriptions are being matched with astrological types: Sagittarians for the long-range, wide-arching planning tasks, Virgos for bookkeeping detail.

[7] • An undetermined number of Americans are discovering ways to make a living or improve their financial circumstance that do not involve job, work, and employment.

A thriving outlaw economy exists, unreported to the IRS, and uncounted in our estimates of the GNP. Edgar Feige, an economist at the University of Wisconsin in Madison, estimates that the underground economy consists of as much as 30 percent of the Gross National Product, an economy of $700 billion (larger than France's entire GNP). This figure includes an estimate of the value of all those transactions not involving the exchange of money such as bartering, trading goods and services—in which wealth is created. Flea markets and garage sales have made merchants and economic outlaws of us all. Millions of Americans are learning the skill of what maverick economist Paul Hawkens calls "disintermediation," cutting out the middleman. When you repair your car, grow a garden, can food, have your baby at home, refinish your furniture, design or build your own house, care for your own health, you join the revolution, you sign the emancipation proclamation that frees you from economic bondage to yet more specialists and experts.

[8] Hard work, honest sweat, and entrepreneurial imagination made America the strongest and most envied kingdom on earth. Why the revolution in paradise? Why the search for new lifestyles, new values? Why are we abandoning the virtues and world view that made us great and prosperous?

[9] The quick and easy answers are economic.

[10] The right-wing priests of the status quo say our problem is that the privileged sons and daughters of the affluent, like welfare recipients, never had to work and are lazy. They want it all now. The "me" generation is spoiled; since they never had to worry about the wolf at the door, they have the luxury of turning inward and meditating on the dove of the spirit or the naval of their own experience. The solution is to get tough, get busy, expand the economy, and get America back to work.

[11] The apocalyptic left says the problem is that we are running out of resources. Energy and materials are more expensive, and economies everywhere are slowing down. No amount of resourcefulness will allow us to continue our pattern of economic expansion. Our only solution is to learn to live small, cut our wants, trim our budgets, produce less, consume less, work less.

[12] Fluctuations in the economy from affluence to stagflation certainly affect the way we think about work. But the deepest motives animating our revolution in work are psychological, or perhaps spiritual.

[13] Yesterday's gods have become today's demons. The Greeks invented the idea of nemesis to show how a single virtue, stubbornly maintained, gradually changes into a destructive vice. Our success, our industry, our habit of work have all produced our economic nemesis. We were the first nation to dream the materialist dream of plenty for all, and to come close to making it a reality. Even in our present moment of economic crisis we are driving to the poorhouse in new automobiles, spending our inflated dollars for calorie-free food, and lamenting our falling productivity in an environment polluted by our industry. Work made us great but now threatens to usurp our soul, to inundate the earth in goods and trash, to destroy our capacity to wonder and to love. The rebels who are trying to overthrow the tyranny of work are, in effect, asking us to meditate on the wisdom of the Greeks, who claimed that Hephaestus (Vulcan) the Blacksmith, the only Olympian god who worked, was born lame.

[14] As western culture, and America in particular, became increasingly industrialized, gradually the meaning and purpose—the reason for which people work—did a flip-flop. The stages in this process were roughly as follows:

1. In the beginning work was a means, never an end in itself. People worked to provide the necessities of life for themselves, and to create leisure to contemplate and enjoy life. Only slaves existed to work.

2. The invention of machines allowed us to produce the necessities of life more easily and, according to Herbert Marcuse, might have freed us from excessive work to enjoy a more erotic and pleasurable way of life

3. However, to keep the machines busy, production increasing, and the economy expanding, we invented a new set of needs. Advertising convinced us that we "needed" and wouldn't be happy without those commodities our factories were producing—cars, radios, TV, hoola-hoops, appliances, and more. To keep artificial needs stimulated, style and model changes were created; it is this year's new thing you need. Before we knew what was happening, all the luxuries became defined as psychological necessities.

4. Our ethic changed from one of production to one of consumption. Our worth gradually became associated with what could be purchased, possessed, and consumed. The size of the toys separated the men from the boys. The important people (who, of course, were defined as "the happy" or fortunate ones) were those with the most expensive things.

5. For the middle class, work became that activity that men (and later women) increasingly engaged in to provide themselves not only with food, clothing, and shelter, but also with the new "necessities"—the large automobile, the suburban home, and the symbolic things that had to be conspicuously consumed to gain status.

6. Our loyalties were gradually shifted from family, friends, and community to work. Identity, especially for the male, became rooted in one's job. The first questions men asked each other were: What do you do? Where do you work? The affluent managers and semi-affluent white-collar workers began to gain their identity, their sense of worth, from that work.

7. The job and the corporation colonized and governed our psyches. They determined our dress, our conduct, where we lived, when we moved, how we measured success, and our friends (or acquaintances and associates). They dictated that we would live in obedience to the clock. They turned us into a nation of what Drs. Friedman and Rosenman called Type A personalities—stressed, chronically struggling, driven.

8. And in the end—the final tyranny—we came to love our chains. According to a *Psychology Today* survey (May 1978) only 29 percent of us would place enjoyment of the work we do as a priority in continuing to work at all. And yet—as Yankelovich found—80 percent of us would go right on working for money even if we didn't have to! As work has come to occupy the center of our identity, to turn the imagination into a factory, we have forgotten that it was for leisure and love that we originally agreed to labor.

[15] The hostility toward work that has developed in this generation comes largely from sons of fathers who were workaholics. The fathers of today's middle-class children lived through and were wounded by the great Depression. Anyone who grew up in the 1940's lives with the fear that the tide

of prosperity might recede again, as it did in 1931, and then there would be no jobs. As a result, most of the men who have risen to middle-management positions devoted themselves to their work and their corporations with religious zeal; the job was the center of their lives. And so a generation of sons and daughters identify "work" as the villain who took Daddy away from them and returned him tired and used-up at the end of the day. A thousand times in the average middle-class home a child eager to play with Daddy was told, "Not now, Daddy's tired" or "Daddy has to go to work." "Work" was the excuse that covered a multitude of sins.

[16] The poet Robert Bly offers a clue to some of the psychological motives behind our hostility toward work: "The boy and his father . . . are the love-unit most damaged by the Industrial Revolution." In primitive cultures fathers initiated their sons into manhood, guided their hands in the use of a bow and arrow or a digging stick, shared the excitement of the hunt, taught them the myths and mysteries of the tribe. In the last two decades the work of the fathers has become so abstract, so remote from the home, so routinized that, for the first time in history, men have abandoned the task and joy of initiating their children.

[17] Instead of time, tenderness, and tacit knowledge of the world, they have given their children the trinkets of affluence. Often in groups I have conducted, I have heard a man break down and sob: "Dad, I never knew you. Where were you? Who were you? You never let me in on your life." The sons have seen the fathers swallowed by the world of work. They have watched as work stole from them the thing they wanted most—Father as the living presence, model, and guide for manhood. As Earl Shorris shows in *The Oppressed Middle*, the corporation man increasingly surrendered his consciousness, his moral autonomy, his private values, to serve the aims of the totalitarian corporation. And the sons lost respect when the fathers sold their souls for the illusion of security.

[18] And the daughters? Daddy was also absent from their lives (which taught them early that they couldn't expect much from men). But little girls had mother as a companion and role model. She touched them, held them when they cried, tended them when they were sick, taught them to bake a cherry pie or make a dress. But they also learned that Mother's task of keeping the hearth was not as valuable as Father's work. His was the kingdom, the power, and the superior dignity. Value was created in the factory, the corporation, and the market-place, not in the home—the real action was in business. Only inferior beings took care of children, raised gardens, and practiced the ancient art of managing a household (the original definition of economics). If you wanted to be important, you had to be involved with the new value-creating process—economics as the production, distribution and consumption of commodities.

[19] By the 1970's women were becoming dissatisfied. Traditionally, the

center of their identity had been in love relationships. As work became more important than love, women experienced a crisis in identity. What Maggie Scarf called "the more sorrowful sex" (*Psychology Today*, April 1979) suffered depression two to five times more often than men. Thirty-two percent of women in the prime of life (30–44) were using prescription drugs for mood elevation. As the desacralization and devaluing of home and hearth continued, a majority of women decided to enter that valuable world of paid work. In the 70's they won the right to measure their worth by money and position in a professional hierarchy and gained equal access with men to the diseases of stress—ulcers and heart attacks.

[20] There are already signs that many women who were liberated in the 70's to enjoy the male prerogatives of sex without love and identities centered around work are coming full circle. The sexual revolution is cooling. The joy of commitment is re-emerging. Many women now in their mid-thirties who are seasoned workers are deciding that their anatomy might have something to do with their destiny and are having children.

[21] Our changing valuation of work is a symptom of our changing view of all of reality. The new iconoclasm is directed against the idolatry of economics, the myth of money, the assumptions that more is better, work makes free (the motto that was emblazoned on the gate over Auschwitz), technology can make us all healthy, wealthy, and wise. Many Americans have reached the top of the success ladder but are beginning to suspect it may be leaning against the wrong wall.

[22] It is too soon to say where the questions and the new quest will lead. It is clear that a civil war may be developing between two philosophies of life, two value systems. And in the chaos that is bound to result from this clash we might best be guided by the words, but not the example, of Freud. It may help us to remember that in his prescription of love and work—*lieben und arbeiten*—he designated love as the first among equals.

THE FUEL OF SUCCESS

It's ambition, and we should stop apologizing for it

by Harry Stein

[1] Rummaging through an old filing cabinet one recent afternoon, I came upon a crumpled sheet of paper labeled, in black ink, "Play-person Data Sheet." The brain raced and the eye scanned the page. Ah, yes, my very own version of the information sheet filled out by every Playboy Playmate of the Month. This one had been composed one rollicking evening several years ago as a girlfriend sat across the room composing hers.

From *Esquire*, August 1981.

Height: 5'9½"
Weight: 145
Sign: Sagittarius
Birth Date: Nov. 25, 1948/N.Y.C.
Goals: To be recognized as a major writer; to make a large amount of money; with above assets; to live comfortably in varying locales with a woman I love and a couple of children.
Turn-ons: Good wine, excellent cigars. In a love interest: brains, wit, unselfishness and sex appeal, a good heart, determination.
Turn-offs: Stupidity, undeserved success, banal thinking, any of a dozen qualities one might associate with Tom Landry.
Favorite Performers: Harpo Marx, Jean-Pierre Leaud, Buster Keaton, Rodney Dangerfield, Louis Armstrong.
Favorite TV Shows: Car 54, The Honeymooners, the original Dick Van Dyke Show.
Favorite Movies: Stolen Kisses, Rules of the Game, Alice's Restaurant, Sunday Bloody Sunday, The Producers, The Cocoanuts, High Noon.
Favorite Activities: Playing softball, interviewing in French, rummaging through interesting historical documents, antiquing.
Ideal Evening: Getting dressed up, lingering for hours over a very fine dinner—including limitless quantities of a quality wine—with four or five close friends; smoking two good cigars over tea as conversation continues.
Special Dream: Holding high political office.

[2] Seeing it again, reading it all with a reasonably detached eye, it all struck me as pretty damn bald. A major writer. High political office. The arrogance of it, the unabashed chutzpah.

[3] It is, alas, all true. I have never made any particular secret of my wish to make a mark with my work. When asked, this is how I put it: "When I am sixty-five or seventy, I'd like to be able to hold a book in my hands that I'm proud of." Nor is such cheek unusual in my business. It was, I think, Norman Mailer who observed what colossal arrogance it takes to put pen to paper in the first place, and to assume that anyone will care what one has to say.

[4] As for my visions of political office (and the office, by the way, was the Presidency), well, that one dates from the Kennedy era. At least a half dozen other junior high schoolers of my acquaintance—all naive and most as prohibitively Jewish as I—shared the same dream. Indeed, I am already far behind in the timetable I set for myself back then; by now I should be in the U.S. Senate, quietly plotting my run for the top spot in '88.

[5] But, explanations or no explanations, so blatant an exhibition of high hopes for oneself always seems unbecoming. Americans tend to be curiously schizophrenic about success; though recognition is prized—and celebrity nearly worshipped—the fact of being obviously on the make is regarded as unseemly.

We may be intrigued by Richard Dreyfuss, but Jimmy Stewart and Gary Cooper remain our ideals.

[6] Indeed, diffidence seems so appealing a trait that we tend to endow those bearing it with an inherent decency. I once spent six months trying hard to get to know an awkward, mild-mannered co-worker, only to finally discover that he was among the greatest slimes I'd ever encountered; it's just that he was a shy slime.

[7] And, of course, it also works very much the other way around. Several years ago, I wrote a profile of a New York politician named Andrew Stein (no relation), who at the time was in the midst of a heated campaign for the Manhattan borough presidency. Now, those of you who are glancingly familiar with Andy Stein are aware of the man's excessive immodesty, of the way he will posture for reporters at the nearest hint of an opportunity, dropping quotable quotes like the Muhammad Ali of the old days (What other official in the land will repeat, whenever asked, that, yes, he is angling to be President?). But, in reporting the piece, I was struck by the reluctance of so many people—including a fair number of other pols—to acknowledge Stein's record on the issues. The ambition was truly all that they could see—though he was actually no more ambitious than most of the rest of them, only less discreet.

[8] The truth is, if the record counts for anything, that aggressive, even grasping, behavior seems to be very much an integral part of our national character. Indeed, in the minds of countless foreigners, it is the chief component of the American stereotype. The very cliches of mainstream existence—"keeping up with the Joneses," "the man in the gray flannel suit," the various sayings of Vince Lombardi—carry with them a connotation of a people incessantly pushing for more, endlessly seeking to impress. In the Sixties, when many young Americans became, in effect, enemies of their government, it was no accident that they simultaneously turned *en masse* against this value system.

[9] By now, of course, the revolution itself has been institutionalized; it is the basis of a counterstereotype. "Well," writes a friend of a friend from Monterey, California, "I went ahead and quit my job at the day-care center, and now I'm taking yoga, aerobic dance, holistic healing, improv classes. At last, a career I can get into!"

[10] But, of course, even those more traditional in outlook frequently have trouble gearing themselves to the emtional rigors of the American working world. Women particularly—under intense, often self-imposed pressure to succeed professionally, yet unprepared by experience to run over people en route to wherever it is they think they should be heading—often find themselves in an unsettling quandary. A woman I know is a junior executive with a fashion concern; her boss, a man, has been pushing her to cozy up to important folk on behalf of the team. "Of course I'm ambitious," she protested to me, "but I don't want to become one of those people."

[11] Nor, heaven forbid, should she. It is my own strong opinion that, if at all feasible (and it is generally more feasible than we allow), one should get the hell out of a lousy work situation and into a less lousy one. I urged the junior exec, whose true passion it is to rummage through thrift and second-hand clothes shops, to open up a store of her own, or to ferret out costumes for theatrical companies, or to do any like thing that will bring in sufficient income. Such work, I reassured her, is every bit as valid as what she was doing. Self-satisfaction, after all, should figure somewhere in the equation.

[12] But, at the same time, it seems to me that ambition and aggressiveness have gotten a bad name in our time. What is indecent, what anyone whose values are reasonably in order should question, is a work situation that demands unprincipled behavior, either in day-to-day functioning or as a prerequisite for advancement. During the period when Watergate was flooding the front pages, it was frequently observed that the win-at-all costs syndrome that had permeated the Nixon White House was merely a reflection of a mentality pervasive in all walks of American life. Obviously, there was some truth to it; most of us have, in our professional lives, run across Haldemans and Ehrlichmans, not to mention countless Magruders and Deans.

[13] However, there are—and it is a measure of how cynical we have become that it needs to be remarked upon—untold thousands in this country who have done very nicely for themselves without sacrificing an iota of integrity. To be sure, their progress in the world is sometimes less easily ascendant than that of those of more flexible morality. A friend told me recently about her father, a gifted teacher of physics at a large university, who in the face of nearly incontrovertible evidence to the contrary continued to insist to his family that brains alone would guarantee his rise in the department. "It took him eight more years to make professor than it might have," she says, "but the day he got the news he brought home a cake with two words on top: YOU SEE."

[14] The very simple truth is that ambition and integrity are no more mutually exclusive than wisdom and wit. Indeed, the impulse to succeed is ultimately what makes human beings create great works and engage in noble deeds. Our problem—and yes, for some it is nearly insurmountable—is to get beyond the psychological flotsam that has become inextricably bound up with the idea of success in this country. It is essential for those driven to succeed to learn, and relearn, that how one gets there is finally more important than the arriving; and for those ill at ease with the whole process to understand that no one is corruptible unless he lets himself be.

[15] I realize that these are notions that run counter to the accepted wisdom of those on both sides of the fence. "Listen," I was reminded by an unapologetically aimless fellow I have known since high school when I mentioned to him the subject of this piece. "Lousy behavior has always paid off in these United States. It's an honored tradition. Look at the robber barons, and the sweatshop owners, and most of the political establishment."

[16] But, as it happened, that very afternoon I was reminded by another tradition from our collective past. In a secondhand bookstore in lower Manhattan, between dusty volumes of Evelyn Waugh and Edith Wharton, I discovered a thin tome by one Frank V. Webster entitled *Tom the Telephone Boy*. It was published in 1909 and it is the story of how Tom, through honesty, diligence, and—a wonderful forgotten word—pluck, outdoes an unscrupulous rival to rise from telephone operator in a law office to whiz-kid attorney. I suspect that seventy years ago it inspired little boys and girls by the score. Hey, if you read it in the right frame of mind, it's still inspiring. It's enough to set a man dreaming of the Presidency.

The article by Annie Dillard makes perhaps the most striking statement of all five articles. It is her opinion that there is no such thing as talent, except in fields where, quite obviously, there are special skills exhibited very early, such as music, math, and chess. In all other areas, especially those where most of us are going to be looking for careers, achievement comes to the people who work hard and educate themselves. It would be much more convenient, Dillard says, to believe that "the people who have made something of their lives" did so because of natural inborn talents that made everything very easy. If talent were the explanation, the rest of us would be "off the hook." But it just isn't so. Hard work and education are the way to accomplishment. Then, as though Dillard wishes to soften the blow, she adds that work isn't as hard as it seems, for it is done out of love. A person doesn't need self-discipline to begin and to carry on a project. Rather, the person simply needs to begin, and the progress of the work will create what amounts to a suction, drawing the person to work more and more until the project is complete. "Come on," she urges, "get to work. Pick a project, select some area, and start to work in it. Soon you will find that love of the project draws you into the work."

Patrick Fenton strikes a sad note in his discussion of the terrible effects his dull job has upon his mind and body. His view contrasts sharply with Hoffer's in the third article.

Eric Hoffer also sets forth a premise which seems to go against generally accepted ideas. The generally held idea is that brilliant people need varied, exciting work in order to thrive and accomplish; dull work will stifle the bright mind. Only dull people can cope with dull work.

Hoffer, however, claims that there is no evidence that achievers live exciting lives. On the contrary, he cites several people who achieved much and lived exceedingly dull lives. He suggests that the eventful life exhausts creative powers and therefore nothing long-lasting gets accomplished. In his own job as a longshoreman, doing dull, repetitive work on the waterfront, he found time for conversation and contemplation, and he produced several very fine books. He concludes that people of character and intelligence can live quite well in spite of dull occupations, and might find that they have more time and energy to devote to thought and to human relations. Having a dull job is not bad, he says, unless you are also a dull person.

Sam Keen discusses what he calls a revolution in Americans' ideas about the importance of work in their lives. Many continue to hold to the "work ethic," a view that says that work is the center of a person's life. People holding this view simply place everything else under work in their list of life's priorities. Love, family, children, recreation, and the arts; all come second to work, which has as its goal the pursuit of money and success.

But some now hold a different view, says Keen. Some now subordinate work to other interests. These people feel that life is richer for the change in values. The people who hold this view have less money, fewer possessions, but more freedom, and they use their freedom to pursue other interests. Keen then discusses the reasons which lie behind that change in values; some of these reasons include dissatisfaction with work itself, reaction against "workaholic" parents, and satisfactions found outside of work.

In the fifth article, Harry Stein discusses the place of ambition in our culture and in the lives of individuals. Americans have always been ambitious, but most have thought a display of ambition is not in good form. Most people have thus hidden their ambition in a display of modesty. Ambition has gotten a bad name among us, says Stein. Most of the time we equate ambition with the kind of ruthless drive to the top that is stereotyped as the way to success in big business and politics. Stein encourages us to admit to ambition when we have it, but not to be pushed into the corner that says all ambitious people are ruthless cut-throat competitors who will do anything at all to get ahead. Many people do very nicely without sacrificing integrity. What ambitious but ethical people must do is avoid jobs where advancement and success depend upon the corruption of the worker.

It is quite possible says Stein, to be ambitious and ethical, successful and yet not corrupted. We need to admit to ambition and to follow it, but to keep it within the bounds of ethical action.

When you have read and outlined each article, write a reaction to the main idea of each one. Then pursue some of the important questions raised by the articles. Among these are the following questions:

1. How important is money to me?
2. Is it important to me to be famous, or at least well-known in my profession or business?
3. Would I sacrifice advancement in my career for the sake of my husband, wife, or children?
4. Do I want excitement in my work?
5. Will work be my primary source of satisfaction in life?
6. Where will it rank it relation to family, religion, recreational pursuits?
7. Is honesty the best policy? Can a person advance in my chosen line of work and still maintain integrity?

The answers to these questions, or at least to some of the questions, should cause you to focus your attention on the subject at hand. You should begin to define ideas about the subject. As you continue to write and ponder these ideas, begin to work on a thesis statement for your essay. As always, your first efforts at formulating a thesis will require some work, some chiseling, and some chipping before the sentence says exactly what you wish it to say. The following statements reflect attitudes toward work as expressed by students and by people in various businesses and professions:

> I will do anything to advance in my career; my wife and children come second, and they know it.

> Most of all in my work, I need a challenge every day to keep me interested. Money is hardly any consideration at all; I figure I can make ends meet somehow. Just give me a challenge.

> I need a very routine job, one that makes few demands on me. I am really interested in being an artist and only need a job to support me while I paint.

> Work is one part of my life, neither much more nor much less important than several other parts. I wish to live a balanced life.

> Although my main interest is music, I'm training to be an electronics technician so that I can support myself no matter what happens to my musical ambitions.

> Since my family is extremely poor, I want very badly to succeed in a ca-
> reer where high income is possible, and I'm willing to make other areas
> of my life secondary priorities.

No single example could accurately reflect your ideas, but you can begin to see some of the possibilities that are open to you. A typical pattern for developing a thesis for this paper might be to find a strong reaction—either agreement or disagreement—to one of the articles. Here is one possible reaction to the article by Annie Dillard.

> This article made me look at my work in high school and college, and I
> realize that I had adopted the position that I had no natural talent and so
> should settle for mediocre performance and look forward to little success
> in business. I've switched to Dillard's position and I have begun to work
> much harder in an area I enjoy, accounting.

This idea could also be joined to some of Stein's ideas on ambition:

> I had little ambition because several of my older friends had laughed at my
> ideas earlier. Now I feel more comfortable about expressing my hopes.

We could produce a worthwile statement of combining these two ideas in the same essay:

> My friends had convinced me that having real ambition was unacceptable
> in our society because reaching lofty goals would require dishonest acts.
> I had convinced myself that I had no genuine abilities, so I had settled on
> a pretty routine career. Now I've changed my ideas and intend to shoot for
> a professional career in accounting.

If this combination of ideas is shortened, it can be developed into a usable thesis statement:

> Convinced that high level achievement required at least some dishonesty,
> and thinking that I had little or no natural ability, I had settled for my third
> choice in careers. I now intend to study for my first choice, accounting.

Another try can make the statement even shorter.:

> Bad advice about ambition and a wrong estimate of my abilities led me to
> aim too low: now, with new ideas, I intend to shoot for a professional ca-
> reer, accounting.

An essay developing this thesis will need to develop points which explain the old and the new attitudes held by this student, and it will also need to show just briefly the circumstances that brought about this change. The following points need to be included:

> The old ideas about ambition.
> The old ideas about her talents.
> New ideas about ambition.
> New ideas about abilities.
> A statement about the new plan.
> A discussion of the way the new ideas developed.

It is simpler to combine some of the items to make the outline of the paper a bit less complex. The following suggests one way to combine the ideas:

> Old and new attitudes about ambition.
> Old and new attitudes about ability.
> A discussion of the development of new ideas.
> A statement of the new plan.

A second method for combining the ideas would be organized in this way:

> Old attitudes about ambition and talent.
> New attitudes about ambition and talent.
> New plan.
> Development of new ideas.

Both of these combined patterns will work quite well for an essay of four to six paragraphs. The only preliminary step remaining is to select an order for presenting the materials. In the first plan, the order of presentation can follow the order of the list as it stands now. In the second plan, a few changes will produce a more logical pattern:

> Old attitudes.
> Development of new attitudes.
> New attitudes.
> New Plan.

With this order established, all that remains is to draft the essay and proceed into the revision process. Work first on the overall organization, and then revise the individual paragraphs, as we discussed in Unit One.

When you write the introduction, remember that you need to

catch the reader's interest and then provide either a direction or a thesis statement for the essay. Here is a workable introduction.

> Coming to college has been a time for me to explore my old ideas and attitudes and test them against the opinions of other people. I've met many new people, and I've done some reading since this year started. All those new contacts, plus a good bit of thinking on my part, have led me to rethink some of my old ideas, especially those that deal with my choice of a career.

For each of the points of development, write a fully developed paragraph that includes a concrete example. If you follow the second suggested pattern, you might find that the paragraph in which you develop the first point becomes too long to be manageable. If this occurs, don't hesitate to split the point into two paragraphs. A sample paragraph developing that first point should start with a topic statement:

> When I came to school I thought that people who were ambitious were in some way committing themselves to cheat or cut corners in order to get ahead. Several of my friends, especially two or three who were a little older than I, were very down on the whole idea of "getting ahead." They were reacting to some of the people in the Watergate scandal who had allowed their ambition to lead them into illegal activities, and they convince me that ambition usually corrupted people. As a result, I had set my sights pretty low and was preparing for a routine sort of job after I got a little college experience.

At this point it becomes clear that treating the rest of that first point in the same paragraph is going to produce a very long paragraph, onethat will be difficult for a reader to manage. It is perfectly correct to shift into a second paragraph at the point where the discussion moves from "ambition" to "talent."

> My lack of high ambition was supported by the fact that I didn't think I have any natural ability or talent. I had watched my sister, who is a natural whiz at math, go right on into college and a career in computer science without, as far as I could tell, ever working very hard at all. Some of my friends in high school seemed to have that same ease at various subjects, and I convinced myself that I just didn't have the stuff to get through a difficult program in college. I knew that I could only get good grades if I worked myself half to death, and sometimes I got really discouraged as I watched those other people sliding through and making better grades than I did. All of those experiences before I even came to college had pretty well convinced me that I'd better find a pretty easy program and settle for any job I could find.

The paragraph that discusses the change in attitude will be a little like a narrative:

When I got to college and began to meet new people and get exposed to some new ideas, I began to rethink my position. One day in a class we read a short essay by Annie Dillard. "There Isn't Any Such Thing As Talent." *(Seventeen Magazine,* June 1979.) . . .

At this point, the paragraph goes on to give a brief summary of Dillard's idea. A little later, the writer mentions the article by Stein.

In another article, Harry Stein defends the idea of ambition, saying that it is perfectly proper and doesn't always lead to corruption. (*Esquire,* August 1981)

Notice the method of citing the sources for those two ideas. The author's name and the title of the article appear in the text; the title of the magazine and the date appear in parenthesis. For a book, the form is quite similar. Put the author and title in the text, and supply in parenthesis the publisher and the date. Note that this same form is used in the essay on the Toyota Starlet.

Paragraph Patterns

A paper such as this one, which treats the examination of old ideas and subsequent changes to new ideas, opens opportunities for several kinds of paragraph development that ought to be useful for other papers as well.

One paragraph might compare the old and new attitudes toward ambition:

In high school I thought that ambition was a bad word. I saw, connected to that word, people whose entire lives were consumed by a desire for power or money, or both. They desired these things so much that they put everything else—mates, children, health, recreation—a very distant second to their careers. They so desired power that they were willing to lie, cheat, and steal to get ahead. My view of ambition was a stereotype of all that was bad about it. Now I see another possibility. People can be ambitious, but keep that ambition from consuming their lives, placing a check on it. They can remember that other areas of life are important and must receive equal time and attention. They can retain their integrity, refusing to compromise themselves and their ethics for advancement. They can, in other words, be ambitious without letting ambition capture them.

Note that the paragraph discusses three characteristics of all-consuming ambition, and then moves to the new view of ambition. The second half of the paragraph mentions the same three characteristics of ambition in the same order, but shows the positive, controlled side of each one. It would also be possible to deal with the characteristics individually, examining the old and then the new versions of the first, second, and the third pairs. In both patterns, this method of development is called *comparison/contrast*.

Another paragraph might treat Annie Dillard's discussion of talent:

> Talent, as something born in us, does not really exist except in rare cases of people who have a special facility for math, music or chess. For all the rest of us, talent really comprises two parts: education and hard work. People who achieve, who appear to be "talented," have educated themselves both in school and in other ways, have trained their minds and provided themselves with background and with skill in a field, and then they have gone to work on a particular project. They have worked hard and long, but not because they were somehow specially equipped for the work. Instead, the project motivated them, drawing them into the work because it became interesting and worth their time and effort in direct proportion to their involvement in the project. Their effort increased as their interest, "love" Dillard calls it, in the project grew. So talent isn't some special inheritance of a lucky few; it is simply education and hard work applied to a project.

Note that the paragraph identifies the concept, the "whole" which it intends to discuss. It next takes up the two parts of that whole, and discusses each part in turn. This pattern of development is called *analysis*.

A paragraph describing the causes of the change in attitude might list and discuss these causes as follows:

> My attitude changed because I had new experiences when I came to college. First, I met some new people, people who showed me other ways of looking at the world. They began to open new possibilities for me, and showed me that everyone else was pretty much like me, people who had to work hard to get anything out of college. Then I began to read. First I read only my assignments, but then I moved to other stuff, magazines and newspapers, especially one or two that had interesting articles of opinion. All these things, new people, college course, and some outside reading helped me to rework my thinking about my college major and my career.

The pattern for this paragraph is called *causal analysis*. These same influences, if treated in chronological order, could detail the steps or the process that led that student to change.

> When I look back over the last few months, I can see pretty clearly how I made my decision. First, I took that class with Mr. Henley, a kind of funny old guy, but he really showed me some new ideas. Then I began to eat lunch with a couple of people from psych class, people from backgrounds I knew nothing about. Next, about mid-October, I was working in the library and picked up a couple of magazines. Two articles really hit me, and I began to tie those ideas in with what I was studying in my classes, especially in psych. Finally, I had to write a paper for one of my classes on changes in careers, changes brought about by technology. All of that research and writing helped me to tie together my thoughts, and the whole semester's worth of experiences worked together to give me a new direction.

This pattern is called *process analysis*.

You will not find yourself thinking of these patterns as you outline an essay or as you do your background writing. Usually you will not think of these patterns at all. Few writers sit down before writing a paragraph and say, "Now that one ought be comparison/contrast." Instead, you will find yourself entering a particular paragraph with an idea in mind or with a question you're trying to answer, and you will see that you are working within an established pattern for such discussions. You might even remember that such a pattern is called, for example, comparison/contrast, but the name isn't really important. It is important to recognize familiar territory, to discover a pattern you have seen before, and to move easily into that pattern when you need it in an essay.

ASSIGNMENT 11

Taking Essay Tests

One of the most practical writing skills a college student can develop is the ability to write essay test answers. As you progress through college, you will probably find that your teachers rely more and more on essay tests to evaluate your work and establish your grade. So it is a good idea to begin practicing such tests now.

Preparation to take an essay test should begin at the beginning of the term, not when the test is about to be given. The subject matter for tests and examinations in a college course comes from three sources:

1. The textbook or textbooks for the course.
2. Lectures and classroom discussions.
3. Outside readings and laboratory work.

From the first day of the course, you should begin to work on the textbook assignments. Read them, underline important points, *and*, in your own words, write an outline of the material. If you are working with more than one book, combine the outlines in a way that makes the information a single unit. Don't underestimate the importance of writing the outlines (along with summaries of important ideas and paraphrases of difficult sections of the book) in your words. Writing is a special way of learning in that it provides control of ideas and allows you to make connections between and among ideas in ways that reading and underlining do not. Be sure to write out the outlines. Do the same kind of work on notes you take in class. Write the notes over again after each class, so that you can organize and clarify them while they are still fresh in your mind. For most people, notes taken on a lecture or discussion are very similar to the rough draft of a paper. The basic ideas are present, but they are probably not expressed as clearly as possible. The notes need to be reworked before they will be meaningful and useful. Remember that the notes will be old, not fresh in your mind, by the time you take the test. The first draft of a set of lecture notes is usually not worth much after several weeks have gone by. The best way to work on improving the notes is to take time to organize and rewrite your lecture notes before returning for the next class session. Organize them and rewrite them so that they will be clear in your mind when you listen to the next lecture. As you rewrite the lecture notes, connect them to the textbook outlines you are developing. Do your best to make the materials a unified whole, a single piece of material for the course.

As you work on the textbooks and lectures notes, you will probably discover that one of those two sources of information contains the outline and provides the control for the course. Some courses provide the basic materials from the textbook and provide additional information and special explanations in lectures and discussions. Others do exactly the opposite: they provide the core of the course in the lectures, and supplement these materials with readings from the texts. If the lectures furnish the outline or control for the course, it is especially important to take good lecture notes and to work very hard at outlining and rewriting your notes.

As the time for the test approaches, gather all the materials you have produced in your studies. Include the revised version of your lecture notes, your textbook outlines, other materials, and the combined lecture notes-textbook notes that give you a unified overview of the course. Review these materials and make an outline to show you the major divisions of the materials.

Within these divisions, make careful note of chronological periods, units or other division, trends, theories, and general conclusions. Pinpoint important concepts and basic ideas. List names of people, events, places, and other important facts that might be useful in taking a test.

When you have produced an outline for the materials covered on the test, write a series of questions that cover the major areas on the test. Try to write questions that are broad in scope. Cover all the important areas by producing seven or eight questions. After you have written the questions, work through the course materials and write an outline of the answer to each question. If the question is difficult or complex, write out the answer. Before you go in to take the test, commit these outlines and answers to memory.

The preparations are a good beginning, but only a strategy for **taking** the test will insure success. When you are sitting in the room with your test in front of you, do two things before you begin to write an answer.

First, read the entire test through very carefully. Read the directions to determine how many questions you must answer and what value each question has. Often you will be allowed to choose the questions you will answer. Sometimes the choice will simply be:

Answer three of the following five questions.

Sometimes the test is more complex, and you will be asked to choose questions from groups of questions:

Answer any two from questions 1 to 4, and any four from questions 5 to 10.

The directions for the test usually include the value for these questions, but it is safe to assume that the two questions out of four are worth more points toward your grade than are the four out of the second group of six.

The rule here is to choose the questions you know the most about, and write your strongest answer first. Then work down to the question about which you know the least. If the questions are divided into groups, answer first the questions from the more valuable group, beginning in that group with the question about which you know the most. Then answer the questions from the less valuable group, from your strongest to your weakest. Try to start where you are strongest and where you will earn the most points.

Second, make brief, careful preparations before you write each question. Follow the first six steps in the writing process to help organize your answers.

Step 1. Identify the subject matter for the question. The answer you write must fit the question. Little or no credit is given to answers that do not answer the question asked.

Step 2. Collect and jot down on a sheet of scratch paper the information you know that will answer the question. You can use portions of the answers you wrote to your own practice questions.

Step 3. Make a definite statement that answers the questions. A test answer needs a thesis just as much as an essay does. Establish firmly what you can say in answer to the question.

Step 4. Select supporting materials from your brief notes. These materials will serve as development for your answer. Since your answer will be relatively short, you need to select only the best supporting materials for each answer.

Step 5 Order the materials in a way that will produce a good paragraph. Your paragraphs should be unified, coherent, and fully developed.

Step 6. Ordinarily, this step is the writing of the rough draft of the paper. Work on this step as if you were producing the final draft; you should not count on having time to revise and recopy the answers to the test. You simply need to be more careful as you write. As you write, weigh your words and check for correctness.

Two brief notes:

1. Be sure to put the number of the question at the beginning of the answer, especially if you have a choice of questions. Don't expect the teacher to recognize an answer without the number.

2. Use the phrasing of the question as the opening sentence for your answer. This technique helps you to get started and focuses the teacher's attention on the question being answered.

Types of Questions

Making up questions to cover the materials included on the test will not seem so difficult if you review the following types of questions. These are likely to occur on essay tests, and you can use the types as the frame work for your questions.

1. *Factual Questions*. These require an identification or a list of facts as an answer. Key words for these questions are *list, name, identify, summarize,* and *trace.* These questions can be answered if you make a list or if you write a few sentences. They require that you remember specific information about the subject and put it in the answer.

Sample Questions:

Name the first three presidents of the United States.
   Answer contains names only.

Name the three most important accomplishments of each president.
   Name the item and write a very brief identifying phrase for it.

Summarize or trace the events that led America into the War of 1812.
   The answer requires a list, plus identification covering each event in chronological order.

2. *Definition and Discussion*. These questions are more difficult than are factual or recall questions. They do not require more than recall of information, but the information required may be extensive and complex. Production of a good answer usually requires that you remember the outline of a portion of your notes. Write a paragraph or paragraphs based on that outline.

Sample Questions:

Define *photosynthesis* and demonstrate its working.

Discuss the physical problems caused by smoking cigarettes.

Define *compound interest* and show how it works.

3. *Relationship Questions*. These questions ask that you establish connections between and among items or areas within the subject matter.

Cause: an explanation of the reasons why something occurs.

What causes inflation?
Why did the United States enter the War of 1812?

Analysis: a discussion of the relationship of a part to the whole to which it belongs, or a discussion of the division of a whole into its parts.

Explain the work of the distributor and the carburetor in an an internal combustion engine.

Discuss the major political positions in America prior to the Revolutionary War.

Comparison/Contrast discussion of like and unlike the qualities of items within the same general class.

How is a butterfuly like a moth? Unlike a moth?
Compare and contrast the political positions of Jefferson and Hamilton.

4. *Evaluation or Criticism*. This is perhaps the most difficult type of question, because an answer requires that you know the criteria for judging or evaluating *and* that you know the subject well enough to compare it to the ideal.

Sample Questions:

Evaluate aluminum as a metal for use in engine blocks. Be sure to discuss both strengths and weaknesses.

Evaluate the county's proposed system of flood control that will use levees, dikes, and canals.

Criticize the performance of George Washington as commander of the American forces.

Although it is difficult in a short section to simulate essay test conditions exactly, the following exercise will help you to develop your skills in that area:

Read the following two articles. For each one, make up a thesis statement, an outline, and a summary. Then develop your own test questions for each article. Cover all areas mentioned in each article, and write all four levels or types of questions.

When you have written your questions, prepare outlines of the answers just as if you were about to be tested on the material. Then look at the test questions that follow the articles, and compare your questions with them. Finally, write out answers to each of the questions on page 189. Write a single, fully developed paragraph for each question.

SYMPATHY FOR THE DEVIL

A more generous view of the world's most despised animal

by David Quammen

[1] Undeniably they have a lot to answer for: malaria, dengue, yellow fever, encephalitis, filariasis, and the ominous tiny whine that begins homing in on your ear just after you've gotten comfortable in the sleeping bag. All these griefs and others are the handiwork of that treacherous family of biting flies known as Culicidae, the mosquitoes. They assist in the murder of millions of humans each year, carry ghastly illness to millions more, and drive not a few of the rest of us temporarily insane. And since they have been around for 50 million years, you can be pretty certain they've had time to figure all the angles.

[2] In fact, judged by sheer numbers, or by the scope of their worldwide distribution, or by their resistance to enemies and natural catastrophe, mosquitoes are one of the great success stories of the planet. They come in 2,700 different species. They inhabit almost every land surface, from arctic tundra to downtown London to equatorial Brazil, from the Sahara to the Himalaya, though best of all they like tropical rain forests, where three-quarters of their species lurk. Mosquitoes and rain forest, in fact, go together like winos and bus stations. And that is what I mean to get at here. However obliquely, that is why we must offer some thanks to the mosquito. But, of course, to appreciate the good they do, you're going to have to hear about the other part first, the treachery. These demons are not without purpose.

[3] They hatch and grow to maturity in water, any entrapment of quiet water, no matter how transient or funky. A soggy latrine, for instance, suits them fine. The still edge of a crystalline stream is fine. In the flooded footprint of an elephant, you might find a hundred mosquitoes. As innocent youngsters they use facial bristles resembling cranberry rakes to comb these waters for smorgasbord, but on attaining adulthood they are out for blood.

[4] It isn't a necessity for individual survival, that blood thirst, just a prerequisite of motherhood. In fact, male mosquitoes do not bite. A male

From *Outside Magazine*, June/July 1981.

mosquito lives his short, gentle adult life content, like a swallowtail butter-fly, to sip nectar from flowers. Like the black widow spider and the mantis, it is the female that is fearsome. Make of that what larger lessons you dare.

[5] She relies on the blood of vertebrates—mainly warmblooded ones, but sometimes reptiles and frogs—to finance, metabolically, the development of her eggs.

[6] A female mosquito in a full lifetime will lay about ten separate batches of eggs, roughly 200 in a batch. That's a tall manufacturing order for the embryonic tissue of one wispy body, and to manage it the female needs a rich source of protein. The sugary juice of flowers will deliver quick energy to wing muscles, but it won't help her build 2,000 new bodies. So she has evolved a hypodermic proboscis and learned how to steal protein in one of its richest forms: hemoglobin. In some species, her first brood will develop before she has tasted blood, but after that she must have a bellyfull for each set of eggs coming to term.

[7] When she drinks, she drinks deeply; the average meal of blood amounts to 2½ times the original weight of the insect. Picture Audrey Hepburn sitting down to a steak dinner, getting up from the table weighing 380 pounds, and then, for that matter, flying away. In the Canadian Arctic, species of the genus Aedes, pressed by the short summer season, emerge in savage, sky-darkening swarms like nothing seen even in the Amazon; an unprotected human could be bitten 9,000 times a minute. At that rate a large man would lose half his total blood in two hours. Arctic hares and reindeer move to higher ground or die. Sometimes solid mats of Aedes will continue sucking the cool blood from a carcass.

[8] Evidently the female tracks her way to a blood donor by flying up-wind toward a source of warmer air, air that is both warm and moist, air that contains an excess of carbon dioxide, or a combination of all three. The experts aren't sure. Perspiration, involving both higher skin temperature and released moisture, is one good way to attract her attention. In Italy it is established folk wisdom that to sleep with a pig in the bedroom is to protect oneself from malaria, presumably because the pig, operating at a higher body temperature, will be preferred by mosquitoes. And at the turn of the century Professor Giovanni Grassi, then Italy's foremost zoologist, pointed out that garrulous people seemed to be bitten more often than those who kept their mouths shut. Experts today aren't sure about that, either, but it's clear the Italians have been working on the problem.

[9] Guided by CO_2 or idle chatter or a distaste for pork or whatever, a female mosquito lands on, say, the earlobe of a human, drives her proboscis (actually a thin bundle of tools that includes two tubular stylets for carrying fluid and four serrated ones for cutting) through the skin, gropes with it until she taps a capillary, and begins an elaborate interaction. Her saliva flows down one tube and into the wound, retarding coagulation of the spilled blood and

provoking an allergic reaction that will cause itching. A suction pump in her head draws blood up the other tube, a valve closes, and another pump pulls the blood back into her gut. That alternate pumping and valving continues quickly for three orgiastic minutes, until her abdomen is stretched full like a great, bloody balloon, or until a fast human hand ends her maternal career, whichever comes first.

[10] But in the meantime, if she is Anopheles gambiae in Nigeria, the protozoa that cause malaria may be streaming into the wound with her saliva, heading off immediately to set up bivouac in the human's liver. Or if she is Aedes aegypti in Costa Rica, she may be drooling out an advance phalanx of the yellow fever virus. If she is Culex pipiens in Malaysia, long, tiny larvae of the filaria worm may be squirting from her snout like a stage magician's springwork snakes, dispersing to breed in the person's lymph nodes and eventually to clog them, causing elephantiasis. Definitely, this is antisocial behavior.

[11] No wonder, then, that in the rogues' pantheon of creatures not only noxious in their essential characters but lacking in any imaginable forgiving graces, the mosquito is generally ranked beyond even the wood tick, the wolverine, or the black toy poodle. The mosquito, says common bias—and on this the experts agree—is an unmitigated pain in the kazoo.

[12] But I don't see it that way. To begin with, the family is not mono-lithic, and it does have—even from the human perspective—its beneficent representatives. In northern Canada, for instance, Aedes nigripes is an important pollinator of arctic orchids. In Ethopia, Toxorhynchites brevipalpis as a larva preys voraciously on the larvae of other mosquitoes, malaria carriers, and then transforms itself into a lovely, huge, iridescent adult that, male or female, drinks only plant juices and would not dream of biting a human.

[13] But even discounting these aberrations, and judging it by only its most notorious infamies, the mosquito is taking a bad rap. It has been victimized, I submit to you, by a strong case of anthropocentric press-agentry. In fact, the little sucker can be viewed, with only a small bit of squinting, as one of the great ecological heroes of planet Earth—if you consider rain forest preservation.

[14] The chief point of blame with mosquitoes happens also to be the chief point of credit: They excel at making tropical rain forests virtually uninhabitable for humans.

[15] Tropical rain forest constitutes by far the world's richest and most complex ecosystem, a dizzying interrelation of life forms and habits and equilibriums. Those equatorial forests—mainly confined to the Amazon, the Congo basin, and Southeast Asia—account for only a small fraction of the earth's surface, but they serve as home for roughly half of the earth's total plant and animal species, including 2,000 kinds of mosquito. But lately, in case you haven't heard, rain forests are under siege.

[16] They are being clear-cut for cattle ranching, mowed down with bulldozers and pulped for paper, corded into firewood, gobbled up hourly

by human development on the march. At the current rate of loss, eight acres of rain forest have gone poof since you began reading this sentence. At that pace the Amazon will look like New Jersey within a generation. Conservation groups are raising a clamor, and a few of the equatorial governments are adopting plans for marginal preservation. But over the past 10,000 years no one and nothing had done more to delay this catastrophe than the mosquito.

[17] The great episode of ecological disequilibrium we call human history began, so the Leakey family tells us, in equatorial Africa. Then immediately the focus of intensity shifted elsewhere. What deterred mankind, at least until this half of this century, from hacking space for farms and cities out of tropical forests? Yellow fever did, and malaria, dengue, filariasis, o'nyong-nyong fever.

[18] Clear the vegetation from the brink of a jungle waterhole, move in with tents and cattle and Jeeps, and Anopheles gambiae, not normally native there, will arrive within a month, bringing malaria. Cut the tall timber from five acres of rain forest and species of infectious Aedes that would otherwise live out their lives in the high forest canopy, passsing yellow fever between monkeys, will literally fall on you and begin biting you before your chain saw has cooled. Tropical forests nurture not only more snakes and bird species than anywhere else on earth, but also more forms of disease-causing microbes and more mosquitoes to carry them. In this sense, the forests are elaborately booby-trapped against disruption.

[19] The peoples of native forests gradually acquired some immunity to these diseases, and their nondisruptive hunting-and-gathering economics minimized their exposure to mosquitoes that favored the canopy or disturbed ground. Meanwhile, the occasional white interlopers, the agents of empire, remained vulnerable. In high colonial days, West Africa became known as "the white man's grave."

[20] So as Europe was being stripped of its virgin woods—as were India and China and the North American Heartland—the rain forests escaped, lasting into the late twentieth century—with at least some chance that they may endure a bit longer. Thanks to what? To ten million generations of jungle-loving, disease-bearing, blood-sucking insects: the Culicidae, nature's guerrilla fighters. And a time, says Ecclesiastes, to every purpose.

TV AS THE NEW RELIGION

by George Gerbner

[1] Whoever tells most of the stories to most of the people most of the time has effectively assumed the cultural roles of parent and school. If that story-telling process also includes teaching us most of what we know in com-

From *The Miami Herald*, Sunday, November 30, 1980.

mon about life and society and, in addition, can speak in every home, it has also replaced the church in its ancient role in the partnership of church and state. That process and power is television.

[2] The only other cultural force before television that transmitted identical messages to every social group and class, so that all shared essentially the same culture, was religion. After more than 10 years of intensive research into its social function, I have concluded that television is best seen and studied as a ritual, as a virtually universal new religion that tends to absorb viewers of otherwise diverse outlooks into its own "mainstream".

[3] These conclusions come from findings of our long-range ongoing research project, called Cultural Indicators, and those of independent investigators in the United States and abroad. They are published in detail in such scholarly quarterlies as the *Journal of Broadcasting*. My colleagues Larry Gross, Michael Morgan, Nancy Signorielli, and I believe the conclusions to be the most coherent data-based theory of television's role in society. Here I will describe the theory in nontechnical terms, illustrate it with some key findings, and point out some of its political, religious and cultural implications.

[4] Television presents a synthetic but coherent world of fact and fiction that most people experience relatively nonselectively. In other media, people choose individual items—an author, a magazine, a subject. But in television, most people do not select particular programs, they just watch TV. Most people watch not by the program but by the clock. The television set is on in the average home for more that 6½ hours a day. Watching has become a ritual, as routine, almost, as brushing one's teeth. For the first time in history, the rich and the poor, the urban and the provincial, the cosmopolitan and the isolated, the very young and the very old share a great deal of cultural imagery in common, although none if it is of their own making.

[5] Relatively few people have witnessed real trials and even fewer have watched surgical operations. But most television viewers have a vivid image of how surgeons work and see an average of 30 cops, seven lawyers and three judges a week—every week—on television. And it is the same with saloons and penthouse apartments, the jailhouse and the White House, and a tightly programmed world of human types, situations and fates. The most recurrent patterns of the ritual, as in any religion, tend to be absorbed into our framework of knowledge; they become assumptions that we make about the world.

[6] What are those patterns? By now we have analyzed about 1,500 programs, more than 4,000 major characters and some 14,000 minor characters appearing in prime time and weekend daytime network television. Basically, on television men outnumber women 3–1, young people comprise one-third of their real numbers, persons over 65 comprise 2 per cent of TV population but 11 percent of the real world's; professionals and law-enforcers greatly outnumber all other working people; crime is about 10 times as frequent as in the real world, and an average of five acts of violence

per hour (four times that many in children's programs!) victimize more than half of all leading characters each week.

[7] What do we learn from TV's world and how do we learn its "lessons"? Conventional research methods investigate the effects of specific programs or viewing habits—with few consistent results. They may demonstrate, for example, that children exposed to a show with violence exhibit more violent behavior afterwards. But if most viewers watch nonselectively, it is useless to look for the effects of individual programs. It's the total pattern that counts. So we measure how much television people watch and relate that to their responses to questions about the world. The questions are based on the most recurrent and pervasive patterns of the world of television. If the heavier viewers respond to our questions significantly more according to the way television depicts things than do the light viewers (given similar living conditions and the same socio-economic group), then that difference reflects the contribution of television to their conceptions of reality.

[8] The synthesis of these findings goes under the heading of "cultivation theory" because it assumes that for most people long-range exposure to television cultivates stable conceptions about life.

To test our theory, we compared the responses of heavy TV viewers to particular questions with those of light TV viewers. We found that in most cases heavy viewers respond more in terms of television's concepts. In other words, television overrode the effects of other factors, such as socio-economic elements. This we call "mainstreaming," because the heavy viewers tend to become absorbed into the mainstream of TV culture.

[9] For example, people of differing income and differing TV viewing habits were asked whether they thought they might become involved in violence—which appears frequently on television. The percentages of those who said they thought that they might were: light viewers with incomes under $10,000, 84: heavy viewers (under $10,000), also 84; light viewers with incomes between $10,000 and $25,000, 68; heavy viewers in that income range, 76; light viewers with incomes over $25,000, 62; heavy viewers (over $25,000), 80. People with higher incomes have valid reasons to think that they are less likely to become involved in violence than do persons with lower incomes; they generally do not live in high-crime areas, for one. So the response percentages should decline as income rises. And indeed, for light viewers, they do. But for heavy viewers, they do not. This suggests that the heavy viewers are absorbing some of the fears of violence generated by the frequent showing of violence on television regardless of income.

[10] Again, groups of people were asked the following question: "Do you agree or disagree with the statement, 'It is hardly fair to bring a child into the world with the way things look for the future' ". It was designed to test assimilation to the negative views implied by the violence on television.

[11] Persons without a high school education, who might fairly be

expected to agree with this philosophy, responded fairly uniformly whether they were light or heavy viewers; 60 per cent of the light viewers agreed with the statement, 58 per cent of heavy viewers. Persons with a college degree, because of their greater chances for advancement, were presumed more likely to have an optimistic outlook and so to agree less with this question. And indeed, among college-educated light viewers, only 12 per cent agreed with it. But of the heavy viewers, 24 per cent agreed. Television was reducing the effects of their college education. They were joining the mainstream.

[12] Further questions demonstrate that heavy viewers consistently exaggerate their risks in life and mistrust strangers more than light viewers do. But TV can also moderate extreme views, can bring them into the mainstream. For most people, television, which is sexist, increases sexism. But among people who are the most traditionally sexist, light viewers retain their old views, but the heavy viewers show less sexism. Mainstreaming implies a kind of homogenization.

[13] Such homogenization seems to take place in more than just the areas of anxiety, insecurity and stereotyping of people. One other area involved is adolescent reading and IQ scores. For example, in most cases, the more viewing, the lower the scores. But in the lowest IQ groups, television viewing leads to some improvement in the scores. This suggests that television's cultivation process is broader than many people assume.

[14] Television also sometimes appears to have an effect upon people different from mainstreaming. This is to reinforce their views. This pheonomenon seems to occur when an issue is extremely relevant to a person's life— more particularly relevant than the more general matters involved in mainstreaming. For example, contrary to real life, persons over 65 are the most victimized group on television. We asked people whether they agreed with the statement that older persons are more likely to be the victims of violent crime than anyone else. Among young people, about 70 per cent of both light and heavy viewers agreed. Among middle-aged people, there was likewise virtually no difference between light and heavy viewers; approximately 74 per cent of both agreed. But among older people, while only 75 per cent of light viewers agreed, 88 per cent of the heavy viewers agreed. Television was re-emphasizing their views. We say that they were resonating to TV and we call this phenomenon "resonance."

[15] We are still trying to define more sharply when mainstreaming occurs and when resonance does. We think, however, that they are not contradictory phenomena, as they may at first appear, but complementary ones, as refinements of cultivation theory.

[16] Considering television as the ritual of a new religion rather than as a selectively used medium, such as books or film, enabled us to isolate its general trends and contributions to conceptions of reality. We have also found that people under 35, the "television generation," are more imbued with its view of life than those who grew up before television.

[17] Understanding the dynamics of television as ritual helps to make some puzzling aspects of the current scene fall into place. Simple, strong, tough measures and hard-line postures—political or religious, or both—appeal to the anxious and alienated who are perplexed by and resistant to change but powerless to prevent it.

[18] The electronic church with its formal trappings of traditional religion speaks to them.

[19] The "moral majority" and its political allies speak to them. The actual majority finds television itself the most attractive choice among different things to do each night.

[20] Its reliable ritual speaks to them—confirming the fears, feeding the hopes, cultivating the assumptions television shaped in the first place—and dominating the cultural climate in which political parties, traditional religions and all other institutions must now find their way.

Questions on "Sympathy for the Devil."
1. Discuss the variety of mosquitoes, their range and habitat, problems caused by mosquitoes, and the way they spread disease.
2. Explain the mosquito's need for blood, and describe in detail the method for extracting it.
3. Discuss the positive contribution the mosquito makes to the ecological system.

Questions on "TV as the New Religion."
1. Define "mainstreaming" and give examples of its effects.
2. Compare and contrast "mainstreaming" with "resonance."
3. Explain the method the author and his colleagues followed to learn the contribution of television to people's views of reality.

Some Notes on the Questions:

You will note that all three questions from "Sympathy for the "Devil" contain a "discussion" element. These questions ask that you find the answer in the text or in your memory, and that you write it out in your own words. Questions 1 and 2 also contain a second element, one which requires that you explain such processes as the way a mosquito spreads disease, and the way the extraction of blood occurs. You must work out each process clearly in your own mind and then record it on paper. This type of answer may be more difficult for you than is simply reproducing the materials from the text.

In the questions from "TV as the New Religion," you will find that only the third question is a discussion question to which the answer is found in the essay alone. Question 1 asks for a definition plus concrete examples listed in the text. You need to join two different sections of the material to produce the answer. Question 2 is a "relationship" question which asks that you put the parts of one idea up against the parts of another. You are expected to show how these parts are alike and how they differ.

Write the answers to the given questions. Each answer should consist of a single well-developed paragraph.

Revision

The previous units covered two parts of the revision process: an examination of the organization and content of the essay as a whole, and a check of individual paragraphs for certain specific qualities. We need to work now on revising sentences and on checking the sentences for correctness. Before we look at these two areas, however, it might be useful to work through the entire revision process on a new essay, reviewing the steps we covered earlier, and then moving to the new steps in the process.

The following example is a typical essay based on the second assignment of Unit Two, in which you were asked to produce a character sketch. This essay has not yet been revised, but it is reasonably successful as a first draft version.

PAUL SCHMIDT, CABINETMAKER

[1] The other guys who worked in the cabinet shop called him "that old grouch" or "the old man." But I always called him Mr. Schmidt, or, later in our friendship, Paul. He taught me all I know about woods and woodworking, and about cabinet making. He was a very special person, and in that special old-world sense of the word, a craftsman.

[2] I met Paul the first day I went to work in the shop as a helper for the summer. I got the job through a friend, and I didn't know two cents worth about wood and woodworking. When we were introduced Paul shook my hand

and then, holding my arm with his left hand, turned my hand over and looked at the palm. "No calluses. That's bad, bad," he said. "But we fix that soon." He was right. He sent me to the storage area to pick up two "absolutely straight" oak planks eight feet long. He sent me four times, to be exact, until I got the two specific boards he had in mind. He was always just like that. Everything had to be letter perfect.

[3] It was a joy and a puzzlement to watch him work. He did everything with immense care and fantastic attention to detail. When he selected the wood for a table top, he didn't pick up the first boards that came to hand. He sorted, discarded, and matched, and then discarded again, until he found the best pattern and match available. When he made a copy of an antique table, every detail had to be authentic, even the joints and corners that no one could possibly see. He measured precisely and carefully and demanded a perfect fit on every joint. But for all his care and attention, he was not a slow worker. He moved surely and never made a mistake. Every move was important and carefully planned, and he had remarkable strength and endurance for a man so old. The first day I worked with him I had to sit down twice to rest while he kept working.

[4] Paul came to America from Germany just about 1930. He had been in apprentice's school when World War I broke out and was drafted into the German Army soon after that. After the war, he finished his training and opened a small cabinet shop. An uncle brought him to America to help run a furniture factory in New York. Paul lasted there three years and left because he couldn't stand assembly line furniture.

[5] He opened his own shop in New York City to build fine custom furniture and cabinets. Once, John D. Rockefeller came to him for a table to be done in four days. Paul laughed and turned him down; it was just not possible to produce a fine table in four days. Four weeks, maybe. But not four days.

[6] He taught me a lot about woodworking, but a lot more about living. I learned to appreciate hard work and careful attention to detail under Paul's direction. I also learned to love fine woods, proper line, and good proportion, and to value craftsmanship above almost everything else.

Remember, the first step in revision is to develop the proper attitude toward the draft. You must view the writing as a first try, an attempt, a preliminary version. Don't let yourself become so attached to the draft that you are unwilling to change, add, cut, and rearrange the materials on the paper. Always assume that the draft is not acceptable. First attempts are never good enough. Only second efforts have the potential to be successful. The first step in revision is to be willing to make changes.

his statement clearly tries to show how hard and long Paul would work. But this paragraph is concerned with his craftsmanship and his attention to authentic detail. That last statement subtracts from the impression of the paragraph. Even worse, the last sentence introduces the writer as an afterthought in a paragraph that mentions only one person, Paul the cabinetmaker. A better last sentence for this paragraph might read like this (beginning with the first clause of the next-to-last sentence):

Every move was important and carefully planned, and he stayed with each task until he finished it to perfection. This dedication was probably a product of his boyhood training as an apprentice in a German cabinet shop.

The mention of his boyhood training also provides a good transition to the next paragraph concerning his early training.

Paul came to America from Germany just about 1930. He had been in apprentice's school when World War I broke out and was drafted into the German Army soon after that. After the war, he finished his training and opened a small cabinet shop. An uncle brought him to America to help run a furniture factory in New York. Paul lasted there three years and left because he couldn't stand assembly line furniture.

References to Paul's early training and arrival in America are close enough to the core idea to be of interest here. The principal difficulty with this paragraph is that it is much shorter and more weakly developed than are the earlier paragraphs. All paragraphs in an essay ought to be approximately of the same length. A paragraph that is a good deal shorter (the two previous paragraphs have eleven and fourteen lines; this paragraph has seven) than the others in an essay is a tip-off for the reader to look for lack of supporting information and details. To find the place that needs more details, read the paragraph and see if any questions come to your mind.

The sentence that triggers several questions reads

An uncle brought him to America to help run a furniture factory.

The last sentence says that he quit after three years. But that three-year period must hold one hundred interesting stories. A young man, a highly trained craftsman, moves to New York from Germany. How does he find life in America? How does a craftsman react to factory methods? Does he speak English when he arrives

An outline of the draft version of the essay, the preliminary step in the revision process, reads this way:

Thesis Statement:
Paul Schmidt was a dedicated, skilled craftsman who taught me much about his craft and about craftmanship.

Paragraph 1.
Introduction and statement of thesis.
Paragraph 2.
My first day on the job gave me a clear indication of Paul's attitudes about work.
Paragraph 3.
His attention to detail and other work habits were impressive.
Paragraph 4.
Paul began his work in this country in a furniture factory.
Paragraph 5.
He opened his own shop and continued to maintain his standards of craftsmanship.
Paragraph 6.
Summary and restatement of thesis.

The actual work of revision begins with a fresh look at the core idea of the essay. Examine that idea to be sure that its statement is genuine, and that it states accurately what the materials collected on the subject suggest. In the case of the essay about Paul Schmidt, the cabinetmaker, the central impression or core idea that comes out of all the material suggests that the man was

1. A dedicated, skilled craftsman who worked hard at his craft.
2. A lover of beautiful woods and well-made furniture.
3. A creator of beautiful works who refused to do less than the best work possible.

The essay must demonstrate these points if it is to be true to the subject and to the core idea. Read the essay again slowly, word by word, point by point. Test the topic statement of each paragraph to be certain that the point made by the paragraph supports or explains some aspect of the core idea. Weigh the order used to present these supporting points. Try a different order to see if the impact of the points can be increased. Remember that you are working with a draft copy, and every part is subject to revision, relocation, or removal from the essay. Then test the paragraphs to see that each statement and each example contribute something to establishing the theme of the essay.

> The other guys who worked in the cabinet shop called him "that old grouch" or "the old man." But I always called him Mr. Schmidt, or later in our friendship, Paul. He taught me all I know about woods and woodworking, and about cabinet making. He was a very special person, and in that special old-world sense of the word, a craftsman.

This paragraph seems satisfactory as an introduction. It introduces the subject: a man. It then specifies a definite area of concern about that subject: his craftsmanship and love of woods and woodworking. This theme is a true reflection of the materials collected about the subject.

Check the second paragraph to see if it supports the theme:

> I met Paul the first day I went to work in the shop as a helper for the summer. I got the job through a friend, and I didn't know two cents worth about wood and woodworking. When we were introduced, he shook my hand and then, holding my arm with his left hand, turned my hand over and looked at the palm. "No calluses. That's bad, bad," he said. "But we fix that soon." He was right. He sent me to the storage area to pick up two "absolutely straight" oak planks eight feet long. He sent me four times, to be exact, until I got the two specific boards he had in mind. He was always just like that. Everything had to be letter perfect.

Note that this second paragraph is written in a primarily narrative style. The writer gets a job working with Paul, goes to work, and finds that Paul does not approve of his lack of calluses. But Paul says, "We fix that soon." The chief impression of the paragraph up to this point suggests that

> Paul likes people who can work hard and thus have calluses.

Thus far, the impression is true to the theme. Paul is indeed a hard worker, and he is a man who expects hard work from others. But the balance of the paragraph, following, "He was right," seems to talk more about a desire for perfection and an attention to detail than it does about hard physical labor. The last four sentences reflect Paul's character accurately,

but they are probably not consistent with the first paragraph.

The entire essay must be true to the theme, but every paragraph must also be consistent within itself. The solution here is to an incident or a statement that can follow honestly the sentence.

> He was right.

A new portion must be substituted for the last four sentences. How was he right? He arranged for the writer to develop calluses. How can the writer show this? Here is a possibility.

> He was right. That first day I sorted lumber, stacking it by lengths and by quality. I moved what seemed like a trainload of furniture around the shop. And to round out the day, I swept the shop and left that floor absolutely dirt-free. He was right about giving me calluses, but he worked harder than anyone.

The next paragraph describes Paul's work habits and his style:

> It was a joy and a puzzlement to watch him work. He did everything with immense care and fantastic attention to detail. When he selected the wood for a table top, he didn't pick up the first boards that came to hand. He sorted, discarded, and matched and then discarded again, until he found the best pattern and match available. When he made a copy of an antique table, every detail had to be authentic, even the joints and corners that no one could possibly see. He measured precisely and carefully demanded a perfect fit on every joint. But for all his care and attention he was not a slow worker. He moved surely and never made a mistake. Every move was important and carefully planned, and he had remarkable strength and endurance for a man so old. The first day I worked with him I had to sit down twice to rest while he kept working.

The paragraph is true to the core statement in that the observations made about Paul claims that he is a craftsman and careful worker. Only the last two sentences fail to establishing the idea of craftsmanship and hard work.

> . . . and he had remarkable strength and endurance for a man so old. The first day I worked with him I had to sit down twice to rest while he kept working.

in New York? Is there one incident from those three years that could help develop the core idea?

If there is a good example or a meaningful incident, it should be written up in two or three sentences, and included before the last sentence. It is often necessary for a writer to collect more materials in this process of revision, in order to have supporting details ready to fill special needs. Imagine that this writer recollected a brief story or comment to use in this paragraph:

> Paul worked hard in that factory, trying to appreciate the methods and the product of mass production furniture manufacturing. But he told me he often walked down the assembly line after the workers were gone pulling off the shoddiest pieces and smashing them on the floor in frustration. Paul only lasted at that factory three years; he could not learn to accept assembly line furniture and its poor workmanship.

If there had been no further comment possible about that period of time, it might have been good to combine Paragraphs 4 and 5 to make one paragraph of a length more or less equal to the other paragraphs. Consider Paragraph 5 before you make the decision to combine two paragraphs:

> He opened his own shop in New York City to build fine custom furniture and cabinets. Once, John D. Rockefeller came to him for a table to be done in four days. Paul laughed and turned him down; it was just not possible to produce a fine table in four days. Four weeks, maybe. But not four days.

Paragraph 5, as it stands in the draft version, is also shorter than the first three paragraphs. Two spots leave questions unanswered and thus require more details.
Sentence 1 says

> He opened his own shop in New York City to build fine custom furniture and cabinets.

Obvious questions arise. What happened? How did he manage this? How big was the shop? How successful? Did he like the work? Again the writer must go back to collect more details. Here is a possible addition to the paragraph:

> In the shop he was "at home" again. He delighted in the work. He hired two other craftsmen and together they earned a reputation for fine work. But they insisted on working up to their standards. Nothing but perfection was good enough for them. Once John D. Rockefeller . . .

The paragraph also needs a summary sentence.

> Paul never compromised on his standards of craftsmanship, even for the rich and famous. He maintained his artistic integrity to the end of his life.

Paragraph 6 provides both a summary and a conclusion for the essay. It does so by listing the impressions that Paul made on the writer. The paragraph is short, but properly so because its only work is to sum up. No examples or anecdotes are needed, and no new ideas should be introduced. The paragraph does its job well.

   A Note on Method. *When writing additional material to be inserted in an essay, don't try to write on the draft itself. Write out each insert on a clean sheet. Identify the location of each by using a number (1) at the beginning of each insert and at the place where it should be inserted in the draft.*

The following is a copy of the essay on Paul Schmidt. Included are the original plus changes and additions. Note that the omitted sentences are in boldface type, the insert marks are in the proper place, and the inserts are written in at the proper place in italics.

> The other guys who worked in the cabinet shop called him "that old grouch" or "the old man." But I always called him Mr. Schmidt, or later in our friendship, Paul. He taught me all that I know about woods and woodworking, and about cabinet making. He was a very special person, and in that special old-world sense of the word, a craftsman.
>
> I met Paul the first day I went to work in the shop for the summer. I got the job through a friend, and I didn't know two cents worth about wood and woodworking. When we were introduced, he shook my hand and then, holding my arm with his left hand, turned my hand over and looked at the palm. "No calluses. That's bad, bad," he said. "But we fix that soon." He was right. [1] **He sent me to the storage area to pick up two "absolutely straight" oak planks eight feet long. He sent me four times, to be exact, until I got the two specific boards he had in mind. He was always just like that. Everything had to be letter perfect.**
>
> 1. *That first day I sorted lumber, stacking it by lengths and by quality. I moved what seemed like a trainload of furniture around the shop. And to round out the day, I swept the shop and left that floor absolutely dirt-free. He was right about giving me calluses, but he worked harder than anyone.*
>
>   It was a joy and a puzzlement to watch him work. He did everything with immense care and fantastic attention to detail. When he selected the wood for a table top, he didn't pick up the first boards that came to hand. He sorted, and discarded, and matched and discarded again, until he found the best pattern and match available. When he made a

copy of an antique table, every detail had to be authentic, even the joints and corners that no one could possibly see. He measured precisely and carefully and demanded a perfect fit on every joint. But for all his care and attention he was not a slow worker. He moved surely and never made a mistake. Every move was important and carefully planned, [2] **and he had remarkable strength and endurance for a man so old. The first day I worked with him I had to sit down twice to rest while he kept working.**

2. *And he stayed with each task till he finished it to perfection. This dedication was probably a product of his boyhood training as an apprentice in a German cabinet shop.*

    Paul came to America from Germany just about 1930. He had been in apprentice's school when World War I broke out and was drafted into the German Army soon after that. After the war, he finished his training and opened a small cabinet shop. An uncle brought him to America to help run a furniture factory in New York. [3] **Paul lasted there three years and left because he couldn't stand assembly line furniture.**

3. *Paul worked hard in that factory, trying to appreciate the methods and the product of mass production furniture manufacturing. But he told me he often walked down the assembly line, after the workers were gone, pulling off the shoddiest pieces and smashing them on the floor frustration. Paul only lasted at that factory three years; he could not learn to accept assembly line furniture and its poor workmanship.*

    He opened his own shop in New York City to build fine custom furniture and cabinets. [4] Once, John D. Rockefeller came to him for a table to be done in four days. Paul laughed and turned him down; it was just not possible to produce a fine table in four days. Four weeks, maybe. But not four days. [5]

4. *In the shop he was at home again. He delighted in the work. He hired two other craftsmen and together they earned a reputation for fine work. But they insisted on working up to their standards. Nothing but perfection was good enough for them.*

5. *Paul never compromised on his standards of craftsmanship, even for the rich and famous. He maintained his artistic integrity to the end of his life.*

    He taught me a lot about woodworking, but a lot more about living. I learned to appreciate hard work and carfeul attention to detail under Paul's direction. I also learned to love fine woods, proper line, and good proportion, and to value craftsmanship above almost everything else.

Paragraph Transitions

With the development of an effective introduction, you arouse the reader's interest, establish the general subject of the essay, and suggest what ought to be expected in the essay. With a solid concluding statement, you sum up the idea or impression of the writing and establish the essay as a completed work. There is still one more service that you need to provide for the reader.

Between each paragraph in an essay there is a physical gap. The gap consists of the white space at the end of the last line of one paragraph and the indentation of the next paragraph. This white space serves a useful purpose, for it tells the reader that the discussion of one idea is complete and that a new idea is beginning. The physical gap between paragraphs is never very large, but sometimes the mental space between paragraphs is a very difficult gap for the reader to bridge. One of your responsibilities as a writer is to provide your reader with an easy transition from one pargraph to the next.

The easiest way to be sure that you have provided good bridges is to examine the union formed by the last sentence and the first sentence of paragraphs in combination. These two sentences ought to provide. a smooth transition from the end of one idea to the beginning of the next. Examine the connections between the paragraphs in the essay on Paul Schmidt. Test their effectiveness and make improvements where needed.

In the original first draft version, the last sentence of the introduction sets the direction for the essay. The sentence establishes that the essay intends to talk about Schmidt. It tells that the writer will show us that Schmidt was, in a special sense of the word, a craftsman. The first sentence of the second paragraph then leads to the beginning of the story, to the first time the writer met Schmidt.

> ... He was a very special person, and in that special old-world sense of the word, a craftsman.

> I met Paul the first day I went to work as a helper for the summer.

The transition between the paragraphs seems adequate. It is natural for the writer to refer to an early recollection. Therefore

> I met Paul

is a fairly natural next step. The transition might be improved if the writer changes slightly the opening of Paragraph 2.

> My first meeting with Paul did a great deal to impress me with his reputation as a demanding boss. The first day I went to work in his shop ...

In the revised version, (see p. 199) Paragraph 2 and Paragraph 3 are joined well.

> . . . He was right about giving me callouses, but he worked harder than anyone.
>
> It was a joy and a puzzlement to watch him work.

The transition is made in that the writer repeats ideas about Schmidt's working habits. The connection can be strengthened by the repetition of a word:

> . . . he worked harder than anyone.
>
> He was not merely a hard worker. He took more pains with his work than any man I've ever met. He did everything with immense care and attention to detail.

The last sentence in the revised version of Paragraph 2 and the first in Paragraph 3 make a good transition:

> . . . his boyhood training as an apprentice in a German cabinet shop.
>
> Paul came to America from Germany . . .

The transition is established by the report of a movement in time and place, from Schmidt's boyhood training in Germany to his later position in this country. The transition is also helped by the repetition of the similar words, *German* and *Germany*.

Between Paragraphs 4 and 5 of the revised version, almost no connection exists:

> Paul only lasted at that factory 3 years;
> . . . he could not learn to accept assembly line furniture and its poor workmanship.
>
> He opened his own shop in New York City.

What is needed is a transitional expression to carry the reader from the statements about Schmidt's old job at the factory to the statements about the new shop. Some repetition of the idea of Schmidt leaving the factory, stated at the end of the previous paragraph, would help to connect the two paragraphs:

> *After he left the factory, Paul* opened his own shop in New York City . . .

Always check the transitions between paragraphs to be sure you have assisted your reader across the gaps that might impede progress through the essay. You can help by:

1. Repeating words or echoing forms of words.
2. Repeating ideas.
3. Using transitional words such as *after*, *next*, *first*, *second*, and others.

Sentence Revision

The process of revision should proceed from the largest elements or concepts down to the smallest. You have just examined the overall organization, the introduction and conclusion, and each paragraph.

There are a few simple checks to test the effectiveness of sentences in an essay. As you recollect from Unit I, sentences should be constructed to answer a series of questions:

1. What happened?
2. Who or what was involved?
3. Answer these questions about the nouns in the sentence:
   (a) Which?
   (b) What kind or quality?
   (c) How much or many?
   (d) Whose?
4. Answer these questions about the action of the sentence:
   (a) When?
   (b) Where?
   (c) How?
   (d) Why?

Use these same questions to revise sentences for effectiveness. In Paragraph 2 of the essay on Paul Schmidt, we read

> I got the job through a friend, and I didn't know two cents worth about woods and woodworking.

What happened, and who was involved? Two things are reported:

> I got the job.
> I didn't know two cents worth about woods and woodworking.

In the first action, *got* is an exceptionally neutral word. Pick a more precise expression by trying some other verbs as replacements.

I obtained the job.

This sounds very formal.

I fell into the job accidentally.

This is more colorful, but is probably not true. The writer felt desperate for a summer job, and so he begged and pressured his friends and relatives.

Choose a verb to suit that truth.

I begged my way into the job.
I hustled the job.
I hustled my way into the job.
I wangled my way into the job.

Wangle means "to manage to get by schemes, trick, persuasion, or in irregular ways." Perhaps this is closer to the idea. Check the thesaurus if no other possibilities come to mind. Check the dictionary to be sure that the chosen word is the right word.

Add information about the nouns:

I wangled the job.

To modify the subject, answer the questions:

1. Which?
2. What kind or quality?
3. How much or many?
4. What size?

What kind or quality of person was "I"? The person may be characterized as desperate for a job, hungry for work, scheming to get a job, and willing to take any job.

An insufficient answer is

Desperate for any kind of job, I wangled the job.

Stop! Repeating *job* is boring. Change the modifying phrase.

> Desperate for work, I wangled the job.
> Desperate for money to go to college, I wangled the job.

The idea here is correct, but try a modification on the word *job*.

> helper's job
> job I didn't especially want

These changes, however, add too much to the sentence. In this case, since *job* is defined in the previous sentence and in the following sentences, it can be left without modification here in this sentence.

Try the other questions:

1. Why? Answered by first modifying phrase.
2. Where? In the cabinet shop; not needed because we know this already.
3. How? Answered in the verb.
4. When? This point is important because of the time relationship to the previous sentence that says:

> I met Paul the first day . . .

The action in the second sentence—*wangled*— happened before the action of the first sentence—*met*. It is important to show this relationship in time. Two choices are available for expressing time:

1. Change the tense from *wangled* to *had wangled*.
2. Add a word or phrase in which you establish the time.

> Early in the spring
> On March 10th
> Earlier

In fact, the exact time is not important to this sentence. The only important fact is that the events described in Sentence 2 happened before those of Sentence 1. Stay with the change in tense, and write *had wangled*. The sentence now reads:

> Desperate for work, I had wangled the job through a friend.

Now apply the same process to the second half of the sentence.

> I didn't know two cents worth about woods and woodworking, and about cabinetmaking.

What happened, and who or what was involved?

> I didn't know two cents worth.

This expression seems effective enough to stand as it is. But the rest of the sentence contains a bumpy, inconclusive combination of words that echoes from Paragraph 1 a sentence about woods and woodworking. This expression must be stated in stronger terms. Try some other ways of saying the same thing:

> About making things out of wood.
> About woodworking.
> About cabinetmaking.

None of these seems effective, but since the sentence starts out with the expression *know about*, the only option is to provide a one-word answer to the question *what* after the word *about*. A complete change in wording is needed:

> I'd never even held a hammer.
> I couldn't tell one wood from another.
> I was all thumbs and couldn't tell oak from pine.

Try the last one and combine it with the first, revised, part of the sentence:

> Desperate for work, I had wangled the job through a friend, and I was all thumbs and couldn't tell oak from pine.

Now the parts are effective, but they don't join properly. The word *and* makes the two parts equal and continuous. Two possibilities are available:

1. Change *and* to *but*.

> Desperate for work, I had wangled the job through a friend, but I was all thumbs and couldn't tell oak from pine.

This change is not of much use, because it focuses attention equally on two parts of the sentence. Try the next option.
2. Change *and* to *although* or to *even though*.

> Desperate for work, I had wangled the job through a friend, even though I was all thumbs and couldn't tell oak from pine.

This version will fit in with the sentences before and after it, and it makes a more effective expression than does the first version.

> I met Paul the first day I went to work in the shop for the summer. Desperate for work, I had wangled the job through a friend, even though I was all thumbs and couldn't tell oak from pine. When we were introduced, he shook my hand and then . . .

The steps in revising sentences for effectiveness are fairly simple:

1. Ask the questions for constructing sentences, to be sure that you have included all necessary details.
2. Try possible ways of joining the parts of the sentence, to make the emphasis in the sentence correct.
3. See that the revised sentence reads smoothly when joined to other sentences in the paragraph.

A Word of Encouragement

As you begin to learn revision, you will find that the work moves slowly. If you will practice the process carefully, you will discover two things:

1. The process itself will become almost automatic and will move more rapidly as you gain experience.
2. Practicing the process of revision faithfully will improve your writing and thus reduce the need for revision.

If you follow the revision process carefully and patiently, you can improve your writing, but in order to benefit from this process, you must resist two temptations shared by every writer.

The first temptation, mentioned briefly before, is to fall in love with a first draft and refuse to revise the paper thoroughly. Occasionally, an inspired effort produces a good first draft, but ordinarily a first draft is in need of much improvement. The old saying is still true:

The only good writing is rewriting.

The second temptation is more subtle than the first. It is very easy to take the advice that says, "That sentence, or phrase, or word is probably good enough. Don't bother to revise it. Skip it. Slide to the next sentence." Hurry, skipping, and careless revision only lead to careless, second-rate writing. Be patient and be thorough, and you will soon be a better writer.

Summary

We have looked at several steps in the revision process. You should use these steps in an order that will let you look first at the whole essay. Then move on to the smaller units of the essay, that is, to the paragraphs and sentences. When you have finished the draft of an essay, set it aside so that you can reduce your emotional involvement with it. Then follow these steps in the order established here:

General Questions for Revision
1. Review the statement of the core idea. Put the preparation sheets on the desk near you, for easy reference.
2. Read the introduction through aloud. Evaluate the introduction.
   (a) Does it interest you in the subject?
   (b) Does the introduction establish the general subject area and then move to a restricted topic?
   (c) Does it provide a statement of the core idea or impression of the essay? If not, does it at least suggest the core idea?
   (d) Does it lay out the plan of the essay for the reader? This is not a necessity, but it is a nice service to the reader.
3. Check the size of each supporting paragraph. A paragraph markedly smaller than the others may need more development. Make a note to check shorter paragraphs carefully.
4. Read each paragraph aloud separately. Answer the following questions about each paragraph:
   (a) Does the paragraph serve to develop, explain, or illustrate the core idea?

(b) Is the paragraph in the most effective position in the essay? Does the main point of the paragraph seem to occur naturally in the order which you originally selected for the essay?

(c) Is the paragraph unified? Does it deal with one subject or idea?

(d) Is the paragraph coherent? Does it read smoothly and carry the reader from start to finish? Note that a break or abrupt change in thought may be a sign that more development is needed.

(e) Do the supporting details, examples, and illustrations develop the idea of the paragraph and only that idea? An illustration may serve the core idea but harm the progress of the essay if it is in the wrong paragraph.

(f) Is the paragraph complete? Does it offer complete development of each point? Do the illustrations and examples make the point of the paragraph clear? Will the reader have any questions about the point of the paragraph when he finishes reading it?

5. Check the transitions between paragraphs. Are the paragraphs tied together by the relationship of the ideas, by repetition of key words, and by transitional words and phrases? Is the movement from paragraph to paragraph easily made?

6. Check the conclusion by asking these questions:

(a) Does the conclusion of the essay leave the reader with a sense of end, of finality?

(b) Does it apologize?

(c) Does it add afterthoughts?

(d) Does it begin a new point?

FURTHER WORK ON REVISION

When you have revised the content and word choice of the sentences in your paper, you need to examine each sentence to be sure that you have formed only complete sentences. Be sure that you have followed the rules and conventions that govern forms of words, punctuation, capitalization, and spelling. Work through the following questions and exercises to be sure that you understand all the concepts. Then apply the questions to your written projects.*

*A review of these concepts and terms is found in the Appendix, p. 233FF.

Completeness

A sentence begins with a capital letter and ends with a period. In order to form a sentence, however, the words between capital letter and period must contain the basic elements of a subject and a verb. Look at each sentence—each unit that you have opened with a capital and closed with a period—and ask the following questions:

1. **Does this unit have a verb?**
2. **Does the verb in this unit have a subject?**
3. **Does each clause in this unit have a subject and a verb?**

Be sure that units beginning with

When	If
Since, because	Who
Although	Whose
In order that	Whom
After	Which, that

all have subjects and verbs.

4. **Is each introductory or modifying clause, such as any of the units listed above, attached to a sentence?**

Such clauses cannot stand alone. They must be part of another unit.

When the rain stopped.
Because I was sick.
Although I tried hard.
The man who drew the cartoon.

Units like these cannot stand alone, but must modify another subject-verb unit.

When the rain stopped, I went fishing.
Because I was sick, I left early.
Although I tried hard, I failed.
I saw the man who drew the cartoon.

Introductory and modifying clauses are not sentences; they are modifiers within sentences. Do not leave them standing alone.

To fix this concept in your mind, practice the following brief exercise. In the following paragraph, you will find sentences and clauses that have no subject or no verb. Keeping to the sense of the paragraph, supply the subjects and verbs as needed:

> The two men walked slowly down the street. Stopped often to look in store windows. Especially stores that contained jewelry or appliances. Because they were security guards and needed to be on guard against possible burglaries. A serious crime wave that threatened both the lives and businesses of the store owners. Hired the guards to protect themselves.

5. Is each phrase connected to a sentence?

The following units contain -*ing* or -*ed* forms of verbs. They cannot stand alone:

> Running down the street.
> Seeing no one there.
> Stored in the small closet.
> The man running down the street.
> Seeing no one there and not wanting to be disturbed.

It is tempting to leave such phrases, standing alone, unconnected to a subject and verb. This is especially true for long phrases. However, these phrases are modifiers that cannot stand alone. They must be connected to a subject-verb combination. You may connect these phrases in the following ways:

> Running down the street, the man tripped and fell.
>
> The man running down the street tripped and fell.
>
> While he was running down the street, the man tripped and fell.
>
> Seeing no one there and not wanting to be disturbed, the girls sat quietly in the lobby.
>
> Stored in the small closet, the toys were completely forgotten.
>
> The toys, stored in the small closet, were completely forgotten.

Be sure to watch for other phrases

> In the long dark corridor.
> Down the dark lonely street.
> With ears standing straight up.

and connect them to sentences if they are standing alone.

In the long dark corridor, the air was damp and smelly.
The policeman walked slowly down the dark, lonely street.
With his ears standing straight up, the dog barked at the children.

Connect the following sentences by joining all the phrases to sentences:

The boy running down the street. Arms pumping. Dodging between parked cars. In the morning, beside the docks, under the bridge. Looking at the ground, with his head down, without looking up. Slammed heavily into a brick wall. Collapsed on the pavement.

6. Have you joined compound sentences correctly?

The sentences—independent clauses—

John left on vacation.
Mary returned to work.

may be joined to become one sentence called a compound sentence. It is not considered proper to join two subject-verb combinations with a comma

John left, Mary returned.

or to join them only with a conjunction such as *and, but, or, for.*

John left and Mary returned.

As another way of joining the two elements, use a semicolon.

John left; Mary returned.

False Compounds

In a compound sentence, both elements are equal. Often you should make one element a modifier and the other element the independent clause. In the compound

I felt sick, and I went home.

the first clause, *I felt sick*, is the cause of the second, *I went home*. The sentence might be more effectively and accurately written:

Because I felt sick, I went home.
I went home because I felt sick.

In many compounds, the sentence needs to show a time relationship. Instead of writing

I found the money, and I took it to the police.

write

After I found the money, I took it to the police.

After you have examined compound sentences, ask this question:

7. **Are the actions or relationships equal in importance, or does one action establish a cause, a time, or another special circumstance for the other action?**

If the clauses are not equal, change the sentence to use the proper special clause.

Rewrite the following compound sentences to show special relationships between the clauses:

After	1. The dog bit the girl, and she became very ill.
Although	2. The man was tired, and he kept on working.
When	3. The storm came, and we left the island.
Because	4. The men worked slowly, and we were late getting home.
While	5. We were in the store, and Joe bought three books.

Modifying Phrases

Reread each sentence in which you have used a verbal phrase to modify a noun. Check the connection between the noun and the modifying phrase. Be sure that the phrase modifies the correct noun. Remember that the structure of the language allows the use of a modifying phrase immediately before or immediately after the noun.

Wearing an overcoat, John left the building and joined Sam.
John, wearing an overcoat, left the building and joined Sam.
The mountaineer, exhausted from the climb, talked quietly to the girl.

If you move the modifying phrase away from one of these two slots, the phrase will probably attach itself to another noun in the sentence:

John left the building and joined Sam, wearing an overcoat.
The mountaineer talked quietly to the girl, exhausted from the climb.

The last two sentences are correct and sensible, but Sam now wears the overcoat and the girl is exhausted from the climb. In each case, the sense of the new sentences differs from the old.

8. **Is each modifying phrase—the *-ing*, or *-ed* form of the verb— in the slot immediately preceding or immediately following the noun it modifies?**

Rewrite the following sentences to make the modification clear:

The man ran up the stairs and out into the fresh breeze, huffing and puffing from the climb.

I watched the dog discouraged by my failures lie down and go to sleep.

Awakened from a sound sleep, the burglar forced me to go into the closet.

The waves, rocking wildly from side to side, threatened to capsize the boat.

Waving his arms and shouting, I watched the policeman directing traffic.

Modifying Clauses

Check all clauses beginning with *who, whom, which,* or *that.* Be sure that they modify the correct noun.

9. **Is each modifying clause—*who, whom, which, that*—immediately following the noun you intended to modify?**

If this is not the case, move the clause to its proper place.

Pronoun/Noun Combinations

Each pronoun must be clearly related to a noun. If the relationship is not clear, the pronoun will not have a clear meaning.
The pronoun *them* in the sentence

A man watched them.

has no real meaning unless the sentence is preceded by another explanatory sentence, such as

Two boys played in the mud puddle, and a man watched them.

In the compound sentence, the word *them* clearly refers to the two boys. Without the noun *boys*, the pronoun *them* has no meaning.

The following two common problems confuse pronoun usage:

(a) The pronoun is separated by other nouns from the noun that gives it
it a meaning.

High in the sky a plane flew in lazy loops and circles. Birds soared by in a
great flock. A single cloud scudded across the sky. Far below, a young
boy lay on his back watching it fly.

What was the boy watching? The plane? The flock? The reference is not clear; therefore, the pronoun *it* has no clear meaning.

(b) The pronoun has no noun to provide its meaning.

Always check the fan belts, the radiator hoses, and the lights before you
drive your car. This will ensure a safe trip.

The pronoun is *this*. What will ensure a safe trip? *This* will. What
is *this*? We don't know, because the only nouns in the sentence are
belts, hoses, and lights. These items do not ensure a safe trip. *Checking* the belts, hoses, and lights ensures a safe trip. The last sentence
ought to read

This check will ensure a safe trip.

or

This procedure will ensure a safe trip.

10. Does each pronoun refer clearly and unmistakably to a noun?

If not, rewrite the sentence to provide clear connections between
pronouns and the nouns they replace. Practice this process by rewriting the following paragraph:

We loaded the food on the boat and hoisted the sails. This took about an
hour. The boat moved easily out of the harbor, the wind blowing fresh from
the east. It heeled over and we took the port tack for about two miles.
After that we turned and ran down the coast. Suddenly we struck a huge
rock and it sank right out from under us.

Other Considerations About Pronouns

Check to be sure that you have not used the word *you* unless
you are writing to another person or quoting someone else's words.

Avoid the use of the word *you* as it occurs in the following example:

The three boys walked slowly up the hill, dragging their feet. You could tell they were very tired.

Say, instead,

I could tell they were very tired

or

It was obvious that they were very tired.

or

Clearly, they were very tired.

11. **Does the pronoun *you* occur when there is no direct statement to the reader or direct quotation using the word?**

If the pronoun occurs incorrectly, rewrite the sentence to eliminate it. Rewrite the following paragraph:

The players showed little interest in the game. One ran so slowly that you could tell he didn't care how it came out. About midway through the third set the umpire warned that they had better perk up or he would call it off. You would think they would be more dedicated to winning.

Form of Pronouns

Check each pronoun to be sure that you have used the correct form. The forms

I
He, she, it
We
They
Who

may be used only as subjects or as complements after forms of the verb *to be*. These forms are expressed by the words *am, is, are, were, have been,* and *had been.* Thus

I saw the man, (not *Me saw the man*).
They came to town, (not *Them came to town*).
This is she (not *This is her*).

The forms

Me
Him, her, it
Us
Them
Whom

may be used as complements after transitive verbs or as complements for prepositions. Thus

He saw me (not *He saw I*).
I saw him running (not *I saw he running*).
We found them (not *We found they*).
After him (not *After he*).
Beside them (not *Beside they*).
In us (not *in we*).

Use the following formula. If the pronoun answers the question
what? after *is*, *was*, or another form of *to be*, use

I, we, they, he, she, who

If the pronoun answers the question *what*? after a transitive verb
or after a preposition, use

me, us, them, him, her, whom

Note that *who* clauses—known as relative clauses—present
special problems. Consider the following examples:

I saw the man who owns the bank.

The word *who* is used, because the pronoun is the subject
of *owns*, but

I saw the man whom you dislike.

takes the word *whom*, because the pronoun is the complement
of the verb *dislike*. Isolate these clauses from the rest of the

sentence. Decide whether the pronoun is a subject, a complement of the verb *to be*, a complement of a transitive verb, or a complement of a preposition. Then choose the proper form.

12. Are all the pronouns in the proper form?

If not, check the formula and make corrections. Try the following exercise on *who/whom* choices:

> The man who/whom ordered the new car wishes to change the delivery date.
> I saw the woman who/whom you saw yesterday.
> We looked for the man to who/whom you gave the money.

Informal writing and most conversational usages will allow you to avoid this problem by substituting *that* for *whom/whom* or by eliminating the pronoun altogether. Note the following examples:

> The man that ordered the new car wishes to change the delivery date.
> I saw the woman that you saw yesterday.
> We looked for the man that you gave the money to.
> We looked for the man you gave the money to.

In questions, use *who* at the beginning of the question.

> Who is that man?
> Who did you see?

Always use *whom* after a preposition.

> To whom can we turn?

Select the proper form of the pronoun in the following:

> John and (I, me) waited for (she her) to bring the men (who, whom) we had seen at the meeting. (They, them) were supposed to tell (we, us) boys about jobs available during the summer. Unfortunately, (they, them) never came, and that left (we, us) without any job prospects for the summer.

Agreement of Subject and Verb

In the present and perfect tenses, the verb ends in *s* when the subject is a singular noun or a singular, third person pronoun. In all other instances the verb ends without an *s*.

He runs   They run
He has run   They have run
The man sees   The men see
The man has seen   The men have seen.

Problems arise when words or phrases separate the subject and the verb:

A wet steamy pile of twigs and branches was our only firewood.
Pile was is the correct subject/verb combination.

Prepositional phrases, including the expressions *together with* and *as well as*, do not affect the number of the verb.

The man, together with his two sons, is arriving tonight.
The boys from home, as well as my sister, are arriving tomorrow.

The pronouns *one*, *each*, *either*, and *neither* are singular:

One of the men is here.
Neither of the boys has arrived.
Each of the girls was surprised.

Some, *any*, and *none* take their number from the noun in the prepositional phrase following them.

Is any of the money gone?
Are any of the boys here?
None of the money is gone.
None of the ships are ready.

Who, *whom*, *which*, and *that* take their number from the noun to which they refer.

The man who owns the car is here.
The women who own the cars are here.

In the expression

She is one of those girls who always look good.

the noun reference for *who* is girls, not *she*. Therefore, *look* must be plural:

girls look

You may use this test to check the form. The sentence can be revised as follows:

Of those girls who always look good, she is one.

Clearly, the verb *look* is plural because it refers to girls. Compound subjects present special problems. Subjects joined by *and* are always plural.

Joe and Tom are here.

When subjects are joined by

either . . . or
not only . . . but also
not . . . but

use the number of the noun closest to the verb.

Either the boys or Mary has arrived.
Either Mary or the boys have arrived.

Special nouns sometimes cause problems. Collective nouns—the names of groups of people or things—such as *group*, *team*, *collection*, or *jury*, are singular:

The team was defeated.

Words that appear plural—*economics*, *politics*, *measles*—are singular:

Measles is a childhood disease.

Nouns signifying weight, measure, time, and money are singular:

Forty dollars is my price.
Five miles is a long distance.

The word *there*, used to open a sentence, can cause confusion.

There was one girl at home. One girl was at home.
There were five girls at home. Five girls were at home.

There is never the subject of a verb. Do not make a verb singular simply because it follows *there*. Find the subject of the verb.

13. Does each subject agree in number with its verb?

Check the guidelines above and make corrections. The following exercises may help you. Choose the correct verb:

The men who own no land possesses/possess no wealth.
The scoutmaster, in addition to the leaders, is/are late.
The men and the boy is/are late.
Either the men or the boy is/are coming.
The faculty is/are divided on that subject.
Some of the boats was/were sunk.
None of the money was/were lost.
There was/were several men in the group.
Neither the dean nor the students has/have arrived.
Not that boy, but those men is/are the owners.

Verb Tense

It is important that you establish the tense of each passage and stay with that tense unless the meaning of the passage demands a change. Do not shift tenses unless you have a good reason. Read the following paragraph and note the shifts in tense:

> The boys walked slowly down the dusty road to school. They seem to hesitate, seemed to be looking for an excuse to turn back. The dust rises slowly under each step. They trudge on, not smiling, not talking much. Finally they arrive at school, throw their books on their desks, and began to work.

It is acceptable to write such a narrative in either past tense or in present tense, but once you choose a tense, you must stay with it to the end of the passage. Thus you can say

The boys walk.
They seem.
The dust rises.
They trudge.

or

The boys walked.
They seemed.
The dust rose.
They trudged.

but you should not shift back and forth as the example paragraph does.

14. **Is your choice of tenses maintained consistently throughout the passage?**

English has three tenses for verbs:

Present	I run
Past	I ran
Future	I will run

and one tense directly related to each tense:

Present perfect	I have run
Past perfect	I had run
Future perfect	I shall have run

The word *perfect* in the tense name means "completed before." Thus, *present perfect* means *completed before this present time.*

I have run three miles this week.

Past perfect means *completed before a past time.*

By this time last week, I had run only two miles.

Future perfect means *completed before a future time.*

By this time next week, I will have run five miles.

15. **Have you made use of these perfect tenses where necessary to show time relationships between two events?**

Verb Forms

Check to be sure that you use proper forms for each verb tense. The present and future tenses present no problems:

They see
They will see

The past tense and the three perfect tenses can present problems because the spelling of some verbs changes in these tenses.

Every verb has three forms. These forms are usually called principal parts:

First	Second	Third
the base	past tense	the past participle
Start	Started	Started

Verbs that simply add *ed* to the second and third parts are called regular verbs. The tenses of all regular verbs are formed in the same way.

Tense	Part	Form
Present	First	They start
Future	Will + first	They will start
Past	Second	They started
Present perfect	Have + third	They have started[1]
Past perfect	Had + third	They had started
Future perfect	Shall have + third	They shall have started

The tenses of all other, or irregular, verbs are formed by using the same pattern, but the principal parts change in spelling rather than by adding *ed*.

Some verbs use the same form for second and third part:

Bend	Bent	Bent
Bring	Brought	Brought
Win	Won	Won

Some verbs change radically in spelling:

First	Second	Third
Be	Was	Been
Drive	Drove	Driven
Come	Came	Come
Begin	Began	Begun
Drink	Drank	Drunk

[1] *Has* for third person singular verbs.

Regardless of the spelling of the three parts, the formula for constructing the tenses remains the same.

Tense	Part	Form
Present	First	They drink
Future	Will + first	They will drink
Past	Second	They drank
Present perfect	Have[2] + third	They have drunk
Past perfect	Had + third	They had drunk
Future perfect	Shall have + third	They shall have drunk

Be sure that you use the proper part to form each tense. The parts of verbs are listed in your dictionary, under the entry for each verb. Somewhere in the entry, usually at the beginning or at the end, you will find the parts of the verb.

Throw	Threw	Thrown
Take	Took	Taken

If you do not find the parts of the verb listed in the dictionary entry, you may assume that the verb is regular and that it forms its second and third part by adding *ed* to the base.

Start	Started	Started

The following list of commonly used irregular verbs may prove helpful to you:

First	Second	Third
Awake	Awaked, awoke	Awaked, awoke, awoken
Be	Was, were	Been
Bear (carry)	Bore	Borne
Bear (give birth to)	Bore	Born
Beat	Beat	Beaten, beat
Begin	Began	Begun
Bend	Bent	Bent
Bite	Bit	Bit, bitten
Bleed	Bled	Bled

[2] *Has* for third person singular verbs.

First	Second	Third
Blow	Blew	Blown
Break	Broke	Broken
Bring	Brought	Brought
Build	Built	Built
Buy	Bought	Bought
Catch	Caught	Caught
Choose	Chose	Chosen
Cling	Clung	Clung
Come	Came	Come
Creep	Crept	Crept
Deal	Dealt	Dealt
Dig	Dug	Dug
Dive	Dived, dove	Dived
Do	Did	Done
Drag	Dragged	Dragged
Draw	Drew	Drawn
Dream	Dreamed, dreamt	Dreamed, dreamt
Drink	Drank	Drunk
Drive	Drove	Driven
Eat	Ate	Eaten
Fall	Fell	Fallen
Fit	Fitted, fit	Fitted, fit
Fly	Flew	Flown
Forget	Forgot	Forgotten, forgot
Freeze	Froze	Frozen
Get	Got	Gotten, got
Give	Gave	Given
Go	Went	Gone
Grow	Grew	Grown
Hang (an object)	Hung	Hung
Hang (a person)	Hanged	Hanged
Hide	Hid	Hidden, hid
Kneel	Knelt, kneeled	Knelt, kneeled
Know	Knew	Known
Lay (put)	Laid	Laid
Lead	Led	Led
Lean	Leaned, leant	Leaned, leant
Lend	Lent	Lent
Lie (recline)	Lay	Lain
Light	Lighted, lit	Lighted, lit
Lose	Lost	Lost
Ride	Rode	Ridden
Ring	Rang	Rung
Rise	Rose	Risen
Run	Ran	Run

First	Second	Third
See	Saw	Seen
Set	Set	Set
Shake	Shook	Shaken
Shave	Shaved	Shaved, shaven
Shine	Shone, shined	Shone, shined
Show	Showed	Showed, shown
Shrink	Shrank	Shrunk
Sing	Sang, sung	Sung
Sink	Sank	Sunk
Sit	Sat	Sat
Slide	Slid	Slid
Speak	Spoke	Spoken
Speed	Sped, speeded	Sped, speeded
Spring	Sprang, sprung	Sprung
Stand	Stood	Stood
Steal	Stole	Stolen
Strike	Struck	Struck, stricken
Swim	Swam	Swum
Swing	Swung	Swung
Take	Took	Taken
Teach	Taught	Taught
Tear	Tore	Torn
Throw	Threw	Thrown
Wake	Waked, woke	Waked, woke, woken
Wear	Wore	Worn
Write	Wrote	Written

The forms of the verb *to be* are very irregular. The six tenses are printed in full below:

Present	I am	We are
	You are	You are
	He is	They are
Past	I was	We were
	You were	You were
	He was	They were
Future	I will be	We will be
	You will be	You will be
	He will be	They will be
Present perfect	I have been	We have been
	You have been	You have been
	He has been	They have been

Past perfect	I had been	We had been
	You had been	You had been
	He had been	They had been
Future perfect	I shall have been	We shall have been
	You shall have been	You shall have been
	He shall have been	They shall have been

The verbs *lie* and *lay* offer unusual problems because of confusion in both spelling and meaning:

a. To lie, an intransitive verb, means to lie down, to recline, to place
oneself in a prone position.

The children lie down for a nap every day at 2:00 P.M.

b. To lay, a transitive verb, means to put or to place.

I am laying the book on the table for you.

The forms are as follows:

to lie		to lay
lie		lay
lay		laid
lain		laid

Present	They lie	They lay
Past	They lay	They laid
Future	They will lie	They will lay
Present perfect	They have lain	They have laid
Past perfect	They had lain	They had laid
Future perfect	They shall have lain	They shall have laid

16. Are all the verbs formed correctly?

PUNCTUATION

Commas are used

1. To separate items in a series.

>   Tom, Dick, and Harry came to town.

2. To set off modifying phrases and clauses at the beginning of
a sentence.

>   Carrying a suitcase, the man hurried off the train.
>   Since I was tired, I took a nap.

3. To set off words, phrases, and clauses that immediately follow nouns or that interrupt the flow of the sentence.

> John Jones, the president, is here.
> The men, because they were tired, took a nap.

Do not separate such a clause at the end of the sentence.

> The men took a nap because they were tired.

4. To set off *who* clauses that add information but do not identify a noun. If the clause follows a proper noun, a name, or a specific identification, set the clause off with commas.

> That is Tom Jones, who is president.
> There is the President of the United States, who will make a speech tonight.
> Today there is a northeast wind, which will bring rain tomorrow.

Do not set off *who* clauses that serve to identify the noun they follow.

> That is the man who is the president.
> There is the man who will make a speech tonight.
> Today there is the kind of wind that will bring rain.

5. To separate the clauses of a compound sentence when the second clause opens with a conjunction.

> Tom left home, and Jim returned.

6. To set off the speaker in dialogue.

> "I think," John said, "that I'll go home."

7. To set off a person addressed.

> John, don't leave us.

8. To set off dates and addresses.

> I was born on March 17, 1947, in Chicago, Illinois.

Periods are used.

1. At the end of a sentence.

> Tom hit the ball.

2. After abbreviations.

> Mr. Jones is here.

Semicolons are used in compound sentences that do not have a conjunction between independent clauses.

> Tom came; John departed.

Question marks are used after a direct question.

> Where is Tom?

Quotation marks are used at the beginning and the end of direct quotations.

> "John is not coming," said Tom.
> "Why," cried Mary, "does he always do that?"

17. **Have you correctly used punctuation marks wherever necessary?**

CAPITALIZATION

We customarily capitalize the first letter of

1. The first word in a sentence or a direct quotation.

> That man stole my wallet.
> Tom shouted, "Stop that thief!"

2. All proper names; that is, all names that stand for a specific person, place, event, period, institution, or region.

> Tom Jones
> Mother
> Boston
> the Depression
> The University of Chicago
> the South

Do not capitalize "mother"—it is not a proper name—unless it stands for a specific person and is replacing the name of that person.

3. Modifiers derived from names.

> American
> the Spanish language

4. Days, months, holidays.

> Saturday
> June
> Thanksgiving

5. A rank or title, and abbreviations that come after names.

> Captain John Smith
> Doctor Johnson
> Jane Jones, Ph.D.

6. Sacred names from all religions.

>   the Bible
>   the Koran

7. Regions, but not directions.

>   I live in the West.
>   We walked west.

8. Specific courses, but not general areas of learning.

>   She is studying physics.
>   Her next course is Physics 211.

18. Are capital letters used where necessary?

Spelling

Spelling is not difficult, but it does require attention to detail. If you wish to become a good speller or to be able to produce papers free of spelling errors, pay very careful attention to the following common spelling errors:

1. Choosing the wrong word from among words that sound alike but are neither spelled the same way nor mean the same thing. Examples include:

accept	cite	its	shone
except	site	it's	shown
	sight		
advice	coarse	later	stationary
advise	course	latter	stationery
affect	complement	lose	statue
effect	compliment	loose	stature
			statute
all ready	consul	past	than
already	council	passed	then
	counsel		
all together	desert	peace	their
altogether	dessert	piece	there
			they're
altar	dining	personal	to
alter	dinning	personnel	too
			two

canvas	formerly	presence	whose
canvass	formally	presents	who's
capital	instance	principal	your
capitol	instants	principle	you're
		quiet	
		quite	

2. Carelessly transposing letters, omitting syllables, or, in general, paying little or no attention to what you put on the paper even though you know how to spell a word.

No set of rules will help, and no piece of advice can correct the fault in this case. Be careful to pay attention to your own words. In addition, start a list of words that you know but regularly misspell. Refer to this list when you edit the final draft of a paper. Be sure that you have spelled all these "lazy error" words correctly.

3. Failing to fix the spelling of new words firmly in your mind. As you meet a new word in your reading or in conversation, write the correct spelling—and the definition—in a small notebook. Try to use these words in your writing. Refer to your list when you need to check the spelling.

No one can do much to make you a better speller, but no one can prevent you from doing it, either. Take the time, pay attention to detail, and do not submit a paper that contains spelling errors.

19. Are all the words spelled correctly?

FINAL FORM FOR PAPERS AND MANUSCRIPTS

The final version of any paper or essay should be typed or neatly handwritten in legible script on standard notebook paper. Be sure that you adhere to the margins—leave one-half inch on the right-hand side. The paper should contain no spelling errors, no strike-overs, no smudges, no marks, and no coffee stains. It should be carefully titled and headed according to your teacher's instructions, and it should be a reflection of the pride and sense of accomplishment that you feel when you submit a paper that is properly worked up from start to finish.

20. Is the form of the paper correct, neat and acceptable?

After you have completed the revision checklist on page 207,

Use These Questions To Check Correctness.

1. Does each unit identified as a sentence unit have a verb?
2. Does the verb in this unit have a subject?
3. Does each clause in this unit have a subject and a verb?
4. Is each introductory or modifying clause attached to a sentence?
5. Is each phrase connected to a sentence?
6. Are compound sentences joined correctly?
7. Are the actions or relationships equal in importance, or does one action establish a cause, a time, or another special circumstance for the other action?
8. Is each modifying phrase— *-ing* or *-ed* form of the verb—in the slot immediately preceding or immediately following the noun it modifies?
9. Is each modifying clause—*who, whom, which, that*—immediately following the noun you intend to modify?
10. Does each pronoun refer clearly and unmistakably to a noun?
11. Does the pronoun *you* occur when there is no direct statement to the reader or direct quotation using the word?
12. Are all pronouns in the proper form?
13. Does each subject agree with its verb in number?
14. Is your choice of tenses maintained consistently throughout the passage?
15. Have you made use of the perfect tenses where necessary to show time relationships between two events?
16. Are all the verbs formed correctly?
17. Is all the punctuation correct?
18. Are all necessary words capitalized?
19. Is all spelling correct?
20. Is the form of the paper correct, neat, and acceptable?

Appendix

Writing is the easiest and the most difficult thing anyone can try to do. By definition, all you need to do is to take a word, join it to another word, and join these to other words until everything is said. But does it really work that way? It does, and it doesn't. Writing is basically the process of combining or using combinations of various things.

> In speech, we combine sounds such as *tell-eh-fon* to make a word, and when we transfer to writing we construct letter combinations that stand for those sounds, and combine them to form the written word, *telephone*.

Then, to express ideas we can combine that word with other words.

> Telephones help us to communicate with each other.

Next, we take that expression, called a sentence, and combine it with other sentences, as many as we want, until we have said everything we need to say about telephones.

When we combine words into sentences, however, we need to follow agreed-upon patterns in those combinations so that others will understand what we want to say. Using the correct words in the wrong combinations will not produce the statement we wish to make.

> Help us with telephones to communicate each other.

produces a statement that makes little sense.

The words in both sentences are the same, but the meaning is destroyed because the combinations of the words are changed.

In English, the basic understanding or rule of language says that the position of a word in a sentence determines what it does and means in that sentence.

Take these three words as an example

dogs   men   bite

and examine possible arrangements:

Dogs bite men.
Men bite dogs.
Bite men, dogs.

Each of these combinations contains the same words, but all three combinations convey entirely different meanings, based on the position of the words in the group. The rule in English is that the basic functions in a sentence come mainly from the position of the words, not from changes in the form of the word. This rule is not true in many other languages. In, for example, Latin, German, and French, endings of words are keys to the functions of these words in a sentence.

Combining words into a specified order constructs meaningful expressions, but putting the proper words into meaningful combinations will not produce effective writing if the combinations are strung endlessly together. These combinations must be separated into groups called sentences, and each sentence must be complete in itself. A sentence must contain certain components that are arranged in specified ways and are separated from other sentences at the point where they form a complete statement. Since the position of the words in the group comprising the sentence designates the function of the parts of a sentence, and since there are only five or six possible functions within any sentence, it is a relatively easy matter to construct completed sentences.

In order to write effectively, you need to be able to use various ways to develop flexibility in the formation of sentences. If you can identify the function of the words in the sentence, you can build sentences effectively, and you can test them to be sure that they are complete and internally consistent. English sentences contain four major components: verbs, subjects, complements, and modifiers.

The following discussion is a review of many things that you already know and use in your speaking and writing. Don't try to memorize any of the material; don't worry if it is not completely clear. Read it carefully twice, and do the exercises as you come to them.

Recognizing Verbs

Verbs perform a basic function in a sentence. They name, describe, or identify the action of the sentence, or they establish connections between parts of a sentence.

Read the following sentences:

We sailed west out of the harbor.
The boat struck a rock.
The water filled the boat.

Look for the word that provides the action in each sentence:

sailed
struck
filled

Here is another set of three sentences:

The man drove the car west on the road.
The car struck a telephone pole.
The pole fell into the river.

Identify the actions

drove
struck
fell

Using all of the following words, write two sentences and under-line with two lines the verb in each:

citizens   mayor   people   elect   policemen   help

It is possible to construct several sentences from this collection of words:

Citizens *elect* the mayor.
Mayor *elects* the people.

Policemen *help* people.
People *help* policemen.
Policemen *elect* the citizens.

Perhaps you found different combinations that produced other sentences. Probably some of the sentences listed above did not ring true, or mean something, to your experiences.

The mayor elects the people.

does not seem to reflect any existing election code, but the combination of words does possess one of the parts of a sentence, a verb.

Elects

Read the following sentences and underline the verbs twice. Remember that the verb answers the questions: *What happens in the sentence? What action occurs?*

The women bought new cars.
The team attempted three field goals.
The chef baked nine pies.
The baby slept for eight hours.
All the students stayed home.

Answers:

bought
attempted
baked
slept
stayed

In the five sentences you just examined, the verbs in Sentences 1, 2, and 3 differ from the verbs in Sentences 4 and 5.
The verbs

bought
baked
attempted

do not produce a complete expression of the action in the mind of the reader. When you read the expression

chef baked

your mind immediately asks "baked what?" The answer is, "pies." When you read the expression

    women bought

your mind immediately asks "bought what?" The answer is, "cars." In Sentences 4 and 5, however, the verbs do not raise the question *what*?

    baby slept
    students stayed

Neither verb allows the reader to ask, "slept what?" or "stayed what?"

The five verbs illustrate two kinds of action-expressions in English. The verbs in the first three sentences

    bought
    attempted
    baked

are incomplete. They require some completion word or complement to express the full idea. Action verbs that require a complement are called *transitive* because they transfer an action to the completion word.

The verbs in Sentences 4 and 5

    slept
    stayed

do not require an answer to the question *what*? and are therefore complete or intransitive; the action does not transfer to a completion word or complement. The ability to identify complete—intransitive—and incomplete—transitive—verbs is important. In order to write complete sentences, you must provide a completion word for every transitive verb.

Test the following verbs by asking the question *what*? after each one to determine whether the action is complete or incomplete. Provide a completion word for each incomplete verb:

    stood
    drive
    loved

follow
chop
build
walk
trim
run[1]

The Rule. Differentiate between complete and incomplete verbs by asking the question *what?* after the verb.

Incomplete—transitive—verbs transfer the action expressed by the verb to a receiver of that action. The receiver of the action is called the "object" of the verb. Observe the following examples:

subject	verb	object
man	saw	the dog
woman	followed	the road
child	chopped	the log
person	built	the house
lawyer	trimmed	the tree

Some verbs, unlike *run* or *hit*, do not indicate action. Instead, they serve as links between the subject and a completion word. They establish a connection between two parts of the sentence. The most common linking verb is *to be*, in all its forms.

John is happy.
The boys were tired.
John Kennedy was the thirty-fifth president.

Other verbs can serve as linking verbs. Among these verbs are *appear*, *become*, *feel*, *look*, *remain*, *seem*, *smell*, *taste*, and *sound*.

John appears happy.
The boys look tired.
John Kennedy became the thirty-fifth president.

Some of these verbs are linking verbs only in certain sentences. The sentence,

I felt the cantaloupe.

[1] Note that run, and some other words, can be incomplete when it means "to operate." My father runs (operates) a drill press in the factory. The verb *runs* must provide an answer (a completion word) to the question, "Runs what?"

obviously has a transfer of action, and differs from

I feel well.
I feel good.

Note that *well* refers to a state of health that represents the opposite of *ill*. *Good* refers to actual bodily sensations ("He felt good all over when she touched his hand").

In addition to expressing the action of the sentence, the verb also establishes the time of the action. The verb can establish three times, or, to use the correct word, *tenses*, for a sentence.

Present	They walk.
Future	They will walk.
Past	They walked.

Present	Today they run.
Future	Tomorrow they will run.
Past	Yesterday they ran.

It is obvious that the use of verb tense alone will not establish a specific time for the action of a sentence.

We drank a cup of coffee.

The expression *we drank* does not establish that at 9:00 A.M., December 20, 1981, we drank a cup of coffee together. *We drank* states simply that the action occurred at a time before the present. The verb *will take* in the sentence

The president will take office.

does not establish that the president will be inaugurated on January 20, 1985.

The verb *will take* states only that the action will occur at some time after the present time.

Therefore, we use the present, future, and past tenses to establish the time of an action in relation to time now.

Present tense time "now" they walk	also express habitual action as in "They walk one mile each day."

Past tense
time before "now"
they walked

Future tense
time after "now"
they will walk

Each of these tenses—present, past, and future—is related to another tense that indicates an action completed before that present, past, or future time.

Present tense	They run (action occurs now).
Present perfect tense	They have run (action completed by present time).
Past tense	They ran (action occurred in past time).
Past perfect tense	They had run (action completed before a past time).
Future tense	They will run (action will occur in future time).
Future perfect tense	They will have run (action completed before a future time).

Observe the time changes in the following sentences:

The men build the houses now. (present tense)
The men have built the houses before now. (before present time)
The men built the houses. (past time)
The men had built the houses. (before past time)
The men will build the houses. (future time)
The men will have built the houses. (before future time)

This relationship can be expressed more clearly if you say

Present—Today the men build are building, a bird house-are in the process of building

Present perfect—Today the men have built a bird house-have completed

Past—Yesterday they built one bird house-completed on that day

Past perfect—Prior to yesterday they had built three bird houses-completed before yesterday

Future—Tomorrow they will build a bird house-occurs in the future

Future perfect—Tomorrow they will have built a bird house-completed before a future time.

Here are six sentences that illustrate tense usage. Try to identify the tense of the italicized verbs.

The women *make* important decisions.
The boy *decided* to buy a bike.
The real estate agents *have sold* three houses.
Before I passed you, I *had run* two miles.
When I get home, I *will have run* four miles.
Tomorrow I *will decide* what to do.

Select the best choice from the following, and fill in the blanks:

We run	We ran	We will run
We have run	We had run	We will have run

Yesterday_____miles.
By next Friday_____three miles.
_____one mile every day.
Next Saturday_____in the marathon.
By last Friday_____seven miles in one week.
_____eighteen miles so far this week.

In the present tense and the present perfect tense, the third person singular form ends with -s.

I run	We run
You run	You (plural) run
He (or she) *runs*	They run

I have	We have
You have	You (plural) have
He (or she) *has*	They have.

Recognizing Subjects

The verb in a sentence expresses an action or establishes a connection in a sentence.

Jane builds a cabinet.
Joan seems happy.

The word or words the verb talks about is called the *subject* of the sentence. In sentences that have verbs expressing action, the actor is usually the subject.

> The man runs.
> Sam walked quickly.
> The women bought the building.

The verbs in these sentences are

> runs
> walked
> bought

To find the subject of these verbs, ask the question *who*? or *what*? about the verb:

> Who or what runs? Man runs.
> (Man is the subject of runs)

> Who or what walked? Sam walked.
> (Sam is the subject of walked)

> Who or what bought? The women bought.
> (Women is the subject of bought)

Subjects of linking verbs can also be located by following the same process.

Locate the verb by asking what happens. Since linking verbs do not express action, a *nothing* answer to the question causes you to look for a linking verb such as

> be   feel   seem   appear

After locating the verb, ask the standard question for locating subjects: Who or what is? Who or what appears?

> John Kennedy was the thirty-fifth president.

Was is the verb. Who or what *was*? John Kennedy *was*. John Kennedy is the subject.

> Sam appears unhappy.

What happens? There is no action. Look for a linking verb. *Appears* is the verb. Who or what *appears*? Sam *appears*. Sam is the subject. The Rule: To locate the verb, look for an action by asking "what happens in the sentence?" If there is no action, look for a linking verb. When you find the verb, locate the subject by asking. "Who or what_____?"

Identify the verb and the subject of the following sentences. Underline the verb twice and the subject once:

The woman drove the truck too fast.
The state trooper gave the driver a ticket.
The students will find the course difficult.
The carpenters had hung three doors by noon.

Kinds of Subjects

Several types of words and word groups can be the subject of a verb.

John Kennedy was the thirty-fifth president.

John Kennedy is a proper noun, a word that names a specific person, place, or thing.

The men own that horse.

Men is a common noun. This type of noun is a word that names a person, place or thing, but does not identify it by a proper name.

They own that horse.

They is a pronoun, a word that stands in the place of a noun.

Note that in the isolated sentence, "They own the horse," *They* has no real meaning. It cannot identify anyone unless there is a noun near it. Pronouns replace nouns; therefore, each pronoun can be used only after the introduction of a noun. Pronouns that can be subjects of verbs are *I, you, he, we, they, who, whoever, anyone,* and *someone.*

Running develops endurance.
Running calms my nerves.

Running is an *-ing* form of the verb *to run*, and is called a verbal noun. In these sentences, the verbal noun identifies or names an action that stands as the subject of *develops* and of *calms*. Be careful to look for the action, or for what happens, in these two sentences.

The actions are

develops
calms

Running is the subject of the verb in each sentence. Words ending in *-ing* can be the verbs of sentences only when they are joined to a form of *to be*, as in

John is running down the street.

Occasionally, you will find two other kinds of combinations as subjects. Note the following example:

To run in the Olympics is the goal.

The form *to* + a verb:

to run
to jump
to cry

is called an infinitive, and can be used as the subject of a verb.

Whoever killed that man was a professional.

In this sentence, the linking verb *was* is the verb. The answer to the question *who or what was* provides the subject. Notice that the answer is not simply *whoever*, but *whoever killed that man*.

Notice also that *whoever killed that man* is simply a less definite and less emphatic way of saying *the killer*.

Whoever killed that man is a combination of words called a *clause*, a group of words that contains a subject—whoever—and a verb—killed—and is designed to perform some function in a sentence.

Identify the verb and the subject of the following sentences. Underline the verb twice and the subject once. Be sure to underline the entire subject.

Walking is good excercise.
Whatever walking I do improves my physical condition.
To win a walking race is my ambition.
A victory in the race is my goal.
Tom won the last race.

Completing the Subject-Verb Combinations

You will recall that certain verbs make a complete statement of action.

John ran.
Mary slept.

Some verbs, linking and transitive, are not complete and must be combined with other words to make a complete expression.

Linking verbs require completion words or complements. Their name suggests that they link or connect two parts, a subject and a completion word.

John Kennedy was president.
James is happy.

There are two possible ways to complete a linking verb.

1. Rename the subject:

Kennedy was president.
Sam is a carpenter.
That was she.

Note that formally correct expression requires that you use only certain forms of pronouns after a linking verb. These pronouns include *I*, *you*, *he*, *she*, *it*, *we*, and *they*. These words are the same forms used as subjects of the verb, and they must be used because you are renaming the subject.

That girl was Mary.
That was she.

2. Name a quality or condition of the subject:

John was tall.
Mary seems tired.
She appeared happy.

Transitive verbs also require completion. You cannot read the expressions

John saw
The women found

without automatically asking *saw what?* and *found what?* after each verb. Several words and word groups can serve as the answer to the question *what?*

John saw the man.
The women found the girls.

Man and *girls* are nouns that, in a position after the verb, serve as complements.

John saw him.
The women saw them.

Him and *them* are pronouns that substitute for nouns. As completion words for transitive verbs, use only the forms *me, you, him, her, us,* and *them*.

John enjoys running.

Here running, the *-ing* form of the verb, is a verbal noun that completes the statement of the verb *enjoys*.

John wants to run.

To run is the object of the verb *wants*, because it answers the question *what?*

Forms such as *to find* are also used to complete special verbs:

He was able to find some money.
We are going to find some money.
We ought to find money here.

The detectives will find whoever killed that man.

The verb of the sentence is *will find*. The subject is *detectives*. Detectives will find whom or what? They will find whoever did that terrible thing. Note that the answer to the question *whom?* or *what?* is not simply *whoever*, but includes the entire clause *whoever killed that man.* Just as in the sentence where a clause is used as a subject (see p. 244), the clause here substitutes for a noun, *the killer.*

Verbs Requiring Two Completion Words

Some verbs, such as *give, show, send,* and a few others, provide two answers to the question *what?*

> John gave me some money.

The verb is *gave.* The subject is *John.* John gave what? John gave money. John gave me. In this sentence, John gave the money to me. When a verb such as *gave* is followed by two complements, the first shows the person to whom the thing was given, and the second shows the thing given.

> Sam gave me a baseball.
> Sam gave a baseball to me.
> The real estate agent showed us a house.
> He showed a house to us.

The construction of a sentence requires only three basic components:

1. A linking verb
2. A subject
3. A complement

> John is rich.

or

1. An action verb
2. A subject
3. A complement

> The men saw a deer.

Except in one case, where only two occur.

1. An action verb
2. A subject

> Tom slept.

The use of these components will allow us to construct sentences but will create only bare statements with little interest or richness. Fortunately, the language contains modifiers that clarify and enrich those bare statements.

In review, the basic elements of a sentence are

| | *subject* | *verb* |
| | The man | slept |

or

| | *subject* | *verb* | *complement* |
| | The woman | is | brilliant |

or

| | *subject* | *verb* | *object* |
| | The man | watched | the dog |

Although these sentences are complete in that they express an action or establish a connection, they lack useful information and interesting details. Details can be added if you use words, phrases, and clauses as modifying elements.

A one-word modifier that can point out additional qualities or characteristics of nouns may be added to a sentence in a position before any noun:

The tired man slept.
The happy man slept.

Such mofidiers, called adjectives, provide information such as

1. Which?
2. What kind of?
3. How many?
4. Whose?

Word groups can also be added before a noun when the noun serves as the subject of a sentence.

The man slept.

A word group called a *phrase*, beginning with either an *-ing* or *-ed* form of the verb and joined with other words, can modify the subject.

Leaning back in his chair, the man slept.
Exhausted by his drive, the man slept.

Such phrases may also modify nouns in other positions in the sentence.

The woman watched the dog sleeping in the chair.

In this example, the phrase *sleeping in the chair* modifies *dog*, because *dog* is the noun in the position closest to the phrase.

Note that a phrase that begins a sentence modifies the noun in the first position. You must use care not to mix modifiers and thus confuse the meaning and, in the process, produce a peculiar image.

Driving down the street, the buildings rose high above him.

subject	*verb*
buildings	rose

A phrase placed before the subject modifies that subject and thus makes the sentence say that the buildings are driving down the street. Phrases placed before a noun modify only that noun.

Clauses that modify nouns can be added to a sentence in the position following the noun.

The man watched the dog.
The man, *who was very tired*, watched the dog.
The man, *who owned the house*, watched the dog.
The man watched the dog *that slept in the chair*.
I want to talk to the man *to whom you gave the money*.
We helped the man *whose house burned down*.

Note that the clauses in brackets, called *relative clauses*, provide information about the preceding noun.

It is also possible to modify the verb in a sentence or a clause. Such modifiers provide answers to questions such as

1. When?
2. Where?
3. How?
4. How much?

The man slept fitfully.
He drank deeply.
The train moved fast.
The girls worked hard.

These one-word modifiers usually follow the verb. Sometimes they may stand for emphasis at the beginning of a sentence.

Quickly, he ran his eyes down that list of numbers.

A word group known as a *prepositional phrase* may also modify a verb by designating special relationships and positions.

The dog ran *under the fence*. He jumped *over the creek* and hid *in a hollow log*. We ran *toward him*. I patted him *on the head*. I was amazed *by his response*. He licked me *on the cheek*.

Prepositions are always joined with nouns that serve as complements or objects of the preposition. Note that when using pronouns with prepositions you must use the object form:

with me
with him, her
with us
with them
with whom

Another modifier, a kind of clause, can be attached to the basic sentence to show relationships such as:

1. Because, since (expresses the reasons why)
    Because we were tired, we went home.
    Since we were tired, we went home.
2. If, unless (expresses the circumstances under which something will occur)
    If you come, I will leave.
3. Although (expresses circumstances in spite of which the sentence is true)
    Although we were tired, we walked another mile.
4. Where, wherever (expresses place or position)
    Where the road ends, you will find the house.
5. In order that (expresses purpose)
    He moved to California in order that he might find a better job.

6. So that, so . . . that (expresses a consequence resulting from the main statement)

    I was so tired that I fell asleep at my desk.

We often use the words *so* or *such* without adding the clause of result. Although this practice is very common, it is technically incorrect because the expression is incomplete.

    We had such a good time (that?)

It is important to join these modifying clauses to another subject-verb combination. Since the clauses are modifiers, they cannot stand alone.

One final kind of modification is possible in English sentences: modifiers that modify other modifiers. In order to extend or intensify modification, we often add words such as *very*, *too*, and words that end in *ly*.

    He is tall.
    He is very tall.
    He is too tall for that desk.
    He is amazingly tall.

The basic components of any sentence are

1. Subject—verb
2. Subject—linking verb—complement
3. Subject—transitive verb—complement

    The boy runs.
    The boy is tired.
    The boy chased the dog.

These three examples are complete statements, and they can stand alone. The structure of the language allows us to modify them in the following ways:

1. One-word modifiers

    The tired boy runs.
    The tired boy runs slowly.

2. Phrase modifiers

    The tired boy wearing the gray shirt runs slowly down the street.
    Searching desperately for his dog, the tired boy runs slowly down the

street. Having searched all day, the tired boy runs slowly down the
street.

3. Clause modifiers

The tired boy, who had been running all day, searched desperately for
his dog.
The boy who owned the dog searched desperately for his pet.

A punctuation note: Relative clauses that are necessary to identify
the noun they modify are not set off by commas. Those that provide useful information but do not serve to identify the noun are
set off by commas.

Because he had lost his pet, the tired boy searched diligently all day
long.
He stopped looking when he found the dog.
After he found the dog, he raced home to tell (in order that he might
tell) his father.

4. Verb modifiers

He cried happily when he found the dog.
He cried for joy because he was happy.

There is one more basic combination available if we wish to
make sentences more lively and effective. It is possible to produce
combined units, called compounds, by joining or doubling basic
sentence elements and by joining complete sentences.

The dogs run.	
The dogs and cats run.	(compound subject)
The dogs and the cats run and jump.	(compound subject and compound verb)
The dogs run, and the cats jump.	(compound sentence)

Note certain differences between the last example and all the
others.

The dogs run is a complete sentence that is joined to another
complete sentence: *The cats jump*. The other three examples join
elements, subject, and verbs in various combinations; the compound
sentence joins one subject-verb combination to a second subject-
verb combination.

The words used to join independent clauses into sentences are
called coordinating conjunctions. There are three such conjunctions
used to join equal elements in a sentence:

1. And (meaning *as well, in addition to, additionally*)
   We went to the show, and Tom joined us there.
2. But (meaning *on the other hand*)
   We went to the show, but Tom did not join us there.
3. Or (meaning *one or the other*, suggesting a choice; *nor* is negative)

Tom will finish the job, or Mary will take over.
Some writers also use *for, yet*, and *so* as coordinating conjunctions.

An important punctuation rule governs the use of coordinating conjunctions. When such conjunctions are used to join independent clauses (clauses that have both subject and verb), a comma is usually placed immediately in front of the conjunction.

Tom came home	, and	his wife left.
(Subject and verb,	Comma and conjunction,	Subject and verb)
Tom came home	and	cooked the dinner

(Subject and compound verb no comma required.)

As a substitute for the comma-conjunction method of joining independent clauses, you may use a semicolon.

Tom came home; Mary left.

The use of compounds highlights one more punctuation problem: the punctuation of lists of three or more items in a series.

We bought salt, pepper, and sugar.
The president, the secretary, and the salesman resigned.

Items in a series are separated by commas, with the last item in the list preceded by a conjunction.

Join the following clauses by using first *and*, then *but*, and finally the semicolon:

I am sick.
Jim is tired.

Sam hid the money.
Jane found it.

Tom ran away from the crash.
Sam ran away from the crash.
Jane stayed to help.